Scientific Evidence: Fingerprints and DNA

Scientific Evidence: Fingerprints and DNA

LIZ HEFFERNAN

First Law

Published in 2006 by
First Law Limited
Merchant's Court,
Merchants Quay,
Dublin 8,
Ireland.
www.firstlaw.ie

Typeset by Gough Typesetting Services, Dublin.

ISBN 1-904480-54-3

The Research for this book was funded by the
Irish Research Council for the Humanities and Social Sciences

A catalogue record for this book
is available from the British Library.

Printed by Johnswood Press

For Conor, Maeve and Rod

Foreword

Scientific evidence has evolved in the criminal investigative process. In the wake of this, scientific evidence has also become a major part of the criminal trial with expert witnesses playing a central role. This is an insightful textbook by Dr. Liz Heffernan which will be of interest to many readers, whether they be practitioners, academics or otherwise. The approach adopted by Dr. Heffernan is to make scientific evidence accessible to the non-scientist. The importance of this textbook is manifest considering the role scientific evidence now plays in the criminal justice process.

Dr. Heffernan begins with a comprehensive look at the relationship between law and science, describing science as a bountiful resource for law both as an academic discipline and in practice. Dr. Heffernan observes both the differences and parallels that exist between law and science, describing law as prescriptive while on the other hand science as descriptive. There is a comprehensive discussion of the role of the expert witness at trial. The standards that should be adhered to are identified and the relationship between the expert witness and the jury is analysed. Later, the author discusses how the concerns that exist in relation to expert evidence which affect judges and juries are often magnified when it comes to expert scientific evidence. The author highlights the judge's role as an important intermediary between the expert witness and the jury. The main focus of the textbook is on fingerprinting and DNA. Dr. Heffernan sets out the various techniques that exist in the collection and analysis of such forensic evidence. There is an examination of the presentation of fingerprint and DNA evidence in court and the importance of preservation of such evidence post investigation but prior to the trial. Fingerprinting, being more clear-cut than DNA testing, is a more common component of a criminal trial. On the other hand, although DNA technology has gained acceptance in criminal investigation, due to its cost and time-consuming nature, the use of DNA technology is normally confined to serious crimes.

Also, in contrast with fingerprinting there is no permanent collection of DNA profiles. Dr. Heffernan discusses the possibility of developing a DNA database. In relation to this, the concerns and policy considerations, human rights or otherwise, are identified.

Dr. Heffernan draws upon a range of references in her discussion of these areas. There is a wide range of case law discussed, along with an excellent discussion on the law in Ireland in relation to the abstracting of forensic evidence under the Criminal Justice (Forensic Evidence) Act, 1990. Dr. Heffernan also examines the situations as they exist in other jurisdictions, in particular England and the United States and makes comparisons with the situation in Ireland. An examination of the proposals set forward by the Law Reform Commission is also included. Dr. Heffernan at various points, throughout the text, highlights how there are numerous dangers associated with the use of scientific evidence at trial, drawing attention to the need for reform in many areas. Although it is recognised that scientific evidence is for the most part reliable, she suggests it should be treated with caution. Concerns are raised that expert evidence may mislead or unduly influence a jury. The problems that are associated with applying technology, which is at the cutting edge of its field, are assessed. Dr. Heffernan emphasises that DNA testing should be conducted in the most professional manner considering its highly probative nature. Furthermore, the reliance on fingerprint evidence in trials is examined, along with the probative value of such evidence. Although expert evidence is treated differently to other evidence at trial, it is fundamental that evidentiary standards be upheld. Scientific evidence must be weighed against other evidence and a conviction should never take place on the basis of scientific evidence alone.

Science in so many ways is fundamental to modern society. It has also become core to the investigation and prosecution of criminals. In such a developing area, a textbook such as this is vital. Adopting a balanced approach to the role of scientific evidence in the criminal process, Dr. Heffernan examines both the negatives and positives of the use of such evidence. This is both a comprehensive and fascinating text that draws together two specialisations into one thorough piece of lucid work which is accessible to a large group of readers. This is a thought-provoking textbook which will be the welcome addition to the shelf of any criminal lawyer and will, no doubt, become an important text in the analysis and understanding of scientific evidence. It is an honour to acknowledge this book as it is an insight into the complex yet intriguing world of scientific evidence.

Paul Carney,
Presiding Judge of the Central Criminal Court,
Adjunct Professor of Law, UCC,
Four Courts
July 24, 2006

Preface

The identification of offenders is a primary concern of the law of evidence. Whereas much judicial and legal academic ink has been spilled over the admissibility in court of conventional forms of evidence, notably confessions and visual identification evidence, less attention has been devoted to the application of forensic scientific evidence, such as fingerprinting and DNA, to the task of criminal identification. The subject necessarily involves a broader consideration of the role of expert evidence in the criminal trial process and, in particular, the evidentiary implications of the law's increased dependency upon scientific means of proof. The dynamic and intriguing field of scientific evidence is strikingly broad and at times dauntingly complex. This book does not purport to offer a definitive account of current law and practice but rather to raise and explore some of manifold issues relating to the interaction of law and science that increasingly influence the administration of justice in our courts.

In carrying out the research for this book, I have been conscious of the limitations of a legal academic analysis of the subject matter. Although I hope the book will interest legal practitioners, the choice of issues to be explored and cases to be analysed was influenced primarily by my interests as an academic. Similarly, the inclusion of some comparative analysis of US law, as opposed to other jurisdictions, is grounded in my particular experience of that jurisdiction. Finally, in the belief that lawyers should endeavour to get to grips with other disciplines applied in the courtroom, the book also contains some discussion of the science underpinning both fingerprint and DNA evidence. As noted in chapters 3 and 6, the relevant discussion does not purport to constitute an authoritative scientific account and should not be construed as such. For a proper analysis of forensic scientific practice, readers should consult the authorities cited in these chapters and other similar sources.

I would like to acknowledge with gratitude the generous funding of the Irish Research Council for the Humanities and Social Sciences which made possible the research on which the book is based. I am most grateful to the Honorable Mr Justice Paul Carney who kindly wrote the foreword. My thanks are also due to Bart Daly and the staff at First Law and especially to Therese Carrick for her tireless efforts in relation to all aspects of the project. I would particularly like to thank Shane Gough of Gough Typesetting Services for his efficiency in typesetting the text and his patience in accommodating last minute changes. I am also grateful to Thomson Round Hall and the Judicial Studies Institute for permission to use certain material in journals published under their respective auspices.

Several individuals gave generously of their time and expertise in responding to questions and/or reviewing drafts. I would particularly like to thank Dr Louise McKenna, Deputy Director or the Forensic Science Laboratory, and Dr Maureen Smyth, Head of the DNA Section, who gave very generously of their time in responding to requests for information and advice, particularly at short notice. I must emphasise, however, that the discussion contained in the book is my own and should not be construed in any aspect as attributable to or endorsed by Dr McKenna, Dr Smyth of the Forensic Science Laboratory. With the same proviso in mind, I would like to acknowledge the invaluable assistance of Detective Sergeant Declan Buckley of the Garda Technical Bureau, Fingerprint Section, in relation to some of the material in chapter 3. I am also grateful to Dr Asim Sheikh, BL, of UCD's School of Medicine also kindly read draft material and made helpful suggestions.

Several other individuals contributed directly or indirectly to the completion of the book. I have greatly appreciated the ongoing support and encouragement of Professor Terry Kiely, Professor Hilary Delany and Professor Paul O'Connor. I am also grateful to Professor William Binchy, Mrs Helen Bradford, BL, Mr Ray Byrne, BL, Mr Ted Henneberry, Dr Paul Anthony McDermott, BL, and Professor Ed Imwinkelried. I would like to acknowledge the benefit of the comments of colleagues in response to papers I delivered at various conferences including the First Annual Conference of the Society of Legal Scholars Ireland, Dublin, February 18, 2006, the Annual Conference of the Socio-Legal Studies Association, Stirling, Scotland, March 30, 2006, and the W.G. Hart Legal Workshop, London, June 28, 2006. Finally, my thanks to Mary Catherine Lucey, Grainne McAuliffe and Mary Thornton. All views expressed in the book and any errors, inaccuracies or omissions are mine alone.

Liz Heffernan
July 21, 2006

Table of Contents

Table of Cases

E

F

G

H

P

R

Table of Legislation

Statutory Instruments

EUROPEAN CONVENTIONS

ENGLAND

Chapter 1

Scientific Evidence[1]

Introduction

There is a longstanding tradition of lawyers and legal scholars reaching outside the law for the support of other disciplines such as economics, sociology and anthropology.[2] The world of science has been a bountiful resource for law both as an academic discipline and in practice. Indeed, the interaction of law and science has been mutually beneficial and just as legislatures and courts have savoured the fruits of scientific discovery they have in turn regulated and encouraged scientific research and development.[3] Relationships between disciplines can be as much a source of controversy as comfort, however, and in the case of law and science the fault-lines and breakdowns have tended to dominate discourse and inform public perceptions. This may explain in part the depiction of the relationship in such negative terms as "love-hate",[4] a "clash of cultures",[5] and a "marriage of opposites".[6] These and similar statements are misleading in so far as they obscure the routine and generally satisfactory application of science in various legal contexts but they have a particular

---

1 This chapter draws in part on the discussion in "Gauging the Reliability of Scientific Evidence in Tort" (2006) J.S.I.J. (forthcoming). The author is grateful to Mr. Tom Daly of the Courts Service for permission to use that material in this context.

2 M. Freeman, "Law and Science: Science and Law" in M. Freeman and H. Reece, eds., *Science in Court* (Ashgate Dartmouth, Aldershot, 1998) 1.

3 The role of the courts in the resolution of scientific and technological disputes is not without controversy however. *See* S. Jasanoff and D. Nelkin, "Science, Technology, and the Limits of Judicial Competence" in W. A Thomas, ed., *Science and Law: An Essential Alliance* (Westview Press, Boulder, Colorado, 1983) 15.

4 P. Roberts, "Science in the Criminal Process" (1994) 14 O.J.L.S. 469.

5 S. Jasanoff, *Science at the Bar: Law, Science and Technology in America* (Harvard University Press, Cambridge, Mass., 1995), p.7.

6 A.K.Y. Wonder, "Science and Law, A Marriage of Opposites" (1989) 29 J. For. Sci. Soc. 75.

resonance when applied to litigation. Whether wittingly or not, the courts have staged some of the most controversial exchanges between law and science.

Scientific evidence is the aspect of the interface between law and science that has provoked most interest in recent years. Courts have long relied on the assistance of scientists when seeking answers to intractable factual issues, a trend which has developed exponentially with the rise of science and technology in modern society.[7] Viewed in this light, the distinctive and ever increasing contribution of forensic science to criminal justice is a contemporary manifestation of a conventional practice. However, it also constitutes a reaction to the demonstrated unreliability of certain traditional forms of evidence, such as eyewitness testimony[8] and confession evidence.[9] Expert scientific evidence is perceived to represent a more accurate, objective and ultimately trustworthy means of proof in criminal trials. The significant role played by science in the investigation of crime, the prosecution and trial of offenders and the exoneration of the innocent seems to belie the image of law and science

---

7 For a historical overview, *see* C.AG Jones, *Expert Witnesses: Science, Medicine and the Practice of Law* (Clarendon Press, Oxford, 1994). Forensic science has not always enjoyed the prominence ascribed to it in the present day. *See e.g.* J.I. Thornton, "Uses and Abuses of Forensic Science" in W.A. Thomas, ed., *Science and Law: An Essential Alliance* (Westview Press, Boulder, Colorado, 1983) 79 at p. 88 ("Despite the near reverence frequently ascribed to science by the general public and the emphatic mandate for increased use of scientific evidence enunciated by members of bench and bar, the law just is not much enamoured with science. In short, despite lip service to the contrary, lawyers frequently perceive forensic scientists as strictly utilitarian tools of the lawyer's trade. The law views forensic science as its handmaiden, and conflicts almost invariably are resolved in favour of the mistress").

8 On visual identification evidence *see generally People (AG) v. Casey (No.2)* [1963] I.R. 33; *People (DPP) v. Cahill and Costello* [2001] 3 I.R. 494; *People (DPP) v. Christo,* unreported, Court of Criminal Appeal, January 31, 2005.; D. McGrath, *Evidence* (Thomson Round Hall, Dublin, 2005), pp.185-208; J. Healy, *Irish Laws of Evidence* (Thomson Round Hall, Dublin, 2004), chap.6; C. Fennell, *Law of Evidence in Ireland,* 2nd ed. (LexisNexis, Dublin, 2003), pp.152-59.

9 On confession evidence *see generally People (DPP) v. Shaw* [1982] I.R. 1; *People (DPP) v. Pringle* (1981) 2 Frewen 57; McGrath, *op. cit.,* chaps. 8 & 11; Healy, *op. cit.,* chaps. 10 & 13; D. Walsh, *Criminal Procedure* (Thomson Round Hall, Dublin, 2002), chap. 9.

"at loggerheads".[10] Nevertheless, there are sound reasons to take seriously the negative characterisations of science in court.

The ubiquity of scientific evidence and its relatively routine application in criminal trials are by no means the only yardsticks with which to measure the success of this interdisciplinary interaction. The marriage of convenience between law and forensic science may say more about the pragmatism of the criminal justice system than the nature and success of the relationship. The disciplines of law and science are characterised by notable differences in ideology, expectation, methodology, language and discourse.[11] The effective use of scientific evidence in court presupposes an ability and willingness on the part of judges and jurors to grapple with the predicate science. The daunting task of gauging the reliability of scientific evidence necessitates an understanding of scientific methodology and the way in which scientific knowledge is developed and validated. That judges are admitting scientific evidence and juries relying on it with greater frequency merely heightens the need to ensure that the practice accords with the highest evidentiary standards and, in the criminal domain, adequately protects the constitutional and conventional rights of the accused.[12]

These general observations preface a more profound reason for caution, namely, the association of science with error in the courtroom and the grave consequence of miscarriage of justice.[13] Forensic scientific evidence is perceived to be more reliable than other forms of evidence and where it is successfully invoked by the prosecution to lead to safer convictions.[14] It has thus been hailed as a bulwark against traditional

---

[10] M. Redmayne, "Expert Evidence and Scientific Disagreement" (1997) 30 U.C. Davis L. Rev. 1027 at p.1035.

[11] *See generally* E.L. Rubin, "Law and the Methodology of Law" (1997) Wis. L. Rev. 521 at p.526.

[12] Notably the right to a trial in due course of law under art.38.1 of the Constitution and the right to a fair trial under art.6 of the European Convention on Human Rights.

[13] *See generally* R. Nobles and D. Schiff, *Understanding Miscarriages of Justice: Law, The Media, and the Inevitability of Crisis* (Oxford University Press, Oxford, 2000), chap.5; C. Walker and K. Starmer, eds., *Miscarriages of Justice: A Review of Justice in Error* (Blackstone Press, London, 1999); B. Woffinden, *Miscarriages of Justice* (Hodder and Stoughton, London, 1965).

[14] Nobles and Schiff, *op .cit.,* p.174.

causes of miscarriages of justice such as fabricated testimony and coerced confessions. Paradoxically, however, scientific evidence has also been castigated as a self-same source of miscarriage of justice. A close examination of the gathering, analysis and presentation of forensic evidence reveals the complexity and subjectivity of these various processes. The potential for error and the scope for scientific variation suggest that the certainty and heightened authority associated with expert scientific evidence may be more apparent than real.[15] The notorious wrongful convictions of the Birmingham Six,[16] the Maguire Seven,[17] and Judith Ward[18] in the English courts were attributed in no small measure to influential scientific evidence which was later discredited. The travesties were compounded by the emphasis placed in the media, and by extension the community at large, on the significance of the forensic evidence as a reliable indicator of guilt.[19] Each of the individuals convicted was falsely imprisoned for several years before regaining his or her liberty at the hands of the Court of Appeal. More recently, the quashing by the Court of Appeal of the murder convictions of parents of cot-death infants has served as a telling reminder of the dangers of undue reliance on scientific evidence.[20] Those dangers may be particularly acute where the evidence of an influential expert stands essentially uncontested and consequently escapes the checks and balances of our adversarial system.

Similar risks arise where the court is presented with a novel scientific technique or an area of expertise which is in a state of rapid development. Frequently, courts face the unenviable task of assessing means of proof which stand at the cutting edge of a particular field of science and which are the source of controversy and disagreement among scientists. In some instances, the disagreement may be sidelined, avoided or even resolved and, consequently, may have no tangible evidentiary effect on the

---

15 P. Roberts and C. Willmore, *The Role of Forensic Science Evidence in Criminal Proceedings*, Royal Commission on Criminal Justice Research Study No.11 (London, 1993), p.143.

16 *R v. McIlkenny and others* (1992) 93 Cr. App. R. 287.

17 *R v. Maguire and others* (1992) 94 Cr. App. R. 133.

18 *R v. Ward* (1993) 96 Cr. App. R. 1.

19 Ironically, once doubt is cast on the reliability of scientific evidence in a given case, media perceptions can easily shift. *See* Nobles and Schiff, *op .cit,* p.175.

20 *R v. Cannings* [2004] 1 W.L.R. 2607; *R v. Clark* [2003] E.W.C.A. Crim. 1020.

proceedings. For example, the scientific evidence may be relatively insignificant when assessed *in tandem* with the other evidence in the trial or, at the other end of the scale, the disagreement among the expert scientists may in and of itself establish a reasonable doubt that would justify an acquittal. In other instances, however, the proffered scientific evidence may lie at the very heart of the prosecution's case and may have enormous probative significance. Whether in the field of pathology, DNA analysis or any other branch of the forensic sciences, the resolution by the court of the disagreement among the expert witnesses may determine the ultimate issue of the guilt or innocence of the accused.[21] In circumstances such as these, serious questions surround the propriety of the criminal court as a forum for the resolution of scientific disagreement. Nor is this conundrum confined to trial courts; appellate courts may be asked to review scientific evidence and to consider the validity of convictions on which such evidence is based in light of new scientific research and discoveries.[22]

Whether those cases in which courts relied erroneously on scientific evidence are exceptional, isolated miscarriages of justice or are indicative of a widespread, systematic malaise is open to debate. Although there is no empirical basis to support the latter proposition, at a minimum an examination of established miscarriages of justice raises troubling questions about the relationship between law and science in the courtroom.

---

21 The sensational conclusion of the criminal proceedings arising out of the death of Brian Murphy outside Club Annabel in Dublin in 2000 provided a recent example of the potential consequences of forensic scientific disagreement. Of the four young men prosecuted, Dermot Laide was the only one convicted of manslaughter. That conviction was subsequently overturned by the Court of Criminal Appeal and in April 2006, the Director of Public Prosecutions entered a *nolle prosequi,* effectively putting to an end any question of a retrial. One of the factors reportedly bearing on the DPP's decision was a report by the State pathologist, Dr. Marie Cassidy, compiled after the trial in which she reached conclusions as to the cause of Murphy's death which differed substantially from those of her predecessor, Dr. John Harbison, who had conducted the post-mortem examination and subsequently testified for the prosecution at trial. See *Irish Times,* April 25, 2006, pp. 6-7 & 18-19; *Irish Independent,* April 25, 2006, pp.1 and 4-5.

22 *R v. Harding* (1936) 25 Cr. App. R. 190; *R v. Jordan* (1956) 40 Cr. App. R. 152; *R v. Lomas* [1969] 1 All E.R. 920; *R v. Campbell* [1997] 1 Cr. App. R. 199; *R v. Hobson* [1998] 1 Cr. App. R. 31.

The travesty of individual miscarriages of justice is further compounded by the precedential value which such cases may wield within the system prior to rectification. Not infrequently, the reception of scientific evidence in a particular case establishes a benchmark in favour of its admission in subsequent cases. Where the reliability of the evidence is a question of law determined by the judge under the rubric of admissibility (as is the practice in the United States), a formal binding precedent is established. But even where reliability is a question of fact bearing on the weight of the evidence (as is the practice on this side of the Atlantic), reliance on science may have a knock-on effect in relation to subsequent cases that are on all fours. The aforementioned cot-death cases in the English courts illustrate this trend.[23]

Law and Science

It is axiomatic that the parallels between law and science are matched and even outstripped by differences that appear at virtually all points on the comparative scale.[24] The engagement of science by lawyers and judges and the correlative embrace of the trial process by expert scientists are complicated by underlying tensions between the respective disciplines. Lawyers and scientists are creatures of their respective cultures; they neither approach litigious issues in the same way nor speak the same professional language.

The search for scientific truth is a markedly different enterprise from the law's inquiry into the guilt or innocence of an accused. Scientific knowledge evolves cumulatively and progressively through a shared commitment among scientists to rigorous evaluation and critical discourse. Claims of universal validity emerge from the construction and deconstruction of scientific theories and the testing and falsification of hypotheses and counter-hypotheses.[25] Litigation, in contrast, is concerned with the particular rather than the general or the universal and the trial is a forum for the resolution of a real and pressing controversy. Courts are

---

[23] *Supra* n.20.

[24] Jasanoff, *op. cit.*, p.7 (noting that the contrasts between law and science are often described in simplistic, binary terms).

[25] *Id.*, p.7.

constrained by the need to secure definitive closure of the underlying dispute within the operational timeframe of the litigation.

Science is descriptive in that scientists seek to explain the world around us through the discovery of scientific truth. Law, in contrast, is prescriptive and is created and applied but not "discovered".[26] Science provides an invaluable window through which to view and understand the workings of the world. Yet science is "unnatural" in so far as it defies the common sense expectations of the non-scientist.[27] It requires a particular mode of thinking, for example in relation to probability or quantification, which may seem counterintuitive to the uninitiated.[28] The law, in contrast, owes much to logic and rational thought and places great store in common sense and objective human experience.[29] Indeed, the social justice imperative of the law often requires courts to exclude relevant and reliable evidence in order to uphold other policies or values. A prominent example is the vindication of the presumption of innocence through the exclusion of prejudicial evidence of an accused's prior criminal record.[30] Conversely, courts occasionally admit questionable evidence where judges

---

[26] Freeman, *op. cit.*, p.2.

[27] L. Wolpert, "What Lawyers Need to Know About Science" in M. Freeman and H. Reece, eds., *Science in Court* (Ashgate Dartmouth, Aldershot, 1998) 289 at pp.289-90.

[28] *Id.*, p.291.

[29] Thornton, *op. cit.*, at pp.86-87 puts the distinction thus: "Law and science on occasion have conflicting goals, each having developed in response to different social and intellectual needs. The goal of law is the just resolution of human conflict, while the goal of science traditionally has been cast, although perhaps too smugly, as the search for 'truth'. Certainly there is nothing intrinsically dichotomous in the pursuit of these goals; the court or jury strives in good faith to determine the truth in a given situation as a way to resolve conflicts. But proof is viewed somewhat differently by law and science, as is the application and the perception of societal values."

[30] On misconduct evidence *see generally Makin v. AG for New South Wales* [1894] A.C. 57; *DPP v. Boardman* [1975] A.C. 421; *B v. DPP* [1997] 3 I.R. 140; *People (DPP) v. B.K.*[2000] 2 I.R. 199; s.1(e) and (f) of the Criminal Justice (Evidence) Act 1924; *Jones v. DPP*[1962] A.C. 635; *People (DPP) v. McGrail* [1990] 2 I.R. 38; *People (DPP) v. Ferris,* unreported, Court of Criminal Appeal, June 10, 2002; McGrath, *op. cit.*, chap.9; Healy, *op. cit.*, chaps.7 & 8; Fennell, *op. cit.*, chaps.10 & 11.

are satisfied that justice demands it.[31] In these and similar instances, the courts might be said to be pursuing the truth but not in the scientist's understanding of the concept.

The differences between law and science can be overstated, of course. By labelling evidence as "scientific", a party may benefit from the popular perception that science is objective, precise and worthy of respect.[32] The reality that scientific evidence does not always meet these lofty benchmarks may cause us to question the special place it occupies within the law of evidence. An obvious justification is the complexity of scientific evidence although it must be conceded that not all scientific evidence is complex. A more pertinent rationale, and one that transcends the evidentiary idiosyncrasies of particular cases, is the reality that scientific evidence necessarily engages the jury's perceptions of science. There may be sounds reasons for questioning the objectivity and accuracy of an expert's evidence in a given case but, unlike other forms of evidence, the jury will likely approach the issue from society's starting premise that science embodies a superior form of thinking. With this in mind, the evidence will doubtless be presented in a manner designed to maximise the benefit of that popular perception.[33] Thus, the likely impact of scientific evidence on the jury has been the primary policy justification for distinguishing it from other forms of evidence. It seems all the more surprising, then, that the distinction has not been supported by indigenous rules and practice in relation to scientific evidence. Despite judicial rhetoric about the need for caution and special treatment, the regulation of scientific evidence remains within the general domain of expert evidence. In England, long-standing proposals for special procedures, such as neutral experts and the pre-trial review of scientific evidence in criminal cases, have floundered in the starting-blocks.[34]

Some writers have questioned the inclusion of forensic science within the traditional, purist classification of science. Forensic science involves

---

[31] Freeman, *op. cit.,* p.4 cites the example of the admission of "unscientific" evidence of battered wife syndrome.

[32] S. Richards, *Philosophy and Sociology of Science: An Introduction* (Oxford University Press, Oxford, 1987), p.7.

[33] For an insightful discussion of these issues *see* Nobles and Schiff, *op. cit.*, pp. 183-85.

[34] See chap.2 *infra*.

the application of the natural and physical sciences to the resolution of issues within the trial process. Unlike other scientists, the forensic scientist has pitched his professional tent within the judicial system and can anticipate the need to defend his scientific conclusions in a court of law.[35] From this perspective, forensic science is more aptly described as a form of practical reasoning than a science *stricto sensu.*[36] Moreover, its explicit function in servicing criminal justice may deprive it of the independence enjoyed by non-law disciplines in the trial process. As Smith explains, "[f]or those used to thinking in terms of the autonomy of scientific communities, forensic practice is striking for the degree to which scientific activity is subservient to legal activity".[37]

It is important to recall in this regard that the intersection between law and science is located not in the abstract but in the tangible setting of the courtroom. Science makes a distinctive contribution to criminal justice and occupies a special place within the trial process in the guise of expert testimony. The context nevertheless belongs to the law and is governed by judges and lawyers on the basis of legal rules, practices and culture. The expert scientist must adhere to court procedures when drafting his written report and testifying in court. Like any other witness, he is subject to the oath and cross examination and, moreover, must tender his expert opinion in the form of responses to counsels' questions.

Lawyers and judges, for their part, must orient themselves to the world of the scientist in order to embrace and assess his contribution to the proceedings. The integration of scientific evidence into the trial thus involves an exchange of distinct cultures which may or may not result in

---

35 Thornton, *op. cit.,* p.86.

36 *See e.g.* A.P.A. Broeders, "Of Earprints, Fingerprints, Scent Dogs, Cot Deaths and Cognitive Contamination – A Brief Look at the Present State of Play in the Forensic Science Arena" (2006) 159 For. Sci. Int. 148, pp.152-53; T. Kiely, *Forensic Evidence: Science and the Criminal Law*, 2nd ed. (CRC Press, Boca Raton, Florida, 2006), pp.1–2.

37 R. Smith, "Forensic Pathology, Scientific Expertise, and the Criminal Law" in R. Smith and B. Wynne, eds., *Expert Evidence: Interpreting Science in the Law* (Routledge, London, 1989) 56. Forensic sciences have also been distinguished from other scientific fields on the basis that they generally have no academic or industrial counterpart disciplines. *See* M.J. Saks and J.J. Koehler, "What DNA 'Fingerprinting' Can Teach the Law About the Rest of Forensic Science" (1991) 13 Cardozo L. Rev. 361, 363.

confrontation in any given case. Certain aspects of the exchange, such as the crucial matter of the degree of proof, are obvious potential flashpoints for cultural misunderstanding.[38] The scientist's inclination to opine in qualified terms sits uneasily alongside the law's emphasis on definitive answers to contested issues of fact. At the end of the day, however, "it is the courts that decide what is and what is not knowledge" for the purposes of the proceedings.[39] The benefits in terms of the court's reception of scientific knowledge generally outweigh the complications that scientific evidence brings to the trial process. The consequences of confrontation and misunderstanding are grave, however, both for the accused and others directly affected by the proceedings and for the legal system as a whole. Questions thus remain as to the steps that can be taken to enhance and control the application of science in the courtroom.

The Criminal Trial

The strict adversarial model that characterises civil proceedings is tempered in criminal trials by the need to safeguard the rights of the accused. Civil trials differ from criminal trials in certain fundamental respects which are reflected in important distinctions in relation to procedure and evidence. The objective of civil proceedings is to determine the rights and obligations of parties and, where appropriate, the allocation of remedies, such as compensation. The court is essentially adjudicating on the merits of a private dispute and, under the common law system, does so on the basis of the adversarial paradigm.[40] Criminal conduct, in contrast, is presumptively the concern of society-at-large and prosecutions are almost invariably brought by the State, through the office of the Director of Public Prosecutions or the Garda Síochána.[41] The State,

---

[38] *See e.g.* G. Williams, *Proof of Guilt* (London, 1958); T. Anderson *et al.*, *Analysis of Evidence,* 2nd ed. (Cambridge University Press, Cambridge, 2005), chap.3.

[39] Smith, *op. cit.*, at p.57.

[40] *See generally* H. Delany and D. McGrath, *Civil Procedure in the Superior Courts*, 2nd ed. (Thomson Round Hall, Dublin, 2005).

[41] A distinguishing characteristic of the Irish criminal justice system is the division of responsibility for the prosecution of offenders among multifarious State actors. *See generally* D. Walsh, *op. cit.,* chap.2.

clearly acting to vindicate the rights of the victim and the community, has a firm interest in the outcome of the case but for the accused there is a great deal at stake: conviction may lead to the loss of livelihood and reputation, the imposition of financial penalties and even the loss of liberty in the form of imprisonment. Criminal trials have a moral resonance which requires of the court something more than the hands-off approach which characterises strictly adversarial proceedings. The purpose of a criminal trial is not to adjudicate between two sides of a dispute (although in practice the systematic back-and-forth between prosecution and defence can leave the onlooker with that impression) but rather to examine the accused's conduct with a view to determining whether he is innocent or guilty of the offence for which he is charged. Another critical distinction is that whereas civil litigants are presumed equal to the task of representation at trial, the accused is dramatically less well equipped than the prosecution, both in terms of resources and experience. A further, more trenchant, concern is the possibility that the State may abuse its power in the investigation, arrest and detention of a criminal suspect.

In response to these moral and practical imperatives, our judicial system incorporates fundamental safeguards, embodied in the Constitution and the European Convention on Human Rights,[42] designed to protect the rights of the accused and counterbalance prosecutorial advantage. Chief among them is the constitutional right to a jury trial for any non-minor offence.[43] A further safeguard is the presumption of innocence which translates in practice into a prosecutorial burden of proving all elements of the offence beyond a reasonable doubt.[44] Thus, on a charge of murder, the prosecution must adduce evidence that establishes all the elements of murder, *i.e.*, both the *actus reus* and the *mens rea*. In addition, the prosecution must *disprove* any viable defence that has been raised by the accused, other than insanity, beyond a reasonable doubt.[45] At a

---

[42] The Convention was signed in 1950 and entered into force in 1953. It was incorporated into Irish law by way of the European Convention on Human Rights Act 2003, No.20 of 2003.

[43] Art. 38.5 of the Constitution.

[44] On the presumption of innocence and the burden and standard of proof, *see generally People (DPP) v. D. O'T* [2003] 4 I.R. 268; McGrath, *op. cit.*, chap.2; Healy, *op. cit.*, chaps. 1 & 4; Fennell, *op. cit.* chap.3.

[45] *See e.g. Woolmington v. DPP* [1935] A.C. 462; *O'Leary v. AG* [1993] 1 I.R. 102; [1995] 1 I.R. 254.

practical level, the disadvantaged position of the accused is ameliorated in part by the provision by the State of legal aid to any person formally charged with a criminal offence.[46] Criminal suspects (*i.e.* persons who have been arrested and detained on suspicion of having committed a criminal offence but not formally charged) are not entitled to State-funded legal assistance as of right, an omission which may bear on the meaningful exercise of the right of access to a solicitor in custodial detention.[47]

The law of evidence has also been crafted with special rules designed to protect the accused from prejudice in the gathering of prosecution evidence and in its presentation at trial. These rights are grounded in various constitutional and international conventional guarantees, such as the right to fair trial,[48] the right to bodily integrity,[49] and the right to privacy.[50] Prominent examples include the law relating to confessions,[51] and the general exclusionary rule governing evidence of an accused's bad character or prior misconduct.[52]

The special characteristics of the criminal trial necessitate a more proactive, interventionist role on the part of the trial judge in ensuring that the accused receives a trial that conforms to these constitutional and human rights imperatives. Thus trial judges are generally more cautious in admitting expert evidence in criminal, as opposed to civil, proceedings and supervise its presentation at trial in a more rigorous fashion. This vigilance finds expression in many and varied aspects of the proceedings. Whereas the civil litigant is generally expected to shoulder his own evidentiary responsibilities in the adversarial process, the judge will intervene in criminal proceedings where he considers it necessary to safeguard the accused's evidentiary entitlements. The presence of a jury in proceedings involving indictable offences also explains the heightened

---

46 *See* Criminal Justice (Legal Aid) Act 1962 as amended; *State (Healy) v. Donoghue* [1976] I.R. 325; R. Byrne and P. McCutcheon, *The Irish Legal System*, 4th ed. (LexisNexis, Dublin, 2001), paras. 9.14-9.28.

47 The introduction by the Department of Justice in 2000 of a scheme to remunerate solicitors for legal advice tendered to clients in police custody is a welcome step in the right direction. *See* www.justice.gov.ie.

48 Art. 38.1 of the Constitution, discussed *infra*; art.6 of the ECHR.

49 Art. 40.3 of the Constitution, art. 3 of the ECHR.

50 Art. 40.3 of the Constitution, art.8 of the ECHR.

51 See n.9 *supra*.

52 See n.30 *supra*.

regulation of expert evidence in the criminal realm. Wary of the danger that an expert witness may unduly influence the jury, the judge may examine more closely the need for expert evidence[53] and, where such evidence is admitted, may curtail the scope of the expert's testimony. Finally, a comparison between civil and criminal practice reveals greater scepticism on the part of criminal trial judges in relation to certain categories of expert evidence. The admission of expert psychiatric evidence is a notable example and has generated an eclectic body of case law and jurisprudence.[54]

The Right to a Trial in Due Course of Law

The constitutional backdrop is a defining, omnipresent characteristic of the Irish law of evidence. More than any other factor, it is responsible for the emergence of an indigenous body of law and practice, for example, similar to but at the same time discernibly distinct from its English counterpart. The Constitution has been at the forefront in affirming the exclusionary nature of the law of evidence. Thus, the courts have routinely held that an item of evidence, however relevant and reliable, is inadmissible if it imperils a constitutional right or principle.[55] An example in relation to forensic scientific evidence is *People (DPP) v. Allen* in which the Court of Criminal Appeal set aside a conviction and ordered a re-trial on the basis of a flaw in the presentation of DNA evidence at trial.[56] The invocation of the Constitution in such an instance might be described as "negative" insofar its effect is to exclude an item of evidence. But the Constitution may also be invoked in an "affirmative" sense to *include* an item of evidence that would be otherwise inadmissible by virtue of an ordinary evidentiary rule.[57] Whether the effect is to exclude

---

53 *See* discussion *infra.*

54 *See e.g.* Healy, *op. cit.,* paras. 12.05-12.11.

55 *See e.g. People (AG) v. O'Brien* [1965] I.R. 142.

56 *People (DPP) v. Allen* [2003] 4 I.R. 295.

57 However, because it cuts across the application of the ordinary rules of evidence, the application in the affirmative sense is rare and controversial. *See e.g. People (DPP) v. Kelly*, unreported, Court of Criminal Appeal, April 29, 2005; *Dunne v. DPP* [2002] 2 I.R. 305; *Ward v. Special Criminal Court* [1999] 1 I.R. 60; *People*

or to include the item of evidence, the intervention of the Constitution may have an important or even determinative influence on the outcome of the proceedings.

Article 38.1 of the Constitution concludes with the expression "due course of law" and, as such, is essentially a guarantee of due process in criminal trials.[58] The text corresponds to the opening words of Article 70 of the Free State Constitution[59] and is "an echo of a clause of the Greater Charter of Ireland granted in 1216".[60] As the Irish courts have noted on several occasions, the provision is an approximate parallel to the due process clause of the Fourteenth Amendment to the United States Constitution.[61] The wording of Article 38.1 is "of very wide import"[62] and has been construed as a judicial mandate to safeguard basic principles of natural justice which include a guarantee of fundamental fairness in the procedural as well as the substantive sense of the term. In short, the guarantee ensures that criminal trials will be conducted in a manner consistent with the basic norms of fair play and fair procedure.[63] Thus, the courts have cited Article 38.1 as a partial justification for the exclusion of prejudicial evidence[64] such as testimony relating to an accused's previous convictions or general misconduct.[65] In a similar vein, the Supreme Court has expressly recognised Article 38.1 as a source of constitutional authority for excluding unlawfully obtained confession evidence.[66] More generally, several courts have treated the constitutional

---

(DPP) v. Shaw [1982] I.R. 1; *People (DPP) v. James T*, unreported, Court of Criminal Appeal, July 27, 1988.

58 *See generally* L. Heffernan and E.J. Imwinkelried, "The Constitutional Right of the Accused to Introduce Demonstrably Exculpatory Evidence" (2005) 40 Irish Jurist (n.s.) (forthcoming).

59 G. Hogan and G. Whyte, *J.M. Kelly, The Irish Constitution*, 4th ed. (LexisNexis, Dublin 2003), p.1039.

60 *Conroy v. Attorney General* [1965] I.R. 411 (*per* Kenny J.).

61 *Id.*; *Goodman International v. Hamilton (No.1)* [1992] 2 I.R. 542 (*per* McCarthy J.).

62 *State (Healy) v. Donoghue* [1976] I.R. 325 at 335 (*per* Gannon J.).

63 *Id.*; *Goodman International v. Hamilton (No.1)* [1992] 2 I.R. 542 at 609; Hogan and Whyte, *op. cit.*, pp.1042-44 and p.1121.

64 *People (DPP) v. Marley* [1985] I.L.R.M. 17.

65 *King v. Attorney General* [1981] I.R. 233; *Director of Public Prosecutions v. Keogh* [1998] 1 I.L.R.M. 72; McGrath, *op. cit.*, p.470.

66 *Re National Irish Bank* [1999] 3 I.R. 145 at 186-87 *per* Finlay C.J.: "It appears

guarantee of a trial "in due course of law" as an implicit justification for overturning convictions secured on the basis of wide ranging species of evidentiary error.[67]

The courts have also invoked Article 38.1 in the aforementioned affirmative sense to support the accused's right not only to challenge the prosecution's attempt to introduce inculpatory evidence but also to present his own exculpatory evidence to the jury. The right to a trial in due course of law safeguards for the accused the right to test the prosecution's evidence by way of cross-examination and to call evidence in his own defence.[68] In addition, the concept of fair procedures in Article 38.1 embraces an accused's right to inspect prosecution evidence which, in turn, presupposes an obligation on the part of the Gardaí to take all reasonable steps to seek out and preserve items of real evidence such as notes of Garda interviews with the accused,[69] CCTV footage,[70] road traffic debris,[71] and fingerprint evidence.[72] Taken together, these cases represent a significant extension of due process rights in the evidentiary domain.[73]

---

to me that the better opinion is that a trial in due course of law requires that any confession admitted against an accused person in a criminal trial should be a voluntary confession and that any trial at which an alleged confession other than a voluntary confession were admitted in evidence against an accused person would not be a trial in due course of law within the meaning of Article 38 of the Constitution …".

67 For recent examples *see e.g. People (DPP) v. Christo*, unreported, Court of Criminal Appeal, January 31, 2005 (visual identification evidence); *Director of Public Prosecutions v. Murphy*, [2005] 2 I.R. 125 (criminal record evidence); *People (DPP) v. Gentleman* [2003] 4 I.R. 22 (corroboration warning).

68 *State (Healy) v. Donoghue* [1976] I.R. 325; *Donnelly v. Ireland* [1998] 1 I.R. 321; *People (DPP) v. McGrail* [1990] 2 I.R. 38 (CCA).

69 *DPP v. Murphy* [2005] 2 I.R. 125.

70 *See e.g. Dunne v. DPP* [2003] 2 I.R. 25.

71 *McGrath v. DPP* [2003] I.R. 25.

72 *Bowes v. DPP* [2003] 2 I.R. 25.

73 While the courts have not yet invoked Art.38.1 to trump a traditional exclusionary rule of evidence, they have hinted at the possibility of doing so at the expense of an evidentiary privilege. *See Ward v. Special Criminal Court* [1999] 1 I.R. 60; *People (DPP) v. Kelly*, unreported, Court of Criminal Appeal, April 29, 2005.

The Expert Scientific Witness

Scientific evidence is presented in court in the guise of expert testimony.[74] The law has long recognised that where litigation touches upon matters calling for special knowledge or expertise, the finder of fact, whether judge or jury, may be poorly equipped to draw accurate inferences from the facts presented. The assistance of one or more experts, qualified to locate the facts in a meaningful context, may be indispensable to the proper resolution of the case.[75] Scientific evidence, broadly defined, encompasses just some of the many species of expert evidence that have become a virtual mainstay of litigation in contemporary practice. As early as 1960, Mr. Justice Lavery made the observation:

> "This is the age of experts qualified to give opinions in every field of human knowledge – whether science, medical or other, in accountancy, finance, handwriting and technical matters in every aspect of manufacturing process and so on. I would certainly not wish to minimise the value of such evidence, but a sense of proportion should not be lost. There are innumerable incidents of everyday life upon which the ordinary person can express a useful opinion and one which ought to be admitted."[76]

The particular incident of everyday life which the learned justice had in mind was drunkenness which he concluded was a subject on which an ordinary person is qualified to express an opinion notwithstanding that a Garda officer or a medical expert might be specially qualified to do so.[77] Some 45 years later, the ubiquity of the expert witness has doubtless far

---

74 On the Irish law of expert evidence *see generally* Fennell, *op. cit.*, chap.6; Healy, *op. cit.*, chap.12; McGrath, *op. cit.*, chap.6; D. Kelleher, "Expert Evidence in Ireland" (1996) 14 I.L.T. 42; P. A. McDermott, "Expert Evidence in Criminal Trials" (2002) 12 I.C.L.J. 16; H. O'Flaherty, "The Expert Witness and the Courts" (1997) 3 M.L.J.I. 3.

75 *Folks v. Chadd* (1782) 3 Doug. K.B. 157; *People (DPP) v. Pringle* (1981) 2 Frewen 57; *L(P) v. DPP*, unreported, High Court, April 16, 2002; *People (DPP) v. Boyce*, unreported, Court of Criminal Appeal, December 21, 2005.

76 *AG (Ruddy) v. Kenny* (1960) 94 I.L.T.R. 185 at 189.

77 *Id.*, Mr. Justice Kingsmill Moore dissenting.

outstripped the expectations of Lavery J. and we are arguably no closer to finding the sense of proportion in relation to expert evidence of which he spoke. Certainly, the learned justice could not have foreseen the level and pace of scientific and technological advance that has taken place in our society in the intervening decades. The consequential application of this burgeoning knowledge in the courtroom has contributed to the rising profile of the expert witness. But because matters of forensic science fall by definition outside the "innumerable incidents of everyday life upon which the ordinary person can express a useful opinion",[78] scientific evidence rarely implicates the overriding concern of the courts, identified by Lavery J., namely whether there is a need for expert opinion in a given case.

(a) The need for expert evidence

The onus on a party to demonstrate that expert scientific evidence is essential to the resolution of the proceedings is the embodiment of the evidentiary touchstone of relevance. Before allowing a witness to testify, or admitting testimony in documentary form, a court must be satisfied that the evidence is relevant to a matter at issue in the case.[79] The requirement reflects the policy concern that the finder of fact, whether judge or jury, should not be unduly influenced by any witness. As Lord President Cooper famously quipped in *Davie v. Edinburgh Magistrates*: "the parties have invoked the decision of a judicial tribunal and not an oracular pronouncement by an expert."[80] Since the task of the expert witness is to assist the court, intuitively, his opinion should relate to a subject outside the ordinary experience of the court. Otherwise the witness is merely drawing inferences which the finder of fact is perfectly capable of drawing and consequently providing an opinion that is just as irrelevant

---

78 (1960) 94 I.L.T.R. 185 at 189.

79 Frequently, the need for expert evidence is recognised by all parties to the proceedings. However, if a party objects to another party's proffer of expert evidence, the latter party must demonstrate that there is a genuine need on the part of the court for the assistance of an expert in relation to a disputed matter. Independent of the parties, the trial judge must be satisfied that the proffered opinion relates to a subject calling for expertise.

80 [1953] S.C. 34 at 40. *See also AG (Ruddy) v. Kenny* (1960) 94 I.L.T.R. 185 at 189.

as that of any other witness. Indeed, an ordinary or lay witness is permitted neither to express opinions nor to draw inferences from the facts which form of the basis of his testimony for the very reason that these functions remain the exclusive preserve of the finder of fact.[81]

Expert evidence constitutes a broad exception to the rule against opinion evidence and is subject to the important caveat, in the form of an admissibility requirement, of a demonstrated need for expertise in the particular case. The law's concern to protect the jury from undue expert influence is particularly acute where the proffered expertise has a scientific hue; conventional wisdom suggests that the danger that a jury will be bamboozled by the high-sounding rhetoric of an esteemed expert is heightened where the opinion is drawn from the impenetrable world of science. Thus, the admissibility requirement assumes particular importance in relation to scientific evidence, as the Court of Appeal explained in *R v. Turner*:

> "An expert's opinion is admissible to furnish the court with scientific information which is likely to be outside the experience and knowledge of a judge or jury. If on the proven facts a judge or jury can form their own conclusions without help, then the opinion of an expert is unnecessary. The fact that an expert witness has impressive scientific qualifications does not by that fact alone make his opinion on matters of human nature and behaviour within the limits of normality any more helpful than that of the jurors themselves; but there is a danger that they may think it does."[82]

In *Turner*, the expertise in question was that of a psychologist who sought to opine on the viability of provocation as a defence to a charge of murder. The Court of Appeal expounded the traditional view that a jury required the assistance of psychiatric opinion to adjudicate a defence of insanity

---

[81] From a practical standpoint, irrelevant evidence, whether lay or expert, suffers the additional taint of being superfluous and a needless drain on the time and resources both of the parties and the court.

[82] [1975] Q.B. 834 at 841 (*per* Lawton L.J.) *See* R.D. Mackay and A.M. Colman, "Excluding Expert Evidence: A Tale of Ordinary Fold and Common Experience" [1991] Crim. L.R. 800.

but not one of provocation. As Lord Lawton put it: "Jurors do not need psychiatrists to tell them how ordinary folk who are not suffering from any mental illness are likely to react to the stresses and strains of life."[83] Parties seeking to introduce forensic scientific evidence generally have far less difficulty crossing this important threshold issue of admissibility. Certainly, in the case of DNA evidence, as opposed to a less well established forensic field, provided that the evidence purports to bear on the issues raised at trial, a court is unlikely to question the need for its admission in a criminal proceeding.

(b) Expertise

The second admissibility requirement that conditions expert evidence relates to the status of the witness as an expert. Before admitting expert evidence, the court must be satisfied that the witness is suitably qualified in the field in question. The witness having been called and having taken the oath, the customary practice is for counsel to open examination-in-chief with a series of preliminary questions pertaining to the witness's qualifications and expertise.[84] Where a party objects to the presentation of expert evidence by challenging the witness's credentials, the trial judge must determine whether the witness is qualified, by virtue of training or experience, to testify in relation to the disputed matter. In a jury trial, that determination may necessitate the hearing of evidence and legal argument in a *voir dire* outside the presence of the jury.

The term "expert witness" is broadly defined. As Murphy J. explained in *Galvin v. Murray*:

> "In general terms, an expert may be defined as a person whose qualifications or expertise give an added authority to opinions or statements given or made by him within the area of his expertise."[85]

The law imposes no stock requirements in terms of qualifications or

---

[83] [1975] Q.B. 834 at 841. *See also Murphy v. The Queen* (1988-89) 167 C.L.R. 94; *People (DPP) v. Kehoe* [1992] I.L.R.M. 481.

[84] *See* Healy, *op. cit.*, p.361.

[85] [2001] 1 I.R. 331 at 336.

experience. In theory, the expert need not have acquired a professional qualification or have undergone specialised education or training.[86] In *R v. Silverlock*, the accused was convicted of obtaining money in the form of a cheque by false pretences. An issue arose at trial as to proof of handwriting. The Court for Crown Cases Reserved held that a solicitor could be treated as an expert in handwriting, notwithstanding that he had acquired the necessary expertise solely through his legal professional experience. Lord Russell stated:

> "It is true that the witness who is called upon to give evidence founded on a comparison of handwriting must be peritus; he must be skilled in doing so; but we cannot say that he must have become peritus in the way of his business or in any definite way. The question is, is he peritus? Is he skilled? Has he adequate knowledge? … There is no decision which required that the evidence of a man who is skilled in comparing handwriting, and who has formed a reliable opinion from past experience, should be excluded because his experience has not been gained in the way of his business. It is, however, really unnecessary to consider the point; for it seems from the statement in the present case that the witness was not only peritus, but was peritus in the way of his business."[87]

This principle remains embedded in the common law[88] but as a practical matter, contemporary society places a premium on formal qualifications and the fact that a witness's expertise has been recognised by respected institutions or entities has a significant bearing on his standing as an expert.

The determination that a witness is qualified to testify depends upon the nature of the subject on which the expert opinion is offered. The

---

[86] O'Flaherty, *op. cit.*, at p.3: "[T]he admissibility of opinion evidence is not confined to those with university degrees or, indeed, expert qualifications."

[87] [1894] 2 Q.B. 766.

[88] In relation to handwriting experts, the principle was endorsed by the Special Criminal Court in *People (DPP) v. Fox*, unreported, January 23, 2002. Although the credentials of the witness were deemed satisfactory in that case, his opinion was excluded on the basis that his methodology was suspect.

witness's particular expertise must be tailored to the specific matter at issue. Whereas a person may be highly qualified and experienced in a particular profession, he may lack the necessary degree of specialisation to testify on the matter at issue. For example, a DNA analyst, though expert in the use of blood to test for DNA, would not necessarily be qualified to testify about the inferences that might be drawn from a spatter of blood found at a crime scene. However, depending upon his training and experience, the DNA analyst might be qualified to testify in relation to hair analysis; although hair analysis is generally perceived as a distinct forensic discipline, DNA methodology may be applied to hair samples provided adequate hair root cells are available for testing.[89] The suitability of the DNA analyst to testify in such circumstances will depend not only upon his expertise but also the precise matter in dispute in the proceedings and the scientific techniques that have been employed in the case. Where the scientific issues are complex, the limits of the witness's expertise may emerge only through the *denouement* of the proceedings. Nevertheless, as this example illustrates, the court must be flexible and pragmatic in making the preliminary determination, assessing the proficiency of the witness in the particular context of the proceedings.

The court's perception of the witness must be informed by evolving notions of expertise within contemporary society. In *AG (Ruddy) v. Kenny*, Lavery J. spoke of the 1960s as "the age of experts" and, several decades later, the label is seemingly used and abused with even greater frequency. O'Flaherty J. writing extra-judicially, has observed: "The categories of situations that would benefit from the evidence of an expert are not closed. But some have to win their spurs before they can properly be accepted as suitable for the reception of expert testimony."[90] The same might be said of emerging fields of expertise which must gain a certain level of acceptance before they are recognised in a court of law. Case law in this jurisdiction suggests that trial judges generally adopt a pragmatic, purposive approach to the question of expert qualifications.[91]

The suitability of proffered witnesses to present expert forensic

---

[89] On hair analysis, *see e.g.* Kiely, *op. cit.*, chap.3.

[90] *Op. cit.*, p.16.

[91] *See e.g. McMullen v. Farrell* [1992] I.L.R.M. 776 (estate agents); *Southern Health Board v. C.H.* [1996] 2 I.L.R.M. 142 (social workers); *Galvin v. Murray* [2001] 1 I.R. 331 (engineers); *People (DPP) v. Gilligan*, unreported, Special Criminal

scientific evidence has been the subject of few reported challenges.[92] This is a reflection of the relatively specialised nature of the forensic sciences and the correspondingly high level of particularised training which witnesses generally possess at this time. However, it may also relate to the relatively embryonic state of forensic trial practice in this jurisdiction and, from this standpoint, the benchmark of expertise may prove a source of contention in the future. It is also worth recalling that forensic evidence is not the exclusive preserve of scientists; the Gardaí undertake the initial tasks of identifying, gathering and preserving the evidence at the crime scene. These preliminary steps in the evidentiary chain of proof may be the subject of close scrutiny at trial. As a consequence, the expertise of an individual Garda officer to testify in relation to such matters may be no less a matter of dispute.

(c) The duties of the expert witness

In *The Ikarian Reefer*, Cresswell J. provided a classic statement of the duties and responsibilities of an expert witness:

> "1. Expert evidence presented to the Court should be, and should be seem to be, the independent product of the expert uninfluenced as to form or content by the exigencies of litigation (*Whitehouse v. Jordan* [1981] 1 W.L.R. 246 at p.256, *per* Lord Wilberforce).
> 2. An expert witness should provide independent assistance to the Court by way of objective unbiased opinion in relation to matters within his expertise (*see Polivitte Ltd v. Commercial Union Assurance Co. Plc.* [1987] 1

Court, March 22, 2002 (assistant Garda Commissioner testifying on the subject of drug trafficking).

92 In *People (DPP) v. Howe,* unreported, October 15, 2003, the Central Criminal Court held that a forensic scientist was not qualified to present statistical DNA evidence. *See* Law Reform Commission, *Consultation Paper on the Establishment of a DNA Database*, LRC 29–2004, pp.240–410. However, this ruling goes against the general trend in favour of admitting the evidence of forensic scientists (as opposed to statisticians) in this regard. *See e.g. People(DPP) v. Boyce*, unreported, Court of Criminal Appeal, December 21, 2005.

Lloyd's Rep. 379 at p.386 *per* Mr. Justice Garland and *Re J.* [1990] F.C.R. 193 *per* Mr. Justice Cazalet). An expert witness in the High Court should never assume the role of an advocate.

3. An expert witness should state the facts or assumption upon which his opinion is based. He should not omit to consider material facts which could detract from his concluded opinion (*Re J. sup.*).
4. An expert witness should make it clear when a particular question or issue falls outside his expertise.
5. If an expert's opinion is not properly researched because he considers that insufficient data is available, then this must be stated with an indication that the opinion is no more than a provisional one (*Re J. sup.*). In cases where an expert witness who has prepared a report could not assert that the report contained the truth, the whole truth and nothing but the truth without some qualification, that qualification should be stated in the report (*Derby & co. and Others v. Weldon and Others, The Times*, Nov. 9, 1990 *per* Lord Justice Staughton).
6. If, after exchange of reports, an expert witness changes his view on a material matter having read the other side's expert's report or for any other reason, such change of view should be communicated (through legal representatives) to the other side without delay and when appropriate to the Court.
7. Where expert evidence refers to photographs, plans, calculations, analyses, measurements, survey reports or other similar documents, these must be provided to the opposite party at the same time as the exchange of reports (see 15.5 of the Guide to Commercial Court Practice)."[93]

Mr. Justice O'Flaherty, speaking extra judicially, has echoed the sentiments of Cresswell J. in more informal terms:

---

[93] *National Justice Compania Naviera S.A. v. Prudential Assurance Co. Ltd (The Ikarian Reefer)* [1993] 2 Lloyd's Rep. 68 at 81-82.

"What then are the essentials for the reception of expert testimony? What discipline should the expert bring to his particular expertise when he comes to give evidence? By what commandments must be abide?

First: the person must be properly qualified in the field in which he says he is qualified. To put it colloquially: he must know his stuff or, if he cannot give an immediate answer, he should say so and point the way to where the answer is to be found. …

Second: the expert should always be a minister or servant of justice rather than act as the hireling of one side or the other. If he can advance his side fairly and properly, well let it be so. If not he should say so. He, like the judge, must make a judgment too, in his case a personal subjective one, whether it is on the reliability of his experiments, the disposition of the experiments or whatever. ….

Third: he should have the confidence to discuss in advance of the trial with the lawyers on the other side of the case his findings, if asked. This most likely will benefit all at the subsequent exposition of the evidence in the course of the trial and may help to speed it up.

Fourth: he should cultivate the gift of being able to explain his conclusions in terms that will be understood by lay people whether they are judges or jurors, or both. …

Fifth: he should be meticulous in his record keeping. …

Sixth: he should never take a chance in pretending to expertise that he has not got. If he does not know the answer to a question, he should say so, or if he needs time to check something or other no one will think less of him for asking for that opportunity.

Seventh: he must always be patient and never lose his temper no matter how stupid or absurd the questions that he is asked may appear to him to be."[94]

---

[94] *Op. cit.*, p.6. It should be noted that just as the expert witness has duties, he also enjoys certain privileges and immunities in relation to his testimony. For example, an expert witness is immune from suit in respect of his oral testimony and any

Although crafted primarily in the context of civil proceedings, these summaries of the expert's duties and responsibilities are apposite for the most part to criminal proceedings.

Tensions Underlying the Role of the Expert Witness

The characteristics of expert evidence sketched briefly above suggest certain tensions underpinning law and practice. The role of the expert witness is routine in the sense that it is commonplace but it is also potentially complex and even uncertain. A closer examination reveals that this aspect of trial practice is both intriguing and paradoxical. There is a contradiction, for example, in the doctrinal classification of expert evidence as an exception to the rule against opinion evidence and the ubiquity of expert evidence in contemporary trial practice. In exploring the tensions underlying the law relating to expert evidence, three matters are worthy of particular mention: the relationship between the expert witness and the jury, the independence of the expert witness, and the presentation of expert testimony in the adversarial trial process.

(a) The expert witness and the jury

The expert witness enjoys a somewhat exalted position in the trial process by virtue of his role in assisting the jury on a matter outside ordinary human experience. Consequently, although the expert must take the oath and deliver his testimony in a manner not unlike the ordinary or lay witness, his evidence is otherwise the subject of special rules and practices. Witnesses must generally limit their testimony to facts within their personal knowledge or perception thereby allowing the jury to carry out their essential function of drawing the necessary inferences from the stated facts. The expert witness, in contrast, assists the jury in drawing those very inferences and, by virtue of this dependency, enjoys wide latitude in relation to the scope of his testimony. He may testify as to matters of opinion and may incorporate secondary material, such as documents, videotapes or the views of other experts, that would otherwise fall foul

---

documents produced in the course of a hearing. *E. O'K. v. D.K.* [2001] 1 I.R. 636; *Meadow v. General Medical Council* [2006] 1 W.L.R. 1452.

of the rule against hearsay.[95] Although orality remains the guiding principle for ordinary witnesses, expert evidence is initially furnished in documentary form and, at least in civil proceedings, there is an emerging trend in the common law world in favour of admitting it in that guise at trial.[96]

Notwithstanding the special treatment that the law affords the expert witness (or perhaps because of it), his relationship with the jury remains complicated and uncertain. It is the function of the jury to determine the course of events to which the legal proceedings give rise and whereas the jury may be guided by the expert's opinion in relation to those events, the task of finding the dispositive facts remains theirs alone. Yet the ease with which the theory is stated belies the complexity of testimonial trial practice. Whether the expert is merely guiding the jury of has strayed into the realm of impermissible direction may be difficult to discern.[97]

The traditional response to this dilemma was encapsulated in the so-called "ultimate issue" rule whereby the witness is free to draw inferences from facts but is precluded from expressing an opinion on the ultimate issues in the case. Examples included the exclusion of opinion that an accused was unfit to drive due to drunkenness,[98] that an accused had intended to commit murder,[99] and that an accused had been provoked by sexual jealousy.[100] The case law on point has been neither clear nor consistent,[101] however, and the precise scope of the rule has long been uncertain.[102]

---

[95] *People (DPP) v. Boyce*, unreported, Court of Criminal Appeal, December 21, 2005. On the rule against hearsay *see generally* McGrath, *op. cit.*, chap.5; Healy, *op. cit.* chap.9; Fennell, *op. cit.*, chap.9.

[96] *See* English Criminal Procedure Rules, Pt.33 (2005) posted at www.dea.gov.uk.

[97] *See generally* M. Redmayne, *Expert Evidence and Criminal Justice* (Oxford University Press, Oxford, 2001), pp.109–112.

[98] *R v. Davies* [1962] 3 All E.R. 97. *But see AG (Ruddy) v. Kenny* (1960) 94 I.L.T.R. 185.

[99] *R v. Chard* (1971) 56 Cr. App. R. 268.

[100] *R v. Turner* [1975] 1 Q.B. 834; *People (DPP) v. Kehoe* [1992] I.L.R.M. 481.

[101] *See e.g. DPP v. A. and B.C. Chewing Gum Ltd.* [1968] 1 Q.B. 159 and *Anderson v. Neville* [1971] 3 All E.R. 1152 (psychiatric evidence on obscenity); *R v. Chard* (1971) 56 Cr. App. R. 268 and *R v. Toner* (1991) 93 Cr. App. R. 382 (psychiatric evidence on intention to kill).

[102] *See* J.D. Jackson, "The Ultimate Issue Rule: One Rule Too Many" [1984] Crim. L. R. 75.

Courts have tended to treat the contexts of expert and non-expert opinion interchangeably and, in justifying the exclusion of expert opinion, have routinely merged the ultimate issue rule with the broad requirement that the opinion pertain to a matter on which expertise is necessary. At its zenith, the rule clearly undercut the admission of expert evidence and was objectionable in theory since the very presence of the expert in the proceedings signals the inability of the finder of fact to resolve the disputed matter. In practice, it required the courts to engage in the Herculean task of identifying those facts and inferences that related exclusively to the ultimate issues in a case and it led to an unwieldy and inconsistent body of case law. For these reasons, the ultimate issue rule has largely been abandoned in contemporary practice,[103] particularly in civil proceedings.[104] The contrary premise, namely that an expert may opine on an ultimate issue, does not always hold true and may depend upon the field of expertise and the evidentiary backdrop against which the expert opinion unfolds.[105] More generally, the spirit of the rule continues to haunt the admission and use of expert scientific evidence in the trial process.[106]

A related source of tension in the relationship between the expert and the jury is the weight or probative value of the expert's evidence. Whereas the need for expert opinion and the scope of that opinion are factors bearing on admissibility, this further issue assumes that the evidence in question has been properly admitted.

The outstanding question is the degree of latitude that the jury enjoys in assessing the value of expert opinion. Typically, the jury must weigh the opinion of two or more experts and, furthermore, must grapple with disagreements among the experts over substance and methodology. Surprisingly perhaps, the need for specialised opinion on a matter outside ordinary human experience — the very rationale for the presence of experts in the proceedings — does not translate into a requirement that the jury accept the expert's conclusions. Rather, the essential function of

---

[103] *See e.g. R v. Stockwell* (1993) 97 Cr. App. R. 260.

[104] *See e.g. F(Orse C) v. C* [1991] 2 I.R. 330. In England the rule was formally removed for civil proceedings by s.3 of the Civil Evidence Act 1972.

[105] McGrath, *op. cit.,* para. 6.14. On the importance of distinguishing the functions of expert witness and jury in relation to DNA evidence, *see* chap. 9 *infra*.

[106] Nobles and Schiff, *op. cit*., p.174.

the expert in *assisting* the jury underpins the general principle that the jury is not bound to adopt the expert's opinion. Where two or more experts disagree, the jury are free to choose between the conflicting opinions.[107] Moreover, the jury are also free to disregard expert opinion altogether and rely instead on the testimony of lay witnesses provided that it is reasonable to do so in the circumstances of the particular case.[108] Although not obliged to accept the conclusions of an expert witness, the jury must lend his opinion due consideration, along with all the other evidence in the case, in reaching a verdict.

Because juries are not required to explain the reasons for their verdicts, there is scant practical guidance in the criminal case law on the factors that may inform the weighing of expert opinion – such as the expert's qualifications, methodology, demeanour, persuasiveness, or the logic of his conclusions – nor the relative weight that may be accorded such factors. The judge's evidentiary instructions to the jury on summing up provide an *a priori* roadmap and further clues are occasionally offered by an appellate court when commenting on the task undertaken by the jury below. Generally speaking, however, the process of weighing scientific evidence is referenced, if at all, only in reports of bench trials conducted in the Special Criminal Court and the civil courts.[109]

(b) The independence of the expert witness

The references by Cresswell J. and O'Flaherty J. above to the expert's duty to the court reflect the traditional doctrinal assumption that an expert's opinion is neutral and unbiased both in substance and appearance. This is consistent with conventional judicial rhetoric which downplays the adversarial character of expert evidence. The reality is that the expert scientist, unlike an ordinary witness, participates in the proceedings in his professional capacity. He is retained by one of the parties and is generally paid for his services. The expert's report and testimony embody

---

[107] *Verveski v. The Queen* [2002] 2 A.J.L.R. 402.

[108] *People (AG) v. Fennell (No.1)* [1940] I.R. 445; *People (AG) v. Kelly* (1962) 1 Frewen 267.

[109] In the context of fraud proceedings, the Oireachtas has responded to the difficulties faced by juries in fathoming complex evidence. The Criminal Justice (Theft and Fraud) Offences Act 2001, No.50 of 2001, facilitates the presentation to the jury of transcripts including documents explaining complicated transactions.

his independent opinion based on his training and expertise in the relevant field yet that opinion is enlisted in the service of a specified party at trial.

In addition to providing the lawyers representing the party with factual data, he performs an advisory function, identifying the strengths and weaknesses of the party's case, and laying the groundwork for a possible plea bargain. The relationship is implicitly partisan and, for example, even where the expert is unable to provide evidence favourable to the party, he may be ethically bound to refrain from making his services available to any other party to the same litigation. In short, an expert witness is identified exclusively with one or other side in legal proceedings and his opinion is expected to support that party's position; though objective and independent in theory, expert opinion is subjective, even partisan, in practice. Whereas this is unquestionably the reality of the civil trial process, it is also the rule of thumb in the less strictly adversarial setting of the criminal trial:

> "For lawyers, jurors and judges a forensic scientist conjures up the image of a man in a white coat working in a laboratory, approaching his task with cold neutrality, and dedicated only to the pursuit of the truth. It is a sombre thought that the reality is somewhat different. Forensic scientists may become partisan.[110]

The subjectivity of expert evidence is a logical incident of the adversarial trial process which some writers associate generally with the failings of science in the courtroom. Alldridge, for example, has argued that the "[t]he most conspicuous dangers of adversarial expertise at trial are that a partisan choice of witnesses will produce experts who are unrepresentative of the range of possible experts, and that the fact that they are being paid will further induce bias."[111] Arguably, these dangers are exacerbated by the system's overriding emphasis on testimony in open court, a process that is costly and resource-intensive and that may reward advocacy at the expense of scientific knowledge.[112]

---

[110] *R v. Ward* (1992) 96 Cr. App. R. 1 at 51 (*per* Glidewell L.J.).

[111] P. Alldridge, "Scientific Expertise and Comparative Criminal Procedure" (1999) 3 E&P 141 at p.149.

[112] *Id.*

The traditional response to criticisms of this kind is to highlight the strengths of adversarialism and the shortcomings of inquisitorial systems of criminal justice.[113] Criticism and counter-criticism in this vein may be overstated and lend itself to crude caricature. In truth, each system is a creature of its own culture and neither may have a monopoly of wisdom on issues of evidentiary probity. As we have seen, the Irish system of criminal justice has relaxed the reins of adversarialism in notable respects. Moreover, in a small jurisdiction such as our own, the regularity with which a limited community of experts may appear in the courts may temper the likelihood that they will become "hired guns." From a common law perspective, however, the difficulties experienced in the use of scientific evidence constitute a cogent reason for exploring the inquisitorially-styled reforms that have been proposed in England over the years and that are discussed in chapter 2.

(c) The presentation of expert testimony

In former times, the expert witness was a black swan, a rare bird treated with a degree of deference by judges and lawyers alike. Experts are now a mainstay of litigation and their function has been woven into the adversarial fabric of the courtroom.[114] The procedures governing the presentation of expert opinion are designed to facilitate its admission and, at the same time, limit and control its role in legal proceedings. The basic principles of fairness and reciprocity that underpin the disclosure

---

[113] On the values of adversarialism *see e.g.* P. Roberts, "Forensic Science After Runciman" [1994] Crim. L.R. 780 at p.781: "[A]dversarialism is centrally concerned to promote accurate fact-finding, in addition to sponsoring certain values which cannot be reduced to inquiries into past events. It is surely plausible to suggest that the truth is more likely to emerge from free, albeit formalised, debate between adversarial opponents than it is to be ferreted out by official inquisition. It is certainly true to say that a procedure which interposes an independent advocate between the defendant and the state *appears* fairer than one which freely mixes the roles of prosecutor and judge and leaves the defendant without effective legal representation. Adversarial procedure is thus designed to cement the legitimacy of the criminal process by promoting the open, fair and consistent administration of criminal justice, in which accurate fact-finding is a significant component" (internal citations omitted).

[114] *See generally* R. Ormrod, "Scientific Evidence in Court" [1968] Crim. L.R. 241; A. Kenny, "The Expert in Court" (1983) 99 L.Q.R. 197.

of evidence apply with particular force in relation to experts. Where one side presents expert evidence, the other side is entitled to respond by cross-examining the witness and by presenting the evidence of its own expert.

The presentation of expert evidence unfolds in two stages. Having been enlisted by a party to legal proceedings, the expert generally compiles some form of written report in advance of trial which typically has an important bearing on plea bargain negotiations. Where the case goes to trial, the expert is invariably called to testify by the party that enlisted his services and, even if not so called, may be subject to cross-examination by the other side. Given the adversarial nature of the process, the expert can anticipate a tough grilling from cross-examining counsel in relation to his qualifications and expertise together with critical rebuttal evidence in relation to the substance of his opinion from the experts retained by the other parties.

Expert opinion embodies the application of the expert's training and experience to the facts of the case. In compiling his written report and delivering his testimony, the expert may base his opinion on facts both within and outside his personal knowledge. Typically, much of the relevant factual information on which the expert relies has been gleaned second-hand. The facts on which his opinion are based must be proved by admissible evidence either by the expert himself or independently. In other words, facts outside the expert's personal knowledge are technically hearsay and, although they may form of the basis of his opinion, they must be proved by other witnesses.[115] This rule is routinely side-stepped in practice by the expedient of asking the witness to couch his opinion in hypothetical terms. During examination-in-chief, counsel elicits the opinion in the form of responses to a series of hypothetical questions. These questions assume facts that have yet to be proved by the party presenting the expert testimony. Consequently, the expert's opinion is intrinsically linked to the promised proof of the facts on which the hypothesis is based.[116]

The expert is permitted to draw inferences from facts and, indeed, the value of expert opinion lies in the inferential light it shines on matters which have left the judge and jury in the dark. However, the insight offered

---

[115] *R.T. v. V.P.* [1990] 1 I.R. 545 at 551; *R v. Somers* [1963] 1 W.L.R. 1306.
[116] *Conley v. Strain* [1988] I.R. 628.

by the expert frequently eschews any firm distinction between fact and inference. By virtue of his skill and training, the expert may be equipped not only to draw inferences from observed fact but also to perceive facts that would escape the lay witness.[117] Attempts to identify the precise point at which the expert departs from the realm of fact into that of opinion are consequently somewhat futile. It is more helpful simply to observe that courts generally adopt a flexible attitude to the testimony of experts on matters within their field of expertise. In particular, experts may marshal a wide range of material in support of their opinions, including the views of their peers.[118]

The basis for the expert opinion – item no.3 on Cresswell J.'s list of the duties of the expert – has been a source of controversy in the Irish courts. It is well established that the facts upon which the expert opines must be supported by admissible evidence. Consequently, during examination-in-chief, the expert is typically asked to explain both the facts and the criteria or standards on which his opinion is based. The premise behind this line of questioning is that the finder of fact should be appraised not only of the expert's conclusions but also of the method by which those conclusions were reached. Armed with this information, the finder of fact is then in a position to test the accuracy of the expert's conclusions and to exercise its own independent judgment on the ultimate issue in dispute.[119] The need for experts to explain the methodologies that underpin their conclusions is heightened in proceedings that depart from the strict adversarial model. Thus, for example, in proceedings relating to the welfare of children, experts have been required to amplify their conclusions with adequate explanations of their predicate methodologies.[120]

Ironically, forensic scientific evidence may also run the converse risk, namely, that the expert will focus in his testimony on the analytical tests that have been employed in the case without placing sufficient emphasis

---

[117] M.N. Howard, "Opinion and Expert Evidence" in M.N. Howard, ed., *Phipson on Evidence*, 15th ed. (Sweet & Maxwell, London, 2000) para.37.10.

[118] *Foyle and Bann Fisheries Ltd v. AG* (1949) 83 I.L.T.R. 29.

[119] *Davie v. Edinburgh Magistrates* [1953] S.C. 34.

[120] *State (D. & D.) v. Groarke* [1990] 1 I.R. 305, [1990] I.L.R.M. 130; *Southern Health Board v. C.H.* [1996] 2 I.L.R.M. 142; *Re N*, unreported, Court of Appeal, March 14, 1996.

on the material that was tested and the conclusions that can be drawn from the tests. For Walker and Stockdate, "[t]he effect is rather like focusing on the making of a cake without being unduly concerned about the quality of the ingredients, what it tasked like and whether it was suitable for the specific purposes for which it had been made."[121]

The realities of the adversarial setting may give rise to other concerns in the context of forensic evidence. Conflicts may arise, for example, between the lawyer and the expert witness in relation to the former's objective of presenting the evidence in the light most favourable to the client. As Thornton explains, the introduction of evidence and the introduction of an interpretation of the evidence are by no means synonymous:

> "Not infrequently, the side wishing to introduce its particular interpretation will treat itself to a scientific 'smorgasbord', selecting this or that morsel for examination by the forensic scientist. The evidence will be selected or rejected with only those items that conform to the arguments of one side actually being submitted for examination. A distinct possibility exists that the results of the examination by the forensic scientist will be skewed. This also is an abuse of science because the scientist is not allowed to consider all alternative interpretations of the evidence. As a result, the ethical standards of the scientist may be challenged by cogent cross-examination."[122]

---

[121] C. Walker and R. Stockdale, "Forensic Evidence" in C. Walker and K. Starmer, eds., *Miscarriages of Justice: A Review of Justice in Error* (Blackstone, London, 1999) chap.6, at p.120.

[122] *Op. cit.,* at p.89.

Chapter 2

The Reliability of Scientific Evidence: Anglo-American Perspectives

Introduction

Concerns about reliability pervade the law of evidence and account for the formulation of many and varied rules and practices. The rule against hearsay is the paradigm safeguard against the reception of suspect evidence[1] but trial practice is replete with other examples such as the issuance by judges to juries of warnings in relation to categories of uncorroborated evidence.[2] The rule against opinion evidence is also rooted in concerns about evidentiary reliability and the exertion of improper external influence over the finder of fact.[3] Although the law gives wide latitude to experts to express opinions, given the cautious tenor of the general rule, it is perhaps not surprising that the reliability of expert evidence is a cause of particular concern.

Although Irish law contains no explicit rule on point, several mechanisms implicitly address the reliability of expert evidence to a greater or lesser extent. The threshold admissibility requirements relating to the need for expert opinion and the suitability of the witness to deliver that opinion reflect an underlying concern regarding the nature and quality of the information presented to the jury. The court's inquiry into the need for expert opinion is conducted primarily in deference to the principle of

---

1 On the rule against hearsay *see generally* D. McGrath, *Evidence* (Thomson Round Hall, 2005), chap.5; J. Healy, *Irish Laws of Evidence* (Thomson Round Hall, Dublin, 2004), chap.9; C. Fennell, *Law of Evidence in Ireland,* 2nd ed. (LexisNexis, Dublin, 2003), chap.9.

2 On corroboration warnings *see generally* McGrath, *op. cit.* at pp.124-185; Healy, *op. cit.,* chap.5; Fennell, *op. cit.,* chap.6.

3 *See* chap.1, *supra.*

relevance and reliability concerns follow secondarily in its wake. In contrast, reliability is the touchstone of the judicial scrutiny of the witness's qualifications. Before bestowing upon the witness the testimonial largesse afforded to experts, the court must be satisfied that the witness has attained the requisite degree of standing in the relevant field of expertise. The courts have adopted a flexible approach, focusing on stock qualifications in the case of the more established professions or, alternatively, reaching *ad hoc*, contextualised determinations when dealing with less established fields. The pragmatism of the exercise coupled with a generally liberal judicial stance to the admission of expert evidence has tended to obscure the importance which Irish law has traditionally placed on expert qualifications as a safeguard against the unreliability of expert opinion. Once the witness's credentials have been recognised by the court, protecting the jury from the influence of untrustworthy expert testimony is left largely to the adversarial nature of the trial process and the testing of evidence through examination and cross-examination.

The ultimate bulwark against unreliable evidence is the common sense of the jury. Because reliability is not a threshold admissibility concern under Irish law, it usually surfaces, if at all, under the rubric of the weight of the evidence. The jury may look to the expert witness for assistance in resolving a disputed matter of proof but they are not unquestioning pupils; they are expected not to blindly accept the word of the expert but rather to careful assess his opinion and weigh it against the backdrop of the evidence as a whole. The task of the jury is eased by the realities of adversarialism since, more often than not, they are effectively asked to choose between two divergent expert opinions. In criminal proceedings, it is essential to recall that the so-called "clash of experts" unfolds not in the abstract but within the tangible setting of litigation and above all the framework of the burden of proof. The apposite inquiry in relation to the ultimate issue at trial is not the jury's evidentiary preference but rather whether the prosecution has adduced sufficient evidence to establish the guilt of the accused beyond a reasonable doubt.

Because the need for close supervision of expert evidence increases exponentially with the jury's dependency on experts, the issue of reliability assumes particular importance when the expertise pertains to a scientific matter. The world of science is typically alien to the judge and jury and the need for expert opinion is easily justified. The danger lies in the possibility that the jury will be overawed by the scientist, blinded by the science itself, or simply predisposed to the notion that science is objective and reliable. When asked to choose between diametrically opposing conclusions offered by eminent experts, the jury may be swayed by form and appearance rather than substance. Nor is the challenge of unravelling expert scientific testimony a matter for the finder of fact alone; lawyers must grapple both with the science and the persona of the expert in order to elicit the expert's opinion through examination-in-chief or, conversely, undermine it through cross-examination. Thus, the concerns ordinarily associated with the practice of judges and juries relying on expert evidence are magnified in the case of scientific evidence.

A further and distinct set of concerns about the reliability of scientific evidence emerge from the scientific as opposed to the legal side of the partnership. Both within and outside the courtroom, a debate has raged over the drawing of distinctions between good science and bad science or, in American parlance, "junk science". The term "science" is broadly defined, covering fields that are often technical and experimental, and the appellation "scientist" may be open to abuse. Against the contested and evolving backdrop of the world of science, disputes over theory, methodology and empirical research are not uncommon. The issue for the courts is how best to ensure that a proffered expert opinion constitutes reliable science as opposed to junk science.

In Ireland, assuming that a need for expert evidence has been established, the party tendering the witness need only show that the witness is a qualified expert. There is no further onus on the party to establish that the expert's opinion has a reliable foundation. Indeed, the courts in Ireland and the United Kingdom, unlike their counterparts in the United States, have shown a marked reluctance to impose any additional requirements for the admissibility of expert evidence.[4] The complexities attending the application of science in the courtroom have not been fully realised in this jurisdiction but are illustrated by the longer-standing experience of the English and American courts. As discussed below, that experience has prompted calls for reform over the years in these respective jurisdictions only some of which have been realised in practice.

---

4 A. Keane, *The Modern Law of Evidence*, 6th ed. (Oxford University Press, Oxford, 2005), p.562.

ENGLAND

Proposals for reforms related to forensic evidence in England can be traced to the high profile miscarriages of justice that resulted from the conduct of certain terrorist trials in the 1970s and 1980s.[5] In several notorious cases, such as the Maguire Seven,[6] the Birmingham Six,[7] and Judith Ward,[8] flawed scientific evidence was identified as a principal cause of the miscarriage of justice. With British justice severely shaken, steps were taken to reform the system, including the appointment of a Royal Commission on Justice chaired by Viscount Runciman.[9] Among the issues which the Commission was asked to address was "the role of experts in criminal proceedings, their responsibilities to the court, prosecution and defence, and the relationship between the forensic science services and the police" and "the arrangements for the defence of accused persons" including "access to expert evidence".[10] Some of the Commission's recommendations in relation to expert evidence are considered below,[11] together with certain other reform proposals which the Commission chose not to endorse. Over a decade later, there has been precious little governmental action on the subject notwithstanding periodic revelations of wrongful convictions secured on the basis of unreliable scientific evidence. In *R v. Dallagher*,[12] for example, the Court of Appeal ordered a re-trial where fresh evidence raised doubts about the

---

5 See authorities cited at chap.1, n.13 *supra* and *see* C. Walker and R. Stockdale, "Forensic Evidence and Terrorist Trials in the United Kingdom" (1995) 54 C.L.J. 69.

6 *R v. Maguire* (1992) 94 Cr. App. R. 133, [1992] 2 Q.B. 936. *See* M. Redmayne, "Expert Evidence and Scientific Disagreement" (1997) U.C. Davis L. Rev. 1027 pp.1039-46; R. Nobles and D. Schiff, *Understanding Miscarriages of Justice: Law, the Media and the Inevitability of Crisis* (Oxford University Press, Oxford, 2000), pp.189-98.

7 *R v. McIlkenny* (1992) 93 Cr. App. R. 287, [1992] 2 All E.R. 417. *See* Nobles and Schiff, *op. cit.*, pp.189-98.

8 *R v. Ward* (1993) 96 Cr. App. R. 1.

9 The Royal Commission on Criminal Justice Report, Cm.2263 (HMSO, 1993).

10 *Id.*, p.iii.

11 *See generally*, P. Roberts, "Forensic Science Evidence After Runciman" [1994] Crim. L. R. 780; M. Redmayne, "The Royal Commission's Proposals on Expert Evidence: A Critique" (1994) 2(4) Expert Evidence 157.

12 [2003] 1 Cr. App. R. 195.

reliability of the prosecution's ear-print evidence. In *R v. Cannings*[13] and *R v. Clark*,[14] the convictions of mothers for the murder of their cot-death infants were overturned on the ground that expert witnesses for the prosecution had presented flawed or incomplete evidence at trial. And in *R v. O'Doherty*,[15] the Court of Appeal for Northern Ireland rejected expert testimony concerning voice identification based solely on auditory analysis, a conclusion diametrically opposed to that of the English Court of Appeal in *R v. Robb*.[16] These cases are symptomatic of underlying tensions in the law relating to expert scientific evidence[17] and point to the wisdom of revisiting the reform agenda first posited in the early 1990s and, moreover, extending it to this jurisdiction.

(a) Trial practice

It is a matter of commonsense that the reliability of scientific evidence depends not only on the manner in which it is presented at trial but also crucially on the pre-trial procedures that govern the gathering, processing and collation of such evidence. A shortcoming in the criminal justice system identified in the *Maguire* and *Ward* cases was the inadequacy of existing practices relating to the pre-trial disclosure of expert evidence by the prosecution to the defence. Disclosure requirements are more rigorous in the present day but it is significant to note that historical difficulties stemmed not only from lax practice but also by "the institutional split between prosecutors and experts" by virtue of which "an expert may not realise the legal importance of disclosing certain evidence, whilst the prosecution may not realise the scientific importance of doing so."[18]

The Runciman Commission endorsed the principle of full disclosure which the law has at least formally imposed on the prosecution by tradition. It emphasised that prosecution forensic scientists are under a

---

13 [2004] 1 W.L.R. 2607.
14 [2003] E.W.C.A. Crim. 1020.
15 [2003] 1 Cr. App. R. 5.
16 [1991] 93 Cr. App. R. 161.
17 *See e.g.* W.E. O'Brian Jr., "Court Scrutiny of Expert Evidence: Recent Decisions Highlight the Tensions" (2003) 7 E & P 172.
18 Redmayne, *supra* n.11 at 158.

strict obligation to disclose to the police all evidence that may be relevant to the case, the police are obliged to pass it on the Crown Prosecution Service, and the CPS, in turn, to disclose it to the defence. The duty is broad in its scope and extends to any information which might assist the defence including tests or experiments of which the scientist is aware that cast doubt on his opinion. Following disclosure, the defence are entitled to access to notes, test results and information about similar evidence discovered in other or related cases.[19] In relation to the defence, the Commission proposed new rules imposing a stricter duty of disclosure. For example, its recommendations included a duty to disclose where the defence does not intend to call an expert to testify in court but does intend to criticise the prosecution's expert.[20]

More controversial were the Commission's recommendations, contained in a separate section of the Report, that the defence be obliged to disclose its case in outline prior to trial. In order to challenge the prosecution's forensic evidence at trial, the defence would have to specify in advance the basis for its objections.[21] These proposals were heavily criticised at the time and have since remained moribund. In an Irish context, requiring the defence to disclose its trial strategy could raise the spectre of an unconstitutional erosion of the presumption of innocence and its placement of the burden of proof on the prosecution.[22]

Aside from the panacea of greater disclosure, the Commission recommended the use of pre-trial conferences between prosecution and defence experts.[23] The underlying objective would be to clarify the evidence by providing the experts with a forum for dialogue and requiring them to identify the areas and extent of disagreement. The Commission also envisioned the possibility of a pre-trial hearing before a judge in cases where the pre-trial conference revealed substantial disagreement.

---

[19] Commission Report, chap.9, para.45.

[20] *Id.*, para.64.

[21] Redmayne, *supra* n.11, p.159.

[22] Roberts, *supra* n.11, at p.786, notes in an English context: "The answer must be that forensic science evidence affords such potential for mischief that a carefully circumscribed sacrifice of this principle – if sacrifice it be – is necessary in the interests of justice. The proposal is strictly limited to this one class of evidence which gives rise to special problems requiring tailor-made solutions. It should not be taken to lend grist to any other mill."

[23] *See id.*, pp.786-87.

The tactic of bringing experts together in advance of trial is sometimes used in practice and may prove constructive in some instances. Equally, in others, it may achieve little in the way of resolving disputes over scientific evidence and may even increase the contested nature of the proceedings. A more promising approach would be the introduction of a formal pre-trial hearing before the trial judge in its own right and not simply as an adjunct to a conference among experts. The Irish courts lack a tradition of pre-trial procedures and operate on the general principle that the resolution of issues relating to the evidence or other aspects of the proceedings may be adequately dealt with during the course of the trial itself. Problems in relation to the evidence, for example, are generally dealt with *ad hoc* during the examination of witnesses or, if the need arises, by way of a *voir dire* or "trial within a trial" outside the presence of the jury.[24] In criminal proceedings, the constitutional imperative of a trial in due course of law[25] coupled with the increasing complexity and cost of litigation have cast doubt on the wisdom of this approach. There is growing support for the use of a pre-trial mechanism as a more effective means of resolving admissibility issues that are disposable in advance of trial.[26]

Moving to the trial phase, the Runciman Commission proposed certain measures in relation to the presentation of evidence. For example, it recommended measures designed to bolster the expert's delivery of his evidence, such as the practice of allowing the witness to clarify his evidence, if disputed, before leaving the witness box, and encouraging him to use visual aids.[27] Where expert evidence takes the form of a report that is not contested at trial, the Commission recommended that the jury be provided with a written summary of the evidence.[28]

---

24 *State v. Treanor* [1924] I.R. 193; *People (DPP) v. Conroy* [1988] I.L.R.M. 44.

25 Art.38.1 of the Constitution; art.6 of the European Convention on Human Rights.

26 *See e.g.* Working Group on the Jurisdiction of the Courts, *The Criminal Jurisdiction of the Courts* (Courts Service, 2003), chap.6, para.774. The Law Reform Commission has added its voice to the debate by recommending the availability of a pre-trial mechanism in cases involving DNA evidence. Law Reform Commission, *Report on the Establishment of a DNA Database* (LRC 78-2005), para.5.24. *See* Chap.9 *infra*.

27 (Runciman) Commission Report, paras.72-73.

28 *Id.*, para.71.

(b) Independent court appointed experts

On the criticisms levelled at the Runciman Commission was that it failed to recommend greater autonomy for trial judges and, specifically, the ability to order the parties to produce further expert evidence either at the pre-trial or trial stage.[29] The Commission also rejected a more far-reaching suggestion in a similar vein, namely, giving trial judges the authority to appoint independent experts.

So-called "independent experts" are found in continental inquisitorial systems of criminal justice but, no doubt because they embody a significant dilution of the adversarial dynamic, are seldom used in common law systems.[30] The justification for the proposal lies in the exceptional nature of forensic evidence and the suggestion that it is particularly ill-suited to an adversarial contest.[31] Adversarialism has been accused of stifling and distorting scientific opinion, emphasising irrelevant considerations such as the appearance and demeanour of the expert and, ultimately, accentuating scientific disagreement.[32] The argument runs that the introduction of a single, independent, court-appointed expert would provide the court with an objective and impartial assessment of

---

29 Redmayne, *supra* n.11.

30 Roberts, *supra* n.11, p.789, n.55 (noting that, except in relation to sentencing, this is the case even in those common law adversarial systems that have made provision for court appointed experts). *See also* S. Gross "Expert Evidence" (1991) Wis. L. Rev. 1113, p.1187 *et. seq.*

31 *Id.*, p.789.

32 *See e.g.* J.R. Spencer, "The Neutral Expert: An Implausible Bogey" [1991] Crim. L. R. 106 and "Court Experts and Expert Witnesses: Have We a Lesson to Learn from the French?" [1992] Current Legal Problems 213, p.224; P. Alldridge, "Scientific Expertise and Comparative Criminal Procedure" (1999) 3 E&P 141; P. Roberts and C. Willmore, *The Role of Forensic Science Evidence in Criminal Proceedings*, Royal Commission on Criminal Justice Research Study No.11 (London, 1993), pp.114-16. Howard has provided a more elaborate summary of the criticisms of the system (in the course of defending it): "The present system is said to be flawed as a result of (i) potential bias of expert witnesses; (ii) risks arising from the expert not being presented with all the data; (iii) the restrictions on the expert's ability to give his (or her) evidence freely because of the way in which evidence is elicited in court; (iv) the dislike of experts themselves of this procedure; (v) unfairness to the defence due to the lack of resources available to it; (vi) absence of any means of controlling the quality of expert witnesses." M.N. Howard, "The Neutral Expert: A Plausible Threat to Justice" [1991] Crim. L.R. 98 at p.99.

the scientific issues raised in the trial.[33] The procedure would unfold roughly as follows. The expert would be appointed from a panel of approved persons, he would draft a report for the court containing an authoritative assessment of the scientific evidence in the case, and he would be available for questioning by the judge. A variation on the theme would permit the expert to be cross-examined by the parties.

In England, the counter-arguments to this proposal have tended to focus on the virtues of adversarialism in general, and cross-examination in particular,[34] as vehicles for testing the probity of alleged facts. The depictions of counsel bullying and cajoling unsuspecting experts into a distortion of scientific truth are not surprisingly dismissed as overstated and misleading.[35] More fundamentally, without the challenge of an adversary the expert is thought to lack the incentive to perform at his best. The court may also be deprived of an adequate professional context in which to locate the expert's opinion; the level of controversy surrounding a particular issue, the objectivity of the expert's views, and the degree of support those views command within the particular scientific community may not be aired and properly tested. Thus, the adversarial system is held up by its proponents as better equipped to expose and address the danger of bias on the part of expert witnesses.[36]

A further concern is the power potentially wielded by an independent expert. The authoritativeness and exclusivity of his opinion carries with it the risk that it may be accorded too much weight by judge and jury. This concern undercuts the objective of the proposal (at least as it was vaunted in the early 1990s in the wake of the high profile English

---

[33] Alldridge, *op. cit.*, pp.151–153.

[34] Wigmore, *Treatise on the Anglo-American System of Evidence in Trials at Common Law* (3rd ed., 1940) vol.5, para.1367.

[35] *See e.g.* Howard *op. cit.*, p.101: "The picture of the suave cross-examiner leading an unwary expert witness into supporting in the witness box the scientific thesis by the opposite party is an attractive one; but it does not accord with reality. If this result ever comes about, it is because there is substantial agreement between the experts, and one or two remaining points of difference can be removed in the course of cross-examination either by exposing a fallacy in one expert's reasoning or by proposing to him a factual context which he has not previously considered."

[36] *Id.*, p.101: "It is slightly mysterious that it should be thought that experts are venal mountebanks when engaged by the parties but transformed into paragons of objectivity when employed by the court."

miscarriages of justice), namely, enhancing the position of the accused by improving the quality of expert scientific evidence. As Howard argued at the time, "[t]here is something rather remarkable about the suggestion that the best way to extend the protection of the accused is to deprive him altogether of the power to employ and call an expert witness on his own behalf".[37] Further difficulties potentially attend the use of independent experts in practice. For example, who will select the panel of experts and what criteria will be applied in the selection? Will the panel necessarily represent the established wing of the particular scientific profession? Who will pay the costs and expenses of the independent expert? What steps are open to the court in the event that the independent expert's opinion is controversial and disputed? On what basis is the judge to instruct the jury in relation to the expert evidence?

The intractable nature of the debate over court appointed experts stems in part from the extreme positions adopted by its proponents and detractors. The tendency to overstate both the strengths and weaknesses of the adversarial and inquisitorial systems respectively is distracting and obscures the possibility of a middle ground. In defending the proposed introduction of independent experts in English criminal trials, Spencer has emphasised the opportunities the system can provide for interaction between the parties and the expert short of cross-examination:

> "Under the French Code of Criminal Procedure, for example, the report of the court expert (or experts) is circulated to the parties, and they then discuss it at a special hearing before the '*juge d'instruction*', which takes places in private, and well ahead of the final trial. The experts can be questioned about their reports, and if the parties are not satisfied by their answers they can ask the *judge d'instruction* to appoint a further expert, or even experts, (with a right of appeal if he unreasonably refuses). ...One of the problems at the Maguire trial was that the defence expert did not manage to produce a piece of vital scientific evidence that seriously undermined the prosecution case until the trial was already part heard, and in consequence this evidence was not properly put before

37 *Id.*, p.99.

> the jury. Under the French system, where the sifting and testing of the expert opinion takes places well in advance, I suspect that this particular catastrophe would have been avoided."[38]

This observation in relation to just one aspect of the procedure serves as a reminder that sophisticated, contextual comparative analysis is essential to a true understanding of mechanisms gleaned from other systems. The feasibility and desirability of introducing court appointed experts can only be assessed by taking onboard the full gamut of safeguards that may be built into such a procedure. At the same time, reform proposals of comparative inspiration should not be imported wholesale but rather tailored to meet the unique, beneficial characteristics of the existing system.

The reality is that the notion of a single, independent expert may work well in some cases but not in others. The practice of the parties agreeing to a single expert is not uncommon and is often encouraged by judges but there may be dangers in translating this practice into an iron-clad rule. A significant difficulty with the proposal, and one overlooked in the literature, is the potential inability of court appointed experts to resolve satisfactorily those cases in which scientific issues are particularly complex and highly contested. In this regard, it is interesting to note that although English law makes provision for the court appointment of single joint experts in civil proceedings,[39] such experts are far less common in complex proceedings and cases involving sharply contested scientific issues.[40]

In Ireland, a possible debate in the future about the introduction of independent experts in criminal cases would necessarily centre on the constitutional rights of the accused. As we have seen, the right to a trial in due course of law under Article 38.1 includes the right of the defence to challenge and test the prosecution's evidence and to present independent evidence. Whether depriving the defence of its existing entitlement to present its own expert witness would violate Article 38.1 is an open

---

38 Spencer *op. cit.*, p.108.

39 Civil Procedure Rules, Pt 35 and Practice Direction. The rules are summarised by Keane, *op. cit.,* pp.572-80.

40 Such as in proceedings for medical negligence. *Id.* p.574 (citing cases).

question. The Supreme Court has previously upheld the constitutionality of video-link evidence notwithstanding its dilution of the right to confrontation.[41] Nevertheless, the introduction of independent experts in criminal trials would represent a far greater intrusion into the preparation and presentation of the case for the defence.

A less radical proposal has recently been adopted in relation to one species of civil litigation. Section 20 of the Civil Liability and Courts Act 2004 permits a court to appoint an expert witness in a personal injuries action over and above experts presented by the parties. The expert, who must be a person "approved" by the President of the High Court in consultation with the President of the Circuit Court and the President of the District Court,[42] shall investigate and give evidence in relation to such matters as the court directs.[43] A party to a personal injuries action is under a duty to cooperate with the expert and, in particular, to furnish him with any report or document prepared by or on behalf of the party and any information used in preparing the report.[44] The party is entitled to cross-examine the expert in relation to any matter on which the expert was appointed to investigate or give evidence.[45] The costs incurred in the appointment of the expert and the carrying out of his investigation shall be paid by such party as the court directs.[46] In explaining the legislative initiative, the Minister stated:

> "The intention behind this provision is that an expert, independent of any expert witness retained by the parties, could be appointed to assist the court. To take a medical example, a court might decide to appoint its own medical assessor, who will testify and be liable to cross-examination, but will give an objective view to the court having listened to the medical experts on either side."[47]

---

41 *Donnelly v. Ireland* [1998] 1 I.R. 321.
42 Civil Liability and Courts Act 2004, s.20(5).
43 *Id.*, s.20(1).
44 *Id.*, s.20(2).
45 *Id.*, s.20(4).
46 *Id.*, s.20(3).
47 Seanad Debates, March 11, col.1808.

Although the Act has entered into force, it will be some time yet before the first of the personal injuries proceedings to which it applies comes on stream. From this speculative standpoint, it is difficult to see how the introduction of independent experts in personal injuries actions will achieve the stated objective in practice. The effect of casting a additional expert opinion into the adversarial mix is difficult to predict. In some cases, a third, independent expert may assist the court in resolving a sharp division between two experts but, in others, he may merely compound the dilemma by increasing the complexity and confusion. Although there is nothing in the section obliging the court to accept the conclusions of the approved person, the pressure to do so will likely be greater under this inquisitorial model. Whether the use of independent experts will operate to the detriment of plaintiffs who are seeking to advance a theory that contradicts orthodox practice is a further concern.[48] The ability of plaintiffs to challenge conventional wisdom in relation to scientific controversies may be compromised if the expert's opinion represents a traditional or established position within the relevant scientific community. Finally, practical issues remain in relation to such matters as the approval and subsequent appointment of experts, potential conflicts of interest, and the assignment of costs.

It remains to be seen whether judges will avail of the services of independent experts in personal injuries actions under section 20. However, given the lacklustre nature of the reform and the lack of clarity surrounding its terms, the impact of the provision may be relatively limited in practice. Nor does section 20 seem a useful precedent for criminal practice not least because the shortcomings noted above would be all the more marked in the context of jury trials. For example, the introduction of a third, independent expert might hamper rather than assist the jury's resolution of a complicated or disputed forensic scientific matter. Alternatively, the jury might afford the opinion of the independent expert undue weight by virtue of his status as a court appointee. In order to safeguard against these eventualities, the task of the trial judge in instructing the jury would become more problematic. A likely overall effect would be an increase in the length and cost of the proceedings.

---

[48] W. Binchy, "The Impact of the New Act on Tort Law" in C. Craven and W. Binchy, eds., *Civil Liability and Courts Act 2004: Implications for Personal Injuries Litigation* (FirstLaw, Dublin, 2005) 44, p.59.

(c) External validation of scientific evidence

At the heart of the debate about scientific evidence is the issue of whether courts are appropriate bodies to be determining questions of science. In Ireland, the trial judge decides whether a proffer of scientific evidence meets the criteria of admissibility and his decision, a finding which need not necessarily be supported by reasons, will be viewed deferentially by an appellate court. The decision to admit or exclude the evidence is generally made without the benefit of information provided by the parties in the form of adversarial expert testimony. Where the evidence is admitted, it will be presented to the jury which will determine its reliability in the context of deciding the guilt or innocence of the accused. Provided that the jury's verdict is not perverse, it will be upheld on appeal.[49] Judges and juries reach these self-same determinations on a daily basis in relation to all forms of evidence. Noting that forensic scientific evidence raises particular problems for courts, some writers have questioned whether judges and juries are suitably qualified to determine such matters, even with the benefit of adversarial or independent expert opinion.[50]

An alternative proposal is the introduction of a system whereby the courts rely on the external validation of scientific methods. Under this model, a judge refers a scientific or technical question to a committee or panel who decide whether a particular technique is sufficiently reliable to be used in legal proceedings. The external panel comprises scientific experts who have been approved for the purpose, in effect, a collectivity of independent court appointed experts. Their function might best be described as certifying or decertifying scientific techniques for purposes of litigation. Like independent experts, this form of extra-forensic validation has an inquisitorial flavour and has been employed in some continental European countries.[51] Alldridge has extolled its virtues in the following terms:

---

49 D. Walsh, *Criminal Procedure* (Thomson Round Hall, Dublin, 2002), p.1194.

50 *See e.g.* Alldridge, *op. cit.*, pp.155–157 (summarising the argument that the decision whether to adopt a novel scientific technique should be regarded as a legislative or executive but not a judicial decision).

51 R. Smith, "Forensic Pathology, Scientific Expertise, and the Criminal Law" in R. Smith and B. Wynne, eds., *Expert Evidence: Interpreting Science in the Law* (Routledge, London, 1989) 56, p.57; N. O'Connor, *Cracking Crime: Jim Donovan–Forensic Detective* (O'Brien Press, Dublin, 2001), pp.70–71.

> "The advantages of having the matter resolved in this way, before the trial, are obvious. The decision need not be affected by the resources of the party litigant, it will be taken by an appropriately skilled body, and it may be relied upon in all litigation. … As to procedure, the rule of law is better satisfied by the existence of such a committee: it would be responsible for all decisions to certify or not to certify, and could be placed under an obligation to give reasons and to behave consistently. …".[52]

An additional advantage is that the committee would be better protected than an individual scientific expert in deciding to certify or decertify a controversial scientific method.

One of the difficulties of this reform proposal is that, although simple in theory, a process of external validation would be far from straightforward in practice. Its introduction would require the importation into the adversarial system of elements of the inquisitorial and academic (or peer review) models of decision-making. Several, far-reaching questions would attend. In what circumstances would a court be permitted, or indeed obliged, to refer a matter to the committee? How would the committee conduct its investigation and deliberations? What degree of fact-intensity would be required of the committee or, to put it another way, to what extent would its findings relate specifically to the facts of the case? Would the parties be able to make submissions to the committee and would they have an opportunity to challenge the committee's findings? Who would bear the costs of the external validation procedure?

Persuasive answers may well exist but the number and depth of these questions indicate the enormity of the implications surrounding the proposal. In England, the Runciman Commission recommended the establishment of a Forensic Science Advisory Council to oversee the provision of forensic services[53] but stopped short of proposing that the body would play a direct role in ensuring the reliability of evidence in criminal cases.[54] Generally speaking, the legal profession has demonstrated a lack of appetite for any such substantial modification of

---

52 *Op. cit.*, p.158.
53 Commission Report, *op. cit.*, para.33.
54 Redmayne, *supra* n.11, pp.161-62.

the adversarial system. Here in Ireland, we might predict a similar response from bench and bar but an additional factor auguring against any such move is the relative paucity of reported cases on forensic scientific evidence. Notwithstanding increased reliance on such evidence in criminal proceedings, coupled with the proposed establishment of a DNA database, Irish practice is considerably less extensive and developed than its English counterpart. It is unlikely that Irish courts would be ready to cede their role as the final arbiters of questions of fact, whether scientific or non-scientific, in criminal trials.[55]

(d) Recent developments

Given the range of measures proposed in England over the years, the lack of movement on the reform agenda is striking. In the wake of controversy surrounding a series of wrongful murder convictions in the English courts of parents arising out of death of their infants due to sudden infant death syndrome (SIDS) or, colloquially, cot-death,[56] the House of Commons has sought to reinvigorate interest in the issue. In March 2005, the Science and Technology Select Committee reviewed the use of science in court[57] and recommended that a Forensic Sciences Advisory Council be established "to oversee the regulation of the forensic science market and provide independent and impartial advice on forensic science". A key function of the proposed Council would be to validate the accreditation of expert witnesses.[58] The Committee also examined the problems

---

[55] The Minister for Justice recently raised the possibility of introducing the Scottish "corroboration" mechanism for ensuring the reliability of scientific evidence whereby each case is assessed by two forensic scientists working independently. The Minister's suggestion was made in response to the decision of the Director of Public Prosecutions to enter a *nolle prosequi* in relation to the retrial of Dermot Laide for the manslaughter of Brian Murphy outside Club Annabel in Dublin in 2000. Apparently a factor bearing on that decision was a pre-trial report of the State pathologist, Dr. Marie Cassidy, which conflicted with the conclusions of her predecessor, Dr. John Harbison. *See Irish Times,* April. 25, 2006, pp.4-6.

[56] *R v. Cannings* [2004] 1 W.L.R. 2607; *R v. Clark* [2003] E.W.C.A. Crim. 1020.

[57] House of Commons Science and Technology Committee, *Forensic Science on Trial*, 7th Report, Session 2004/05.

[58] A significant step was the establishment in 2000 of the Council for the Registration of Forensic Practitioners which provides an independent, non governmental system of accreditation. *See www.crfp.org.uk.*

associated with scientific disagreements between expert witnesses in criminal jury trials. The various solutions proposed in the early 1990s were re-canvassed before the House Committee and currently await a response from government.[59]

THE UNITED STATES

The reliability of scientific evidence has generated surprisingly little jurisprudence in Ireland and the emergent discourse has been cautious and indirect. In criminal proceedings, the reliability of expert evidence tends to surface, if at all, under the rubric of the weight of the evidence. Conflicts among expert witnesses are by no means uncommon and the law leaves it up to the finder of fact, invariably a jury, to decide which expert opinion they should follow, if at all. Assuming that the relatively basic requirements for the admissibility of expert evidence are met and that the jury are properly instructed by the trial judge, a reasonable determination by the jury on the facts presented will almost invariably be upheld on appeal. The modest regulation of expert scientific evidence embodied in the Irish system prompted Professor Edward J. Imwinkelried, a leading authority on the law of evidence, to propose that the Irish courts follow the American lead by introducing reliability as a formal admissibility requirement.[60] This represents a more radical proposition that the reforms proposed, and those actually adopted, in England. In order to gain an understanding of how the American requirement operates in practice, it is first necessary to chart its historical development.

(a) *Frye* and *Daubert*

The debate in the United States about the reliability of scientific evidence[61] is usually traced to the landmark decision of the U.S. Court

---

[59] Parliamentary Office of Science and Technology, *Postnote: Science in Court*, October 2005, No.248.

[60] E.J. Imwinkelried, "'Junk Science' in the Courtroom: Will the Changes in the American Law of Expert Evidence Influence the Irish Courts?" (2004) 26 D.U.L.J. 83.

[61] *See generally* K.R. Foster and P. W. Huber, *Judging Science* (MIT Press,

of Appeals for the District of Columbia Circuit in *Frye v. United States.*[62] At issue in the case was the admissibility of a systolic blood pressure test, a forerunner of the polygraph or lie detector test. In upholding the trial judge's decision to exclude the evidence, the court stated:

> "Just when a scientific principle or discovery crosses the line between the experimental and demonstrable stages is difficult to define. Somewhere in this twilight zone the evidential force of the principle must be recognized, and while the courts will go a long way in admitting expert testimony deduced from a well recognized scientific principle or discovery, the thing from which the deduction is made must be sufficiently established to have gained general acceptance in the particular field in which it belongs."[63]

The "general acceptance" test became the dominant standard for the reception of scientific evidence in federal and state courts for the next 70 years. It requires a party calling an expert witness to demonstrate that the scientific theory or technique on which he relies has been endorsed by a substantial majority of specialists in his field.[64] Although the court did not articulate a policy rationale for what was to become a national standard, the *post hoc* justification for *Frye* was that it guaranteed the reliability of scientific evidence by banning novel, avant-garde theories in favour of tried, tested, well established techniques.[65] The specific concern to which *Frye* was directed was the competency of lay jurors to critically evaluate expert scientific evidence. The effect of the test is to place in the hands of the relevant scientific community the determination of whether the predicate science is valid and reliable. The D.C. Circuit explained in a later case: "The requirement of general acceptance in the scientific community assures that those most qualified to assess the general

---

Cambridge, Mass., 1999); E.J. Imwinkelried *et al., Courtroom Criminal Evidence* (3rd ed., Lexis, Charlottesville, Virginia, 1998), chap.6.

62 293 F. 1013 (D.C. Cir. 1923).

63 293 F. at 1014.

64 Imwinkelried, *op. cit.,* p.84.

65 *Id.*

validity of a scientific method will have a determinative voice."[66] As Imwinkelried notes, the consequences of the test were far reaching:

> "*Frye* represents a step beyond general deference to experts. In effect, *Frye* delegates the decision to the pertinent community of experts. The dispositive question is whether a substantial majority of them accept the theory as valid. Unless they do, testimony based on the theory is automatically inadmissible; even if the attorney proffering the testimony can point to experimentation supposedly verifying the theory, the jurors and judges are deemed incompetent to properly evaluate the research data."[67]

Although widely applied, *Frye* was the subject of ongoing controversy. Some courts, fearing the loss of valuable, reliable evidence, began to limit the scope of the test, for example, by refusing to apply it to evidence presented as "non-scientific" expertise and to evidence from so-called "soft" scientists, such as mental health experts. The result was a patchwork quilt of admissibility practice in which *Frye* could be seemingly applied with rigour or not at all.

In 1993, the decision of the United States Supreme Court in *Daubert v. Merrell Dow Pharmaceuticals, Inc.*[68] signalled a seachange in the American law on expert scientific evidence. The case was one of many challenges brought by plaintiff children against the defendant pharmaceutical manufacturer alleging that limb defects registered at birth had been caused by the plaintiffs' mothers' ingestion during pregnancy of the anti-nausea drug Bendectin. The plaintiffs presented the evidence of 8 experts who based their conclusions that the drug can cause human birth defects on animal studies, chemical structure analyses, and the unpublished reanalysis of previously published human statistical studies. The federal trial court determined that this evidence did not meet the *Frye* general acceptance standard for the admission of expert scientific evidence and granted summary judgment in favour of the defendants. The Court of Appeals for the Ninth Circuit affirmed citing *Frye* as the

---

66 *United States v. Addison,* 498 F.2d 741, 743-44 (D.C. Cir. 1974).

67 *Op. cit.,* at p.87.

68 509 U.S. 579, 113 S.Ct. 2786, 125 L.Ed.2d 469 (1993).

applicable standard. The U.S. Supreme Court declined to follow suit and instead announced a new standard for the admissibility of scientific evidence.

The lynchpin of the Supreme Court's judgment was the enactment by Congress in 1975 of a statutory codification of the rules of evidence for the federal courts. Federal Rule of Evidence 702, governing expert evidence, provided:

> "If scientific, technical, or other specialized knowledge will assist the trier of fact to understand the evidence or to determine a fact in issue, a witness qualified as an expert by knowledge, skill, experience, training, or education, may testify thereto in the form of an opinion or otherwise."[69]

Blackmun J., speaking for the majority of the Court, noted that the federal rules had superseded the common law of evidence and concluded that nothing in the text of Rule 702 nor its drafting history supported the assertion that Congress had intended to incorporate a general acceptance standard. He continued:

> "... [A] rigid 'general acceptance' requirement would be at odds with the 'liberal thrust' of the Federal Rules and their 'general approach of relaxing the traditional barriers to 'opinion' testimony.' Given the Rules' permissive backdrop and their inclusion of a specific rule on expert testimony that does not mention 'general acceptance,' the assertion that the Rules somehow assimilated *Frye* is unconvincing. *Frye* made 'general acceptance' the exclusive test for admitting expert scientific testimony. That austere standard, absent from and incompatible with the Federal Rules of Evidence, should not be applied in federal trials."[70]

The displacement of the *Frye* test by the Federal Rules did not leave the matter unresolved, however. Blackmun J. confirmed that the Federal Rules oblige a trial judge to ensure that any scientific evidence admitted at trial

---

69 F.R.E. 702 (1975).

70 509 U.S. 579 at 588-589 (internal quotations and citations omitted).

is both relevant and reliable. In the latter regard, Blackmun J. derived a new standard from the text of Rule 702 itself, "which clearly contemplates some degree of regulation of the subjects and theories about which an expert may testify."[71] Focusing on a methodological definition of the term "scientific knowledge," he posited a standard of empirical validation:

> "[I]n order to qualify as 'scientific knowledge,' an inference or assertion must be derived by the scientific method. Proposed testimony must be supported by an appropriate validation – i.e., 'good grounds,' based on what is known. In short, the requirement that an expert's testimony pertain to 'scientific knowledge' establishes a standard of evidentiary reliability."[72]

The majority opinion of Blackmun J. is itself illustrative of the complex terrain which the Supreme Court had opened up to the federal trial courts. The opinion contains a rich tapestry of references to scientific sources, including the works of scientists, scientific philosophers, and medical experts. In his dissenting opinion, Rehnquist C.J. doubted that the Federal rules imposed on federal trial judges "either the obligation or the authority to become amateur scientists".[73] Blackmun J., in contrast, expressed his confidence that federal judges "possess the capacity to undertake this review".[74] Emphasising that the inquiry is a flexible one, he offered, by way of guidance, the following non-exhaustive list of factors which a trial judge might take into account in determining admissibility:

> (1) Whether the theory or technique can be tested;
> (2) Whether the theory or technique has been tested;
> (3) Whether the theory or technique has been subjected to peer review and publication;
> (4) Whether the theory or technique has a known or potential rate of error;

---

71 *Id.*, at 589.
72 *Id.*, at 590.
73 *Id.*, at 600-601. Rehnquist C.J. was joined by Stevens J.
74 *Id.*, at 593.

(5) Whether the theory or technique has been generally accepted within the relevant scientific community.[75]

The *Daubert* decision revolutionised expert evidentiary practice and its far-reaching effects were soon felt throughout the federal and state courts.[76] It is a great deal broader in its application than the pre-existing *Frye* standard. Whereas the general acceptance test had been directed primarily at novel science, *Daubert* requires proponents of all forms of scientific evidence to empirically validate their theories. The fact that a technique is well established within the scientific community may be a factor but it is still incumbent on a party to lay the necessary foundation for its admission at trial. It is ironic, therefore, that *Daubert* may have lowered the bar for the admission of novel scientific techniques but raised the benchmark overall for the broader constituency of scientific evidence. The scope of the *Daubert* standard is also more expansive in so far as Blackmun J. favoured a definition of science that was sufficiently broad to cover soft as well as hard science.[77] The practice of exempting categories of experts from the admissibility inquiry which had become so prevalent under *Frye* was in any event foreclosed by the subsequent decision of the U.S. Supreme Court in *Kumho Tire Co. Ltd. v. Carmichael*.[78] Breyer J. delivering the opinion for the Court, held that the need to demonstrate reliability was not limited to scientific testimony but applied to any form of expert knowledge proffered pursuant to Federal Rule 702.[79]

Controversy over expert scientific evidence has not abated in the

---

75 509 U.S. 579 at 593-594.

76 *Frye* remains the governing standard in a minority of the States. Imwinkelried, *op.cit.*, pp.85-86.

77 *Id.*, pp. 99-100.

78 526 U.S. 137, 119 S. Ct. 1167, 143 L.Ed.2d 238 (1999).

79 In 2000, F.R.E. 702 was amended to incorporate *Daubert* and *Kumho*. It now states: "If scientific, technical or other specialized knowledge will assist the trier of fact to understand the evidence or determine a fact in issue, a witness qualified as an expert by knowledge, skill, experience, training, or education, may testify thereto in the form of an opinion or otherwise, if (1) the testimony is based upon sufficient facts or data, (2) the testimony is the product of reliable principles and methods, and (3) the witness has applied the principles and methods reliably to the facts of the case."

United States. *Daubert* has had the beneficial effect of raising standards in relation to the admissibility of such evidence but it has created in the process a highly contestable and contested element of trial practice. If *Frye* required judges to defer to the views of the relevant scientific community, *Daubert* reversed that trend and, over a decade later, opinions are divided on the suitability of judges as assessors of scientific validity. Of course, general acceptance remains an element within *Daubert's* foundational mix and the suggestion has been made that the difference between the two standards is far greater in theory than in practice depending upon how judges interpret the terms "scientific knowledge" and "general acceptance".[80]

American practice has the merit of rendering explicit and transparent the reception of scientific evidence and raising the standard for its admission. Moreover, *Daubert* has spawned a national discourse among judges, lawyers and academics which has arguably enhanced the consistency and predictability of the law in this field. At the same time, it has made the reliability of expert evidence a mainstay of pre-trial admissibility practice. Experts continue to dominate American trial practice but the battle lines are now drawn at admissibility. Although juries adjudicate the majority of criminal and civil trials in the United States, they are not privy to admissibility contests of this kind; the determination whether to admit scientific evidence lies in the hands of the judge and, consequently, the jury will never read or hear scientific evidence that has failed to pass the judge's *Daubert* inquiry. Where scientific evidence is admitted, it then becomes the source of a further contest between the parties in the context of the weight of the evidence. Thus, under *Daubert*, expert scientific evidence remains a complex, contested and costly aspect of trial practice.

(b) An Irish *Daubert*?

The *ad hoc* approach to the reliability of expert scientific evidence that characterises Irish practice provides courts with a degree of flexibility. There is a danger, however, that the absence of a prominent gatekeeping function on the part of trial judges may facilitate the admission of scientific evidence regardless of its reliability. In a system that emphasises trial, as

---

80 Foster and Huber, *op.cit.*, pp.226-228.

opposed to pre-trial, procedures, the assessment of scientific evidence is left in the hands of the jury at the close of the proceedings. When instructing the jury, the judge summarises the scientific evidence, along with the other evidence in the case, pointing to strengths and weaknesses and explaining the limits of the jury's inquiry. However, by virtue of the secrecy of jury deliberations, the manner in which juries assess scientific evidence and their conclusions in relation to the weight of that evidence remain within the realm of speculation. By its nature, a regime that is both *laissez faire* in relation to the admissibility of scientific evidence and closed-door in relation to its ultimate use raises the spectre of inconsistency and unpredictability in practice. The consequences may include unnecessary complexity at trial and an inescapable toll in terms of the cost of the proceedings. Viewed against this backdrop, Imwinkelried's suggestion that Ireland incorporate a *Daubert* admissibility requirement seems an attractive alternative that holds the promise of systematic, rigorous scrutiny of expert scientific evidence, increased certainty in expert practice, and overall savings in terms of costs.

The difficulties involved in introducing a *Daubert* admissibility requirement in the Irish courts become apparent, however, when one begins to unearth the complexities of trans-Atlantic comparative analysis. Although the Irish and American systems have a great deal in common, they are also characterised by marked differences which have a significant bearing on the present discussion. The volume of American litigation is staggering and is fed by a miscellany of factors including population, geography, language and culture. The rules of evidence are codified and, as such, provide the starting point for an explicit discourse among judges concerning virtually every aspect of the law of evidence which is facilitated by the widespread use of databases by courts nationwide. In short, the extensive, detailed debate in the United States over expert scientific evidence is indicative of the penetrating reach of litigation in that jurisdiction and the extent to which evidentiary issues are contested and judicially determined.

A more trenchant objection to a *Daubert* admissibility requirement lies in procedural differences between Irish and American trial practice. American federal trial practice contains important mechanisms designed to encourage the resolution of proceedings in advance of trial. In particular, the federal rules of evidence require judges to examine the reliability of expert evidence and in cases involving forensic scientific evidence this frequently necessitates the convening of a pre-trial evidentiary hearing. Indeed the general emphasis in American practice on pre-trial procedure is such that by the time that a case comes on for trial in a federal courtroom, many of the contestable issues relating to the evidence have already been the subject of challenge and adjudication. Of course, any evidence deemed admissible will be further challenged before the judge and jury during the course of the trial but solely in terms of its weight rather than its admissibility.

Irish trial procedure contains no equivalent, threshold, pre-trial mechanisms for the resolution of proceedings. Nor does the system generally emphasise pre-trial practice in a manner akin to its American counterpart. Even if the courts were amenable to the introduction of a *Daubert* admissibility requirement, which is doubtful, it must be conceded that the Irish system would be far less procedurally accommodating. Whereas Irish courts routinely assess the need for expert evidence and the credentials of the expert witness as matters of admissibility, the proposed inquiry into the reliability of the evidence would likely be considerable more lengthy and complex.

None of these factors represents an insurmountable challenge to the introduction of a *Daubert* admissibility requirement. Nevertheless, coupled with the general reluctance on the part of judges in this jurisdiction (and, indeed, in other common law jurisdictions such as England and Canada) to introduce new admissibility requirements, they suggest a pessimistic outlook for this particular reform.[81]

This may be room, however, for a compromise position, namely, the use by courts of *Daubert*'s empirical validation requirement as a standard for assessing the weight of scientific evidence in deciding the ultimate issues in a case. This could be done with relative ease in civil cases where judges sit without juries and decide issues of fact as well as law. If judges were to begin to refer systematically to such a standard and, for example, to apply the non-exhaustive *Daubert* factors, lawyers would doubtless follow suit in constructing cases, and experts in detailing their methodologies and formulating their conclusions. This would not require

---

[81] Alldridge, *op.cit.*, p.155 argues that sooner or later it will be necessary to take the American lead and adopt a test to identify appropriate scientific evidence. However, he questions the American conclusion that courts are appropriate bodies for the application of that test.

any dramatic change in existing civil practice but it would likely have the welcome, beneficial effects of clarifying law and practice and raising standards in relation to expert scientific evidence. The application of a reform of this kind in the criminal realm would be less straightforward, however, and at a minimum would require the use by judges of clear and consistent instructions to juries on summing up.

Chapter 3

Fingerprinting

Introduction

Of the various forensic techniques used to establish facts in a court of law, fingerprinting or dactyloscopy is the oldest and also the most embedded in the public consciousness. First developed in the late 19th century, the classification of the ridge patterns on the palm side of the fingers and thumbs has become a defining, universal aspect of crime detection in the modern age. A form of physical evidence, fingerprints discovered at a crime scene are used primarily by law enforcement to link a suspect to a crime.[1]

The process comprises several distinct stages. Scene of the crime officers use highly specialised equipment and techniques to visualise and lift the prints and subsequently preserve them for purposes of examination. A fingerprint expert then compares the prints with prints taken from the suspect. This involves classifying the finger-ridge patterns of both sets of prints under a recognised classification system and then establishing a point-to-point comparison. The use of computerised systems that can digitally record prints and search databases for potential matches has eased and expedited the expert's task in this regard. The expert's determination of a fingerprint match, or the absence of same, may be used as an investigative tool to identify, confirm or eliminate a suspect from an investigation. The fingerprints serve an additional, evidentiary function where the expert subsequently presents his opinion at trial as to the inferences that may be drawn from the presence of the prints at the crime scene.

Fingerprints are by no means the only impression that may be left at a crime scene whether by an individual or an object: footprints, ear prints

---

[1] Fingerprints may also serve other ends such as identifying an offender as the holder of previous convictions for purposes of sentencing, tracing the movements of the victim of an abduction, or identifying a corpse.

and lip prints are among a miscellany of impressions which may ultimately be offered in evidence at trial. Nevertheless, fingerprinting remains the doyen of identification by virtue of the confidence which courts have placed in the reliability of its scientific premises. Although fingerprint testimony represents the subjective opinion of the expert, fingerprint experts have traditionally tendered statements of identity in more positive and assertive terms than experts in other forensic fields such as hair, fibre and soil.[2] This authoritative tone has inspired judicial confidence but the willingness of courts to admit fingerprint evidence also rests on certain important assumptions about the predicate science itself: first, that fingerprints are unique in that no two fingers have yet been found to possess the same characteristics; second, that fingerprints are permanent and will remain unchanged during an individual's lifetime; third, that fingerprints may be transferred to surfaces; and, fourth, that fingerprints may be systematically classified.[3] These virtues explain a preference for fingerprints over other impressions as a means of establishing identity and, by extension, the use of fingerprinting techniques in the detection and analysis of such other impressions.[4]

At the same time, the use of fingerprints in the forensic process is subject to obvious limitations. The function of fingerprinting as an investigative tool is limited to identifying a suspect or confirming or refuting the identity of a suspect. The technique is of little or no use in situations where law enforcement has not identified a suspect and a search of a computer database, such as a database recording the prints of previous

---

2 T. F. Kiely, *Forensic Evidence: Science and the Criminal Law* (CRC Press, Boca Raton, Florida, 2001), p.223.

3 *See generally* R. Saferstein, *Criminalistics: An Introduction to Forensic Science*, 7th ed. (Prentice-Hall, Upper Saddle River, New Jersey, 2000), chap.14; S. H. James and J.J. Nordby, eds., *Forensic Science: An Introduction to Scientific and Investigative Techniques* (CRC Press, Boca Raton, Florida, 2003), chap.15; C. Champod, C. Lennard, P. Margot and M. Stoilovic, *Fingerprints and Other Ridge Skin Impressions* (Boca Raton, Florida, CRC Press, 2004); Interpol 14th International Forensic Science Symposium, Lyon, 19-22 October 2004, Review Papers (N. Nic Daéid, ed.), pp.6-21 (hereinafter IFSS 2004). The basic fingerprint patterns are genetically determined and are influenced by various factors including race. G.A. Vignaux and B. Robertson, *Interpreting Evidence: Evaluating Forensic Science in the Courtroom* (Wiley & Sons, Chichester, West Sussex, 1995), p.139.

4 P. C. Giannelli and E.J. Imwinkelried, *Scientific Evidence*, 3rd ed. (Lexis Law Publishing, Charlottesville, Virginia, 1999), p.740.

offenders, fails to reveal a match. In other words, fingerprints do not assist in the investigation of the manifold facts other than identity that are relevant to the commission of the crime. The one extended or collateral issue on which some fingerprint experts have been willing to opine is the age of an impression, *i.e.* whether the prints are fresh or whether they have been present at the crime scene for some determinable time. Even here, however, experts are divided as to the certainty with which such pronouncements may be made.[5]

The use of fingerprint evidence is also affected by conditions in investigative practice. Prints recovered at a crime scene tend to be partial rather than full impressions which limits the range of available ridge characteristics and, consequently, the extent of the expert's fingerprint comparison. The location of prints at a crime scene can create further difficulties. Where the prints appear on surfaces such as blood, that have independent forensic value, particular care must be taken to ensure that the retrieval of the prints does not alter or disturb the underlying surface.

Reliance on fingerprint evidence has waned somewhat in contemporary practice in response to two significant developments. First, whereas fingerprints remain the preferred form of impression evidence, the dominance of fingerprinting as a general method of criminal identification has been eclipsed by the advent of DNA. Because DNA resides and may be detected in the full range of tissue and bodily fluids, it is a more ubiquitous and flexible forensic source than fingerprints. In addition, DNA analysis constitutes a more sophisticated and, ultimately, discerning process than fingerprint analysis. Finally, the expert testimony of the DNA analyst may be perceived to be more objective than that of the fingerprint expert.[6] The second contemporary development cuts to the very heart of fingerprinting as an evidentiary tool. Assumptions about the infallibility of fingerprint identification have been called into question in recent years. The revelation of errors in certain cases coupled with empirical studies on the proficiency of fingerprint experts[7] suggest the need for greater caution on the part of courts in assessing the admissibility of fingerprint evidence. These developments dovetail with an emerging

---

5 *Id.*, p.283; Kiely, *op. cit.*, pp.226-229.

6 Law Reform Commission, *Consultation Paper on the Establishment of a DNA Database,* LRC 29-2004, para. 1.11.

7 Giannelli and Imwinkelried, *op. cit.,* pp.740-41.

trend within the fingerprint profession of critically re-evaluating the scientific foundation for fingerprint identification.[8]

Origins and History

Throughout the centuries, fingerprints have been have been employed by societies across the globe for multifarious purposes. The use of finger impressions for the ceremonial sealing of contracts is said to extend to China in the third century B.C. and, more remotely, ancient Babylon in the twentieth century B.C.[9] The origins fingerprinting as a criminal investigative tool are customarily traced back to the scientific endeavours of certain individuals in the second half of the nineteenth century. In 1858, William Herschel, a British administrator in India, began the practice of recording the handprints of local inhabitants on contracts as a means combating fraud. Herschel sought but was denied permission to employ his fingerprinting technique in the jails but, over the next two decades, he continued to conduct limited experiments designed to demonstrate the unchanging characteristics of fingerprints.[10] In 1880, Henry Fauld, a Scottish missionary physician based in Japan, published a series of articles in the journal *Nature* advocating the use of fingerprints in the detection of crime. Herschel responded and an open correspondence between the two men ensued[11] which sowed the seeds for the first textbook on the subject, *Finger Prints,* published by the biologist Francis Galton in 1892.[12] Galton's pioneering work explored the anatomy of fingerprints and presaged the modern science of fingerprint identification. It was Galton who developed the first rudimentary system for the classification of fingerprints based on the three fingerprint patterns – loops, arches and

---

8 Champod *et al*, *op. cit.*, p.204.

9 A. A. Moenssens, *Fingerprints and the Law* (Chilton Book Co., Philadelphia, 1969), p.1. *See also* G. Lambourne, *The Fingerprint Story* (Harrap Ltd, London, 1984), chap.1; N. O'Connor, *Cracking Crime: Jim Donovan–Forensic Detective* (O'Brien Press, Dublin, 2000), pp.89–99; D. Campbell, "Fingerprints: A Review" [1985] Crim. L. R. 195.

10 Moenssens, *op. cit.*, pp.28-33.

11 *Id.*, pp.36-37 and 52-53.

12 *Id.*, p.41. The following year, Galton published a supplement entitled *Decipherment of Blurred Finger Tips.*

whorls – which remains the touchstone of contemporary systems. Galton is also credited with first positing the notion that fingerprints are unique and unchanging.[13]

The development of fingerprinting as a criminal investigative tool was by no means the preserve of the English, however. Working independently and simultaneously, experts in other countries were proposing and testing means of human identification. The most elaborate of such systems, known as anthropometry, was introduced in France by a senior police officer, Alphonse Bertillon in 1883. Bertillon's theory was that the basic dimensions of the human skeleton remain unchanged during adult life; by recording in detail a dozen or so anatomical measurements, such as height, width of head, and length of foot, law enforcement officers could compare the physical profile of current suspects with recorded data in the hope of finding a match. The recording of fingerprints was later used in conjunction with anthropometry[14] and eventually overtook the Bertillon system as the most convenient and accurate means of criminal identification.[15]

Fingerprinting innovations were also causing ripples in the Americas. In 1891, Dr. Juan Vucetich, an Argentinian police officer, developed a fingerprint classification system that is still used in most Spanish-speaking countries today.[16] The following year, a judicial precedent was set when the system was used to secure the conviction of Francesca Rojas, for the murder of her two sons.[17] In the United States, fingerprinting was introduced by the New York Civil Service Commission in 1901 to certify applications to the civil service.[18] At the 1904 World's Fair in St. Louis, several American police officials were instructed in the technique by

---

[13] Saferstein, *op. cit.,* p.396.

[14] An example is Bertillon's investigation into the murder of Joseph Reibel in Paris in 1902 which culminated in the conviction of Henri Scheffer. Moessens, *op. cit.*, p.33.

[15] Saferstein, *op. cit.*, p.396 notes that the Bertillon system began to fall into disfavour in the early 20th century due to two revelations: the propensity for error in the taking of measurements by persons not adequately trained in the task and, in 1903, the inability of the system to clearly distinguish William West, a convict at Fort Leavenworth prison, from an inmate of similar appearance.

[16] Moenssens, *op. cit.,* p.7.

[17] *Id.,* pp.31-33.

[18] Saferstein, *op. cit.,* p.396; Moessens, *op. cit.,* pp.7-9.

detectives from New Scotland Yard and, in the years that followed, fingerprinting was adopted by the police departments in all the major cities.[19] In 1924, the Identification Division of the newly formed Federal Bureau of Investigation established a centralised fingerprint collection with the receipt of over 8 million files, mostly from Leavenworth Penitentiary.[20]

In late nineteenth century England, Galton's discoveries emerged against a backdrop of dissatisfaction with existing methods of identifying criminals. The details of recently released convicts, including distinctive physical marks, were published annually in a Habitual Criminals Register maintained in London.[21] Though useful in its day, the detailed and elaborate Register was too cumbersome and imprecise to satisfy the needs of the Metropolitan Police. The Register failed to distinguish the habitual criminal from the first-time offender and led in practice both to erroneous identifications and failures to identify previous offenders. A committee chaired by Charles Troup of the Home Office was charged with exploring the possible introduction of either the Bertillon system or Galton's fingerprint system. Ultimately, the committee recommended a compromise in the form of a proposed Anthropometric Registry within Scotland Yard which would combine the five major measurements of the Bertillon system with the use of fingerprints.[22]

The strength of Galton's contribution lay in the identification of distinctive ridge patterns on the palm side of the fingers and thumbs; its weakness was the lack of a systematic means of classifying and filing fingerprints on a large scale. The development of a versatile, standardised classification regime was essential if the promise of fingerprinting was to be realised in criminal investigative practice. This lacuna was filled by the seminal work of Edward Henry, Herscehel's successor in India, who laid the foundation for the contemporary classification systems employed in England, the United States and Canada. Building on Galton's tripartite division of fingerprint patterns (into loops, arches and whorls),

---

19 Saferstein, *op. cit.*, p.396; Moessens, *op. cit.*, p.9.

20 Kiely, *op. cit.*, p.219. Today, the FBI collection houses over 250 million files of prints recorded for criminal and civil purposes. *Id.*

21 Under the Habitual Criminals Act 1869 and later the Prevention of Crimes Act 1871. *See* Lambourne, *op. cit.*, p.41.

22 *Id.*, p.49.

Henry converted ridge patterns on all ten fingers and thumbs into a series of letters and numbers arranged in the form of a fraction.[23] The code, which enabled experts to locate a set of prints in one of 1,024 possible categories, provided an effective and efficient, standardised means of reducing the number of a suspects in a criminal investigation. Adopted by Scotland Yard in 1901, Henry's system underscored the potential superiority of fingerprinting over the Bertillon system as a means of criminal identification. The transition from anthropometry to dactyloscopy was also secured through the efforts of French scientist, Edmond Locard. Having spent several years comprehensively reviewing both identification methodologies, Locard determined that the future lay in fingerprinting. Whereas the optimum utility of Henry's system turned on the availability of a full set of fingerprints, Locard recognised that the impressions retrieved from crime scenes are typically only single or even partial prints. It was Locard who formulated in 1914 the first response to the perennial question of the minimum number of ridge characteristics or minutiae that are necessary to support a fingerprint identification.[24]

Early Common Law Cases

India was the location in which fingerprint pioneers William Herschel and Edward Henry developed their theories and conducted their empirical studies. It was also one of the first jurisdictions in which the embryonic science received legislative and judicial recognition. In 1899, section 45 of the Indian Evidence Act 1872 was amended to facilitate the admission in court of expert opinion as to the identity of finger impressions.[25] Fingerprints had been in use as a criminal investigative tool for some time when the first cases upholding its admissibility as a form of evidence were reported in the early years of the twentieth century.[26]

The first reported English decision on the subject was the 1915 case

---

[23] Saferstein, *op. cit.*, p.402. Henry's book entitled *Classification and Uses of Fingerprints* was published in 1899.

[24] Champod *et al*, *op. cit.*, p.26.

[25] Cited in Moessens, *op. cit.*, p.31.

[26] *Emperor v. Sahdeo* 3 Nagpur L. Rep. 1 (India) (1904); *Emperor v. Abdul Hamid* 32 Indian L.R. [Calc.Ser.] 759 (1905) cited in Moessens, *op. cit.*, pp.34-36.

of *R v. Bacon* in which the appellant, having been sentenced to 15 months hard labour, submitted that his eight previous convictions were not properly attributable to him. On the evidence of a fingerprint expert, the court was persuaded that the appellant had indeed collected these previous convictions while operating under a number of assumed names.[27] There followed in 1907, the case of *Coleman v. Rex* in which the admissibility of fingerprint evidence at trial was discussed for the first time.[28] The accused was convicted of burglary, the sole evidence against him at trial being an expert comparison of his fingerprints with latent prints found on the glass pane of a window of the house which had been burgled. He contended that the recording of his fingerprints by the police constituted compelled testimony against interest and that it violated the privilege against self incrimination. The court demurred on the basis that the accused had consented to the procedure and held that the prints were akin to a voluntary confession. Two years later, the Court of Appeal handed down a landmark decision in *Rex v. Castleton*.[29] Here also, the charge was one of burglary and the prosecution evidence consisted solely of a fingerprint allegedly left by the accused on a candle found at the scene of the crime. On appeal against conviction, the Lord Chief Justice recognised the admissibility of expert fingerprint comparison as a species of evidence. Moreover, the court rejected the accused's contention that the fingerprint evidence, standing alone, was an insufficient evidentiary edifice on which to rest his conviction. This holding was echoed in the 1912 Australian case of *Parker v. Rex*[30] in which the Supreme Court of Victoria noted the general acceptance of fingerprint evidence and determined in the case before it that the fingerprint comparison had constituted in itself sufficient evidence to go to the jury.

In the United States, the 1911 decision of the Illinois Supreme Court in *People v. Jennings*[31] was the first judicial landmark on the admissibility of fingerprint evidence. Thomas Jennings was charged with the murder

---

27 [1915] 11 Crim. App. R. 90. *See* Campbell, *op. cit.*, p.196.

28 [1907] Trans. L.R. (Sup. Ct.).

29 [1909] 3 Crim. App. R. (Cohen) 74. For a discussion of the case see (1911) 1 J. Crim. L. & Criminology 848.

30 [1912] 14 C.L.R. 681, 3 B.R.C. 68. *See also Hamilton v. H.M. Advocate* [1934] S.C. (J) 1; *H.M. Advocate v. Rolley* [1944] S.C. (J) 154.

31 252 Ill. 534, 96 N.E. 1077 (1911).

of Clarence Hiller who had been shot in his home by an intruder. The prosecution's case at trial was that, in the early hours of a Monday morning, Jennings had entered the house through a kitchen window from which he had first removed the window screen. The back porch, adjacent to the window, had been painted on the Saturday prior to the shooting, and the imprint of four fingers of a left hand was found on the railing of the porch in the fresh paint. Officers from the identification bureau of the Chicago Police Department removed the railing in the early morning after the murder and enlarged photographs were made of the prints. Eyewitnesses identified Jennings and he was arrested and fingerprinted. He had also been fingerprinted the previous year after he had been returned to the penitentiary for a parole violation. These impressions were enlarged for the purpose of comparison with the enlarged photographs of the prints on the railing. Included in the array of prosecution evidence at trial was the testimony of four fingerprint experts that, in their opinion, Jennings's prints matched the prints on the railing. Jennings was convicted of murder and one of the many grounds on which he appealed was that the trial judge had erred in admitting the fingerprint evidence. His challenged was directed not at the techniques whereby the fingerprints had been retrieved, visualised or compared but rather at the admissibility of the evidence *per se*.[32] His argument was simply that nothing in the common law or statute authorised the admission of this information as evidence in a court of law.

The Illinois Supreme Court acknowledged that the admissibility of fingerprint evidence was a question of first impression in the United States. Nevertheless, standard scientific authorities had discussed the use of fingerprints as a system of identification and had concluded that experience had shown it to be reliable. The use of the technique had become widespread in both American and foreign police departments and, in particular, had achieved notable success in England. The court recognised that fingerprinting represented novel scientific evidence but drew an analogy with other means of proof, such as photographs, X-rays and microscopy, which though initially approached with scepticism were now routinely admitted in courts of law. In the present case, each of four expert witnesses had considerable experience in fingerprint identification at the behest of law enforcement and each had testified as to the scientific

[32] Kiely, *op. cit.*, p.221.

basis for their conclusions. On the basis of their evidence and the authorities to which it had been referred, the court concluded:

> "We are disposed to hold from the evidence of the four witnesses who testified, and from the writings we have referred to on this subject, that there is a scientific basis for the system of finger print identification, and that the courts are justified in admitting this class of evidence; that this method of identification is in such general and common use that the courts cannot refuse to take judicial cognizance of it. Such evidence may or may not be of independent strength, but it is admissible, the same as other proof, as tending to make out a case."[33]

In addition, the court determined that "the classification of finger print impressions and their method of identification is a science requiring study". As such, it constitutes a field of expertise outside the common experience of persons in ordinary walks of life and one in which the trial court and jurors were properly assisted by expert opinion.[34]

Jennings was followed in 1918 by the decision of the Supreme Court of Nevada in *State v. Kuhl*[35] confirming the admissibility of palmprints as a form of identification evidence. Kuhl was convicted of the first degree murder of a mail stage driver and sentenced to death. The prosecution's evidence was entirely circumstantial and included the testimony of expert witnesses that the bloody impression of the palm of a human hand found on an envelope in one of the rifled mail sacks had been made by Kuhl. On appeal, Kuhl's challenges to the admission of the palmprint evidence and the use by the expert witnesses of a projectoscope and photographic enlargements at trial were roundly rejected. The Supreme Court held that there is no basic difference between fingerprints and palmprints and that experts schooled in the former are competent to deliver opinion evidence on the latter. As is the case with other forms of expert evidence, the weight to be attributed to such testimony is a matter for the jury to determine. As regards the expert's presentation at trial, the court concluded

---

33 252 Ill. 534 at 549.

34 *Id.,* at 549.

35 42 Nev. 195, 175 Pac. 190 (1918).

that it was within the discretion of the trial judge to permit the use of technical equipment to illustrate the proffered opinion.

In *Kuhl,* the Supreme Court of Nevada observed *obiter dicta* that the sole of the human foot bears the same, unchanging ridge patterns that exist on the palm of the hand. The use of footprints as a means of criminal identification was the subject of considerable dispute among experts[36] and it was not until 1938 that a higher court, the Supreme Judicial Court of Massachusetts, upheld the admissibility of footprint evidence in *Commonwealth v. Bartolini.*[37] Again, the comparability of footprint identification with the scientific technique of fingerprinting provided the necessary justification for judicial recognition of this novel form of evidence.

The Scientific Basis of Fingerprint Evidence[38]

(a) Fingerprints

The term "fingerprints" refers to the distinctive areas of friction ridge skin which appear on the palm side of human fingers and thumbs at the end joints. These areas are characterised by clusters of ridges and furrows which form the three basic fingerprint patterns first identified by Galton, namely, loops, arches and whorls. Each of the three categories subdivides into more specific sub-categories, such as plain or tented arches, radial or ulnar loops and, within the most complex whorl category, plain, central pocket or accidental whorls.[39] In the case of loops and whorls, the individuality of prints is further underscored by the presence of so-called core and delta features.[40] From an evidentiary point of view, the key to

---

36 Moessens, *op. cit.,* p.207.

37 299 Mass. 503, 13 N.E. 2d 382, *cert. denied* 304 U.S. 562 (1938).

38 The discussion in this section does not purport to constitute an authoritative scientific account and should not be construed as such. Readers should consult the forensic scientific authorities cited herein and similar sources elsewhere.

39 R. Gaensslen and K.R. Young, "Fingerprints" in S.H. James and J.J. Nordby, eds., *Forensic Science: An Introduction to Scientific and Investigative Techniques* (Boca Raton, Florida, CRC Press, 2003), p.278; Saferstein, *op. cit.*, p.401.

40 Gaensslen and Young, *op. cit.*, p.278.

fingerprint identification lies in yet other definable, unchanging[41] ridge characteristics known as minutiae which appear either individually or in combination in three basic forms: a dot (a short ridge), an ending ridge (a ridge ends abruptly) and birfucation (a ridge splits in two).[42]

Friction skin ridges are dotted with pores through which sweat glands secrete perspiration. A fingerprint impression is formed when the skin touches a surface on which the perspiration and any accompanying oils are deposited, duplicating the ridge pattern.[43] Most prints are deposited in this fashion and are classified as "latent prints" because they are ordinarily invisible to the eye and must be rendered visible by a form of physical or chemical treatment or illumination.[44] In contrast, prints that have been left on materials such as blood, ink, paint or grease ("visible" or "patent" prints) or on soft materials such as butter, putty, wax or soap ("plastic prints") typically do not require such additional methods of enhancement.[45]

(b) Latent fingerprint enhancement

The processing of latent prints has benefited from extensive scientific research and technological development over the past several decades. A multiplicity of methods for developing, enhancing and visualising pints are available depending upon the nature of the surface encountered at the crime scene.[46] Powder dusting is one of the oldest physical methods of fingerprint detection for hard surfaces such as glass, metal or tile. Fine-grained particles of powder adhere to the fingerprint residue creating a

---

[41] It is impossible to change one's fingerprints and extremely difficult to obliterate or obscure them. Saferstein, *op. cit.*, p.400 cites the example of gangster John Dillinger who applied corrosive acid to his fingers in an unsuccessful attempt to destroy his prints.

[42] Gaensslen and Young, *op. cit.*, p.279.

[43] E.R. Menzel, "The Development of Fingerprints" in E.J. Imwinkjelried, ed., *Scientific and Expert Evidence,* 2nd ed. (Practising Law Institute, New York, 1981), p.621; W.R. Harrison, "The Detection of Fingerprints on Documents" (1958) Crim. L.R. 591, p.51.

[44] *Id;* Saferstein, *op. cit.*, p.400; Champod *et al*, *op. cit.,* pp.106-07.

[45] *Id.*, p.406; Gaensslen and Young, *op. cit* at p.285. For a discussion of the Lisdoonvarna "glove of flesh" case in which prints were retrieved from a layer of flesh left inside a glove in the wake of a fire, *see* O'Connor, *op. cit.*, p.91.

[46] IFSS 2004, *op. cit.*, pp.14-20 (citing scientific references).

contrast between the ridges and background that may be further enhanced through the use of a magnetic brush.[47]

In the case of porous surfaces such as paper, cardboard and fabrics, chemical techniques are preferred. The classic example is iodine fuming whereby an object or surface suspected of housing latent prints is exposed to iodine fumes.[48] Fats and oily substances in the print residue absorb the iodine vapours resulting in a brownish stain.[49] A prevalent chemical technique for the visualisation of latent prints involves the use of the agent ninhydrin which reacts to the amino acids in the fingerprint residue by forming a purple-blue colour. The ninhydrin solution is typically sprayed onto the porous surface from an aerosol can and the prints appear within hours or, in the case of weaker prints, days.[50] In the case of porous surfaces that have been wet at one time, a silver nitrate based chemical known as "physical developer" has gained widespread use.[51] Super glue enhancement is another popular chemical technique, particularly as an initial step in the development of latent fingerprints. Based on the interaction between super glue fumes and print residue, the technique is operationally similar to iodine fuming and produces a friction ridge impression that is off-white in colour.[52] Unlike other chemical techniques,

---

47 *Id.*, p.287; Menzel, *op. cit* at pp.621-22; Saferstein, *op. cit.*, p.406; Giannelli and Imwinkelried, *op. cit.*, pp.743-44; Champod *et al*, *op. cit.*, pp.136-38.

48 Champod *et al*, *op. cit.*, pp.149-50.

49 The result may be achieved by placing the surface and iodine crystals in an enclosed tank, by spreading the iodine vapour onto the surface using a fuming pipe. The effect, in either case, is only temporary. *Id.*, pp.744-45; Menzel, *op. cit.*, pp.622-23; Saferstein, *op. cit.*, p.407; Gaensslen and Young, *op. cit.*, p.288. Similar results may be achieved using the chemical agent silver nitrate with particular effect on paper surfaces and untreated wood. Silver nitrate is expensive, however, and can produce destructive results. Champod *et al*, *op. cit.*, p.153. Consequently, the method is no longer in widespread use. Gaensslen and Young, *loc.cit.;* Menzel, *op. cit.,* pp.623-24.

50 Ninhydrin is sometimes used as a preliminary step and the ninhydrin-developed prints subsequently treated with other chemicals or illuminated with a specialised light source. Gaensslen and Young, *op. cit.,* pp.288-90; Saferstein, *op. cit.*, p.408; Giannelli and Imwinkelried, *op. cit.*, p.745; Menzel, *op. cit.,* pp.624-25. For a more detailed scientific discussion see Champod *et al*, *op. cit.,* pp.114-120 and 124-28.

51 *Id.,* pp. 131-33; Saferstein, *op. cit.*, p.409; Gaensslen and Young, *op. cit.*, p.290.

52 Gaensslen and Young, *op. cit.*, p.290. For a more detailed discussion of scientific variations on this theme, known generically as cyanoacrylate fuming, *see*

super glue enhancement has the merit of developing prints on non-porous surfaces such as metals, electrical tape, leather and plastic bags.[53]

In addition to physical and chemical processes, fingerprint experts rely on special forms of illumination to visualise latent prints whether initially at the crime scene or subsequently in the laboratory.[54] The greatest innovation in this regard was the advent of laser illumination which capitalises on the florescent capabilities of fingerprint residue; components found in perspiration absorb the light and reemit it in wavelengths longer than the illuminating source.[55] The discovery of florescent inducing chemicals and the development of coloured filters enabled fingerprint experts to achieve the same results using alternative, less expensive, high-intensity light sources such as quartz halogen.[56] Operating alone or *in tandem* with other processes, special illumination techniques are a flexible and efficient means of facilitating fingerprint examination both at the crime scene and in the laboratory.

It is important to emphasise the dynamism and versatility of latent fingerprint visualisation as a field of expertise. These are just some of the more commonly used techniques and each is subject to multiple variations. The field is in a constant state of flux adapting to the fruitful results of widespread, on-going research.[57] Furthermore, the appropriate method for detecting fingerprints depends crucially on practical factors including conditions at the crime scene and the location of the suspected prints. In responding to the challenge, the fingerprint expert will likely employ a combination of techniques, whether conventional or novel, in a logical sequence.[58] Because each technique has its strengths and

---

Champod *et al*, *op. cit.*, pp.138-42. Vacuum metal deposition is another useful technique that has recently been applied to the detection of fingerprints. *Id.*, pp.145-47.

53 Saferstein, *op. cit.*, p.409.

54 Champod *et al*, *op. cit.*, pp.112-13.

55 *Id.*, p.410.

56 Saferstein, *op. cit.*, p.410; Menzel, *op. cit.*, pp.634-38.

57 For example, autoradiography (which involves labelling the fingerprint residue with a beta-emitting radioisotope) is another technique. Giannelli and Imwinkelried, *op. cit.*, p.747.

58 The application of some chemical agents, for example, may rule out the subsequent use of others. For example, if several chemical techniques are used on the same surface, the proper sequence would be iodine fuming, followed by ninhydrin and, finally, physical developer. *Id*; Champod *et al*, *op. cit.*, pp.147-48.

limitations, the choice of the appropriate methodology must be tailored to fit the peculiarities of the particular case.[59]

(c) Recording and preserving fingerprints

Locating and visualising fingerprints is just the first step in an investigative progression that may lead ultimately to the presentation of fingerprint evidence at trial. The successful completion of the journey from crime scene to court depends crucially upon the preservation of the evidence at each stage along the route. A print detected at the crime scene must be properly recorded and preserved if it is to be subjected to expert fingerprint examination; the examiner, in turn, must safeguard the authenticity of the print if it is to be offered as a means of proof in court.

Movable objects suspected of housing latent prints are often submitted directly to the laboratory for examination;[60] where the object is immovable by virtue of its nature or location, enhancement and development techniques must be administered at the scene. In either instance, the conventional practice is to photograph the impression as it is found at the crime scene. This permanent record of the print provides a safeguard against both the accidental destruction and the deliberate fabrication of fingerprint evidence.[61] Indeed, photography, by means of special equipment and film, is a constant feature of the forensic process and should be used before the application of each and every fingerprint development technique. After the impression has been photographed in its original location, the object is removed for further examination or, in the case of an immovable object that has been dusted with powder, the prints are "lifted" from the surface by means of an adhesive tape and

---

[59] Certain surfaces present special difficulties for fingerprint experts. The development of latent prints on skin is a case in point. *See e.g.* Menzel, *op. cit.*, pp.625-26; Giannelli and Imwinkelried, *op. cit.*, pp.750-51; Champod *et al*, *op. cit.*, pp.154-60.

[60] The objects are ordinarily covered in cellophane or placed in protective cellophane bags and labelled at the crime scene.

[61] Giannelli and Imwinkelried, *op. cit.*, p.752 (discussing an evidence tampering scandal in the New York Sate Police Department in the mid-1990s). For a general discussion on fabrication and error *see* Champod *et al*, *op. cit.*, pp.193-201. *See also* IFSS 2004, *op. cit.*, pp.12-13; *Chiori v. United Kingdom* (1999) E.C.H.R., App. No. 44926/98.

transferred onto a card.[62] Lifting provides a second, permanent record of the print and facilitates the transportation of the impression from the crime scene to the laboratory.

Computer technology has added a new dimension to these conventional methods of recording and preserving fingerprints. Digital imaging is now used to increasing effect as a method of enhancing prints lifted from a crime scene. The process enables the fingerprint expert to convert an image into a digital file which may then be manipulated through the application of computer software. Weak or imperfect prints may be enhanced to facilitate a more complete and detailed analysis; portions of an image may be magnified for purposes of specific examination; and background colours that interfere with the analysis may be removed.[63] Digital imaging also allows the fingerprint expert to compare two images simultaneously so as to identify common features.[64]

The other significant function increasingly performed by digital technology is the recording by law enforcement officers of the fingerprints of suspects for purposes of comparison with prints found at a crime scene. Inking is the traditional method of choice and involves the recording on card of several complete sets of a suspect's fingerprints. The standard FBI operating procedure calls for three rows of inked impressions: the first two rows contain rolled impressions whereby each fingertip and thumb-tip is lightly inked and rolled from side to side onto the card and the third row records smaller, flat impressions of two or more fingers made simultaneously.[65] Prints are now recorded using LIVESCAN systems which can capture the fingerprint image and store it digitally. The information may then be printed on standard cards or linked to an

---

[62] Saferstein, *op. cit.*, p.414. The card is produced in a colour that provides a contrasting background to the powder. An adhesive-backed clear plastic sheet attached to a coloured cardboard backing may be used to the same effect. *See also* Giannelli and Imwinkelried, *op. cit.*, p.753.

[63] Saferstein, *op. cit.*, p.417.

[64] *Id.*

[65] Federal Bureau of Investigation, *The Science of Fingerprints* (1977), chaps. 9-10 cited in Gianelli and Imwinkelried, *op. cit.*, p.754, n.71. Special techniques have been devised for exceptional situations such as abnormal or deformed fingers, fingerprints worn down for example from heavy manual work, and fingerprint decay following death. *Id.*, pp.754-56.

automated electronic system which searches a database of fingerprint records for a match.[66]

The Automated Fingerprint Identification System, commonly known as AFIS, has been in operation in Ireland since 1995. Plans are currently underway to update the existing AFIS system with the latest, cutting-edge technology. The equipment used by the Fingerprint Section of the Garda Technical Bureau includes LIVESCAN technology which will likely replace the traditional inking method for the taking of prints from suspects in garda stations in the future. Special crime scene vehicles, fitted with digital cameras and scanning equipment, enable the Gardaí to capture fingerprints and other impressions at crime scenes. The Gardaí currently operate three Livescan units around the country and that number will probably increase significantly in the coming years. The extended use of LIVESCAN will in time permit the transmission of electronically recorded fingerprints via ISDN lines from remote sites to work stations in the Fingerprint Section. Thus, the future of the recording and processing of fingerprints is inextricably linked to evolving computer technology.[67]

(d) Fingerprint classification

The key to the use of fingerprints for purposes of identification is a sound system of classification that assists the expert in comparing prints obtained from a suspect with prints found at a crime scene. The systems operated by law enforcement authorities in common law jurisdictions are generally rooted in the code first devised by Edward Henry at the close of the nineteenth century. Henry assigned numerical values to the presence or absence of friction skin ridge characteristics (loops, arches and whorls) on each individual finger and thumb. The key determinant was the presence or absence of whorl patterns on individual fingers: a finger having a loop or arch pattern was assigned a value of 0 whereas the presence of a whorl pattern was valued at 1, 2, 4, 8 or 16 depending upon the finger on which it was located. Henry paired the fingers and thumbs

---

66 *Id.*, p.753.

67 Communication with the Garda Technical Bureau, Fingerprint Section. *See www.garda.ie*. For the statutory basis of electronically recorded fingerprints, *see* s.11 of the Criminal Justice (Miscellaneous Provisions) Act 1997 (No.4 of 1997).

in sequence and arranged them in a series of fractions (e.g., right index over right thumb and left middle over left index). Each number gleaned from a particular finger or thumb was inserted as the numerator or denominator of the corresponding fraction. The values obtained were then totalled, and 1 added to both the numerator and denominator, to produce a single fraction. To this so-called "primary" classification were added secondary and final classifications based on finger-specific characteristics.[68]

Though groundbreaking in its day, the Henry formula suffered from two major shortcomings: first, it assumed the availability of a complete set of ten fingerprints and, second, it could accommodate no more than 100,000 sets of prints. The latter limitation was cured through the expedient of extended forms of classification.[69] The former proved more intractable, however, because the system could not accommodate single or partial prints which are by no means uncommon in crime scene investigation. In such cases, a ten-finger file will be useful only when a suspect is known; a manual trawl through the repository of files in search of a matching single or partial print would be time-consuming and ultimately impractical. For this reason, some law enforcement authorities developed supplementary systems for filing five-finger impressions or single finger impressions.[70] However, it was only with the gradual transition from manual to electronic systems in the 1980s and 1990s that a more complete and satisfactory solution was found. Just as in other areas of forensic science, such as DNA and ballistics, the application of evolving computer technology has become an essential aspect of the classification and retrieval of fingerprints.

Automated fingerprint identification systems use scanning devices to

---

[68] The patterns of the index fingers are the basis for a secondary classification and the ridge count and/or whorl tracings of the index, middle and ring fingers the basis for a subsecondary classification. A final classification is based on the pattern of the little fingers. For a detailed description of the system *see* Giannelli and Imwinkelried, *op. cit.*, p.762-66; Menzel, *op. cit.*, pp.648-52; Saferstein, *op. cit.,* pp. 402-04.

[69] Such as the second subsecondary classification and the special loop extension. Giannelli and Imwinkelried, *op. cit.*, p.765.

[70] Such as the Battley single-print system. *Id.*, p.766. However, single-print collections are effective only when the number of individuals on file remains relatively small. Saferstein, *op. cit.*, p.404; Campbell, *op. cit.,* p.197.

convert images into digital files which record and store fingerprint minutiae in all their detail. High speed computer processing is then used to search an electronic database of fingerprint files for a possible match. Files may be searched for complete sets of prints or for single prints and thousands of comparisons may be made in a single second. The comparison is based on the degree of correlation between the minutiae of the respective prints which is measured using numerical values. Consequently, the computer produces not a single match but rather a list of the prints on file that have the closest correlation to the prints which are the subject of the search.[71]

As noted above, the use of the AFIS and LIVESCAN computer systems is central to the work of the Fingerprint Section of the Garda Technical Bureau. The impact of technologies such as these on criminal investigation in general and the work of the police and fingerprints experts in particular has been both dramatic and profound, particularly in cases where conventional investigative techniques have failed to produce a suspect whose prints may be compared to those found at the crime scene.[72] The technology is neither precise nor limitless, however, and does not obviate the exceptional need for the manual recording and searching of prints, for example, where the original fingerprint image (the subject of the computer scan) has been incorrectly recorded[73] or the quality of a latent print is too poor for digital encoding.[74] Technological difficulties include programming computers to take account of practical factors, such as distortion caused by the lifting and laying down of a latent impression.[75] Moreover, from a law enforcement perspective, access to fingerprint databases and the sharing of fingerprint information has been frustrated by the incompatibility of systems operated in different jurisdictions.[76]

(e) Fingerprint identification

Identification is the final step in the forensic development of fingerprints.

---

71 Saferstein, *op. cit.*, pp.404-05; Gaensslen and Young, *op. cit.*, pp.284-85; Giannelli and Imwinkelried, *op. cit.*, pp.770-73; Menzel, *op. cit.*, pp.65-55.

72 Gaensslen and Young, *op. cit.*, pp.284-85.

73 Giannelli and Imwinkelried, *op. cit.*, p.773.

74 Saferstein, *op. cit.*, p.405.

75 Giannelli and Imwinkelried, *op. cit.*, p.771.

76 Saferstein, *op. cit.*, p.405.

Although intrinsically linked to the classification of prints, particularly through the application of computer technology, identification is a distinct concept and very much the preserve of the fingerprint expert.[77] From an evidentiary standpoint, the processing of fingerprints from the crime scene to the laboratory is but a prelude, however intricate, to the fundamental task of identification. It is the opinion of the fingerprint expert as to identity that constitutes the evidence presented at trial. The images of the fingerprints, whether manually, photographically or digitally recorded, and a description of the expert's methods of examination may be used to illustrate and underscore his conclusions. The means of proof, however, is the expert's testimony as to the inferences that may be drawn from the presence of fingerprints at the crime scene.

The heart of the expert function is a comparison of fingerprints found at a crime scene with those of a suspect, a process that may be undertaken manually, as is the case here in Ireland, or by means of a combined computer and manual examination. Contrary to the popular view, fingerprint comparison is not a precise science and rarely, if ever, produces an exact match. The expert essentially opines on the correlation between the respective prints and his conclusion that the impressions were made by the same person is based on similarity rather than exactitude.[78] Indeed, experts have long been divided over the degree of similarity between two impressions that is necessary to support an identification.[79] For example, of the numerous potential points that may be applied to the comparison of ridge characteristics, the standard currently applied in court in Ireland is 12 points as opposed to the traditional American standard of eight to ten points and the former English standard of 16 points. The trend is increasingly away from exact numbers and the English Home Office, for example, has since adopted a more floexible, non-numerical

---

77 *See generally* Champod *et al*, *op.cit.,*.chap.2.

78 As Champod *et al*, put it, *op. cit.*, p.35: "It is axiomatic than no two fingerprints are identical; indeed, no two entities of any kind can be identical to each other. The crux of the matter is not the individuality of the friction skin ridges but, rather, the ability of the examiner to recognize sufficient information for the disclosure of the identity from a small, distorted latent fingerprint fragment that may reveal only limited information in terms of quantity or quality."

79 Campbell, *op. cit.,* p.199.

standard.[80] Opinions also differ regarding the extent of detail which the analyst should consider and the factors that should be used in evaluating the detail.[81]

The Fingerprint Section of the Garda Technical Bureau operates a rigid protocol to ensure the reliability of a fingerprint match. A garda officer must undergo five years' specialised training in order to qualify as a fingerprint expert. A match determined by an expert must be verified independently, by way of "blind identification," by two other experts, and subsequently confirmed by the inspector in charge. Where a match is determined by a non-expert, *i.e.* an officer who has not accumulated five years' training, blind identification by three experts is required.[82]

Saferstein notes the difficulty in establishing "meaningful guidelines for defining the uniqueness of a fingerprint" in the absence of "a comprehensive statistical study to determine the frequency of occurrence of different ridge characteristics and their relative locations."[83] He concludes that "the final determination must be based on the experience and knowledge of the expert, with the understanding that others may profess honest differences of opinion on the uniqueness of a fingerprint if the question of minimal number of ridge characteristics exist."[84] Thus, the testimony of the fingerprint expert is sometimes perceived to be more subjective than that of other forensic experts, such as DNA analysts. Champod *et al.* couch the state of contemporary practice in the following terms:

---

[80] Even in its heyday, the English numerical standard was not applied rigidly. A 1983 addendum to the 16 point standard stated that in extremely rare cases an experienced expert could opine on an identification that did not meet the standard. Champod *et al.*, *op. cit.*, p.13. On American practice *see Kiely, op. cit.*, p.223; Menzel, *op. cit.*, pp.652-54.

[81] Giannelli and Imwinkelried, *op. cit.,* pp.766-69; Champod *et al*, *op. cit.,* pp.27-31.

[82] Communication with the Garda Technical Bureau, Fingerprint Section.

[83] Saferstein, *op. cit.*, p.398.

[84] *Id.,* p.399. In 1973, the International Association for Identification adopted a resolution to the effect that "no valid basis exists for requiring a predetermined minimum number of friction ridge characters which must be present in two impressions in order to establish positive identification". This resolution was endorsed by members of the international fingerprint community at a conference in Israel in 1995. *Id*; Champod *et al*, *op. cit.,* pp.29-30.

> "The individualization process cannot therefore be reduced to counting minutiae; each identification represents a unique set of circumstances, and the judgment of the value of concurring features between a mark and a print depends on a variety of conditions that automatically exclude any minimum standard. It is not justifiable (or even scientific) to reduce the issue of fingerprint individuality to numbers of corresponding minutiae alone. The identification process is a holistic assessment, balancing both quantitative (number of minutiae) and qualitative aspects (general pattern, type of minutiae, pores, edges) visible to the mark."[85]

The qualified terms in which these and other scientists extol the certainty of fingerprint identification reflects renewed critical interest in the field. Various factors, including developments in research and technology, and the spillover effect of the debate over the introduction of DNA evidence,[86] have prompted the fingerprint profession to analyse the scientific foundations of identification through a more critical lens.[87] The importance of this scientific trend to the law relating to fingerprint evidence cannot be overstated but its impact has yet to be felt in legal practice. The complexity of fingerprint identification as a contemporary applied science is generally overlooked by lawyers and judges. Although some courts, especially in the United States, have begun to approach fingerprint evidence with new-found scepticism, the vast majority adhere to the traditional view that "fingerprint evidence, when competent, relevant, and material, and when presented by qualified experts, is admissible for the purpose of establishing identity of an individual."[88]

---

[85] *Id.*, p.30.

[86] J.L. Mnookin, "Fingerprint Evidence in an Age of DNA Profiling" (2001) 67(1) Brooklyn L. Rev. 13. On the combined use of DNA and fingerprints see IFSS, *op. cit.*, pp.20-21. *See also* S.A. Cole, "Fingerprint Identification and the Criminal Justice Sustem: Historical Lessons for the DNA Debate" in D. Lazer, ed., *DNA and the Criminal Justice System: The Technology of Justice* (MIT Press, Cambridge, Mass., 2004) 63.

[87] Champod *et al*, *op. cit.*, pp.204-05; S.J. Gutowski, "Statistics and Evidence in Field and Identification Sciences" (Nov. 2001) Forensic Science Bulletin 16; D. Fairhurst, "Is Fingerprint Examination a Science?" (2003) 29 (113) Fingerprint World 139.

[88] Moessens, *op. cit.*, p.112.

The long-standing acceptance of the scientific foundation for fingerprint evidence has led courts in some jurisdictions to take judicial notice of the fact that fingerprints provide a means of positive identification.[89] It also explains the dearth of reported cases involving challenges to the reliability of the predicate science.[90] Moving forward, these aspects of legal practice may well be subject to change, as the law catches up with nuanced developments in dactyloscopy.[91]

(f) Estimating the age of fingerprints

One of the most disputed issues in relation to fingerprints is the accuracy and reliability of testimony relating to the time-frame within which an impression was made at the crime scene. Courts in the United States have occasionally permitted fingerprint experts to offer opinions to the effect that pints are recent or a specified number of days old.[92] These determinations are based on various scientific techniques including fingerprint luminescence and liquid chromatography. Age determination is complicated by environmental and physiological factors, however, and the efficacy of any of these techniques remains the subject of controversy.[93]

---

89 *Id.,* pp.112-13.

90 Kiely, *op. cit.*, p.225.

91 *See generally*, H.H. Kaufman, "The Expert Witness, Neither *Frye* nor *Daubert* Solved the Problem: What Can Be Done?" (2001) 41(1) Science and Justice 7; R. Epstein, "Fingerprints Meets *Daubert*: The Myth of Fingerprint "Science" is Revealed" (2002) 75 S. Cal. L. Rev. 605; E.J. Imwinkelried, "Fingerprint Science" (2002) 26 Nat. L.J. 18; D.H. Kaye, "Questioning a Courtroom Proof of the Uniqueness of Fingerprints" (2003) 71(3) Int'l Stat. Rev. 521.

92 Giannelli and Imwinkelried, *op. cit.*, p.774 (citing cases).

93 *Id.,* pp.775-76; Menzel, *op. cit.,* pp.645-46. Campbell commented in 1985, *op. cit.*, at pp.200-01: "In general, whilst it may be possible to say that a mark is recent because of its location and the conditions under which it was found, dating of fingerprints is not possible". For a more recent, detailed discussion *see* Champod *et al*, *op. cit.,* pp.187-93.

CHAPTER 4

The Recording of Fingerprints[1]

THE CONSTITUTIONAL BACKDROP

A criminal defendant enjoys a panoply of rights and privileges under the Constitution, statute, the common law, and the European Convention on Human Rights. Fingerprint evidence, no less than any other means of proof tendered by the prosecution, is generally inadmissible if procured in breach of these basic protections.[2] In terms of constitutional protection, the rights of most immediate relevance are the right to bodily integrity and the right against self incrimination.[3] The former comes within the unenumerated personal rights guaranteed by Article 40.3[4] and is enjoyed by suspects and prisoners alike.[5] It protects the individual from deliberate physical interference with his person including torture and inhuman or

---

1 This chapter is a version of "The Recording of Fingerprints: Legal Aspects" (2006) 28 D.U.L.J. (forthcoming). The author gratefully acknowledges the permission of Thomson Round Hall to use the material in this context.

2 By virtue of the exclusionary rule relating to improperly obtained evidence, a trial judge must exclude unconstitutionally obtained fingerprint evidence and has a discretion to admit such evidence where there are extraordinary excusing circumstances or where the evidence was obtained through illegal rather than unconstitutional means. *See People (AG) v. O'Brien* [1965] I.R. 142; *People (DPP) v. Kenny* [1990] 2 I.R. 110 , [1990] I.L.R.M. 569; D. McGrath, *Evidence (*Thomson Round Hall, Dublin, 2005), chap.7; J. Healy, *Irish Laws of Evidence* (Thomson Round Hall, Dublin, 2004), chap. 11; C. Fennell, *The Law of Evidence in Ireland,* 2nd ed. (LexisNexis, Dublin, 2003), chap.4.

3 The retention of fingerprints also raises potential privacy issues under art. 40.3.1 of the Constitution and art. 8 of the ECHR. *See e.g. McVeigh v. U.K.* [1983] 5 E.H.R.R. 71. *But see also R (S and Marper) v. Chief Constable of South Yorkshire* [2004] 4 All E.R. 193.

4 *Ryan v. AG* [1965] I.R. 294.

5 *State (Richardson) v. Gov. Mountjoy Prison* [1980] I.L.R.M. 82.

degrading treatment[6] and, in the context of the criminal justice system, operates *in tandem* with guarantees of due process and fair procedures.[7] However, the right to bodily integrity is by no means absolute and the State is obliged to protect it only so far as is practicable having regard to the common good. There is scant guidance in the case law as to how far the right extends in the general context of custodial detention, much less the specific context of fingerprinting.

The Gardaí lack any general power to take fingerprints and may do so only with the consent of the person concerned or pursuant to some specific statutory authority. Although the taking of fingerprints without consent and beyond the limits of the legislative power is unlawful,[8] it is not necessarily an unconstitutional interference with the right to bodily integrity. Commentators have suggested that the unlawful taking of intimate bodily samples for forensic testing would *per se* interfere with the right to bodily integrity.[9] But the extension of this principle to fingerprinting is questionable given that the procedure is non-invasive and involves neither pain nor physical harm.[10] A circumstance far more likely to infringe a suspect's right to bodily integrity would be the taking of fingerprints by the Gardaí through the use of excessive physical force. The unconstitutional infliction of actual bodily harm through excessive force would surely warrant the exclusion of the fingerprint evidence regardless of whether the Gardaí were purporting to act on foot of statutory authority.[11] An exception would apply only where the prosecution could demonstrate the existence of extraordinary excusing circumstances and even then the evidence would be admissible not as of right but at the discretion of the trial judge.[12]

---

6 *State (C) v. Frawley* [1976] I.R. 365. *See also* ECHR, art.3.

7 *State (Healy) v. Donoghue* [1976] I.R. 325 at 348-49 (*per* O'Higgins C.J. citing Arts. 34 and 38).

8 Indeed, such conduct would be actionable as a common law assault.

9 *See e.g.* D. Walsh, *Criminal Procedure* (Thomson Round Hall, Dublin, 2002), p.470 (citing E.F. Ryan and P.P. Magee, *The Irish Criminal Process* (Mercier Press, Dublin, 1983), p.135).

10 Walsh, *op.cit.*, pp.470-71. *See also Raninen v. Finland* [1997] 26 E.H.R.R. 563 (unnecessary handcuffing did not violate art.3).

11 *See Ribitsch v. Austria* [1995] 21 E.H.R.R. 573, para.38 (prohibiting any unnecessary use of physical force on a suspect).

12 *See e.g., People (AG) v. O'Brien* [1965] I.R. 142 at 170 (*per* Walsh J.); *Freeman v. DPP* [1996] 3 I.R. 565. None of the examples of extraordinary excusing

The contours of constitutional protection are even less well defined in relation to the application of the right against self incrimination to custodial fingerprinting. The right comprises a disparate group of immunities[13] including the right of a suspect not to answer questions and the right of an accused not to be compelled to give evidence or make incriminating statements at his trial.[14] It is most commonly associated with the right to silence, grounded in Article 38.1 (trial in due course of law)[15] and Article 40.6.1 (freedom of expression)[16] and the exclusion of confessions procured in breach thereof.[17] In each of its various guises, the right not to incriminate oneself is qualified and may be restricted proportionate to the need to further a legitimate State aim such as the prevention and detection of crime or the protection of the rights of others. Whether the right extends to fingerprint evidence and, if so, how far it extends, are questions of first impression in this jurisdiction. As the discussion below indicates, the courts have been reluctant to equate fingerprint evidence with confession evidence and, by extension, afford to the former the special protections applied to the latter. At a minimum, however, the right against self incrimination reinforces the absence of any general police power to take and record fingerprints and serves as a reminder of the need for the Gardaí to act within the strict limits of lawful authority.

Certain other constitutional rights may bear indirectly on the recording

---

circumstances cited in the case law (such as the imminent destruction of evidence or the need to rescue a victim in peril) are apposite to the taking of fingerprint evidence.

13 *R v. Director of Serious Fraud Office, ex parte Smith* [1993] A.C. 1 (*per* Lord Mustill).

14 *See generally* McGrath, *op.cit.*, p.623 *et seq.*

15 *Re National Irish Bank* [1999] 3 I.R. 145, [1999] 1 I.L.R.M. 321; *Heaney v. Ireland* [1994] 3 I.R. 593, [1994] 2 I.L.R.M. 420 (HC). *See also* art. 6 of the ECHR.

16 *Heaney v. Ireland* [1996] 1 I.R. 580, [1997] 1 I.L.R.M. 117 (SC). *See also* ECHR, art.10.

17 The bulk of the case law concerns constitutional challenges to statutory encroachments on the right to silence. In addition to *Heaney* and *Re National Irish Bank, see e.g. Rock v. Ireland* [1997] 3 I.R. 484, [1998] 2 I.L.R.M. 35; *Lavery v. Member in Charge Carrickmacross Garda Station* [1999] 2 I.R. 390. *See also Heaney v. Ireland* [2001] 33 E.H.R.R. 1; *Saunders v. United Kingdom* [1996] 23 E.H.R.R. 313; *Funke v. France* [1993] 16 E.H.R.R. 297.

of fingerprints and, moreover, may do so with significant evidentiary effect. For example, if fingerprints are obtained from a suspect during the course of an unlawful detention, evidence in relation to those prints will be generally excluded at trial as a remedial consequence of the underlying violations of the rights to liberty[18] and privacy.[19] Aside from these or other specific examples, it is important to recall the omnipresence of the constitutional right to a trial in due course of law[20] in relation to the admissibility of all forms of evidence in the Irish courts.

The Statutory Authority to Fingerprint

The authority of the State to record and store fingerprints is governed by an assortment of statutory provisions.[21] In each instance, the authority is specific and limited and, consequently, its statutory remit should be narrowly defined. From a practical standpoint, the most significant of the statutory powers are housed in the Criminal Justice Act 1984.[22] Under section 4 of the Act, a person who has been arrested without warrant on suspicion of having committed an offence may be detained at a Garda Síochána station for a defined period if the arresting Garda officer has reasonable grounds for believing that the person's detention is necessary for the proper investigation of the offence.[23] Section 6 delineates certain

---

18 Art. 40.4.1; *People (DPP) v. Madden* [1977] I.R. 336 (confession evidence). *See also* ECHR, art.5.

19 Art. 40.3.1; *DPP v. Kenny* [1992] 2 I.R. 141; *People (DPP) v. Davis* [2001] 1 I.R. 146. *See also* ECHR, art. 8.

20 Art. 38.1; *Re National Irish Bank* [1999] 3 I.R. 145, [1999] 1 I.L.R.M. 321; ECHR, art.6.

21 *See generally,* Walsh, *op.cit.*, pp.340-45; Law Reform Commission, *Consultation Paper on the Establishment of a DNA Database* (LRC CP 29–2004), paras. 4.03-4.12. In the United Kingdom, the authority of the police to fingerprint suspects is couched in terms similar to the Irish Acts in s.61 of the Police and Criminal Evidence Act 1984 as amended and paras. 3.1 to 3.6 of the Code of Practice and Identification (Pt D). *See* M.N. Howard, ed., *Phipson on Evidence* (15th ed., Sweet & Maxwell, London, 2000), para.14-31; N. Ebisike, *An Appraisal of Forensic Evidence in Criminal Proceedings* (Greenway Publishers, London, 2000), p.18.

22 *See generally* K.Boyle and M.Lawless (1984) I.C.L.S.A. 84/22-01.

23 S.4 originally provided for detention for an initial period of up to six hours from

Garda powers in relation to a person so detained including the power to search, photograph and fingerprint. The latter power is specified under section 6(1)(d) which states that a member of the Garda Síochána may "take, or cause to be taken, his fingerprints and palm prints".

Section 4 of the 1984 Act applies to any offence for which a person of full age and capacity may be punished by imprisonment for a term of five years or a more severe penalty.[24] By virtue of section 7 of the Criminal Law Act 1976, the power to fingerprint was extended in identical terms to persons detained under section 30 of the Offences Against the State Act 1939 and section 2 of the Emergency Powers Act 1976. The power was similarly extended to persons detained under the Criminal Justice (Drug Trafficking) Act 1996 by section 2 of that Act. Section 11 of the Criminal Justice (Miscellaneous Provisions) Act 1997 provides for the electronic recording of fingerprints and palm prints taken under any enactment.

The legislative intent behind these various provisions was to facilitate the taking of fingerprints from persons suspected of serious offences; detention under the cited statutory provisions relates for the most part to offences attracting severe penalties although it may apply exceptionally to offences subject to minor penalties.[25] This is a justifiably proportionate restriction that accords with general international practice.[26] It is echoed in current calls for the retention of a strict limit on the taking of forensic

---

the time of arrest which could be extended for a further period not exceeding six hours at the direction of an officer not below the rank of superintendent. Special provisions apply in relation to persons below the age of 17 years. S.9 of the Criminal Justice Act has amended s.4 of the 1984 Act by providing for the possibility of a further 12 hours detention in certain circumstances. The origins of the Act can be traced to the *Report of the Steering Group on the Efficiency and Effectiveness of the Garda Síochána* (the Garda SMI Report) (No. 1997) at sec.4 (Legal Framework); and the *Report of the Expert Group Appointed to Consider Changes in the Criminal Law Which Were Recommended in the Garda SMI Report* (Leahy Report) (1998). The Act was signed into law by the President on July 16, 2006. Commencement orders have yet to be issued.

24 Provided that the offence is not one for which the person has already been convicted.

25 See P. O'Connor, (1990) I.C.L.S.A. 90/34.04; LRC Consultation Paper, *op. cit.*, p.87.

26 Although s.62(2)(a) of the English Police and Criminal Evidence Act 1984, as amended, is less restrictive and permits the taking of forensic samples from persons suspected of "recordable offences".

samples to persons suspected of serious offences.[27] Although this would not necessarily involve any substantive change in the law, a reformed legislative regime might benefit from a more explicit statement of this fundamental principle.

These various statutory provisions apply exclusively to situations of investigative detention which occurs at the commencement of the criminal process prior to a suspect being formally charged.[28] The Gardaí are also empowered by section 28(1) of the 1984 Act[29] to take a person's fingerprints at the culmination of court proceedings or after they have been processed through the criminal justice system. The provision applies to a person who has been prosecuted for an indictable offence and placed on probation or a person convicted of an indictable offence and otherwise dealt with. In either situation, the person concerned is not in custody and the provision effectively allows the Gardaí to require the person to attend within seven days (of the making of the probation order or the conviction) at a named Garda station or other convenient place to have his fingerprints taken.[30]

---

27 *See, e.g.,* Irish Human Rights Commission, *Observations on the Scheme of the Criminal Justice Bill 2003* (January 14, 2004), pp.32-33; Irish Council for Civil Liberties, *Human Rights Compatibility of the Establishment of a DNA Database* (ICCL Position Paper, Oct. 2003), p.11. *See also* Law Reform Commission, *Report on the Establishment of a DNA Database* (LRC 780–2005), para. 2.47 (recommending no change in the current position).

28 Note also that under s.51 of the Criminal Justice Act 1994, the Minister for Justice may nominate a district court judge to receive evidence, including fingerprint evidence, which has been requested by authorities in a foreign jurisdiction in connection with a criminal investigation or proceeding in that jurisdiction. *See Brady v. District Judge Haughton,* unreported, High Court, July 22, 2003.

29 As substituted by s.12 of the Criminal Justice (Miscellaneous Provisions) Act 1997.

30 Refusal to comply with a requirement under the provision is an offence. *See* s.28(4). *See generally* Walsh, *op.cit,* pp.343-44. *See also* the Penal Servitude Act 1891 (Measuring and Photography of Prisoners) Regulations 1955 (extending to persons on remand); and s.19 of the Criminal Justice (Miscellaneous Provisions) Act 1997 (allowing the Minister for Justice to make prison rules for the taking of fingerprints).

Statutory Safeguards

The defining characteristic of the statutory regime relating to the taking of fingerprints is the absence of any requirement of prior consent on the part of the suspect.[31] It is sufficient that the suspect has been lawfully detained in Garda custody under one of the predicate statutes. There is also no statutory requirement that the suspect be cautioned prior to the recording of his fingerprints. Whereas this is consistent with the absence of a consent requirement, it would be desirable, nevertheless, if the legislation explicitly required the suspect to be told in ordinary language that his fingerprints are being taken pursuant to statutory authority and the purpose for which they are being taken.[32]

Unlike most of the other powers incidental to arrest that are specified in the 1984 Act, the power to fingerprint is subject to an authorisation requirement. Under section 6(2), the fingerprints of a suspect may be taken only on the authority of a member of the Gardaí not below the rank of superintendent.[33] The Act is silent, however, as to the factors that should inform the decision to grant or withhold the necessary authorisation. There is no explicit requirement, akin to the equivalent statutory provision governing the authorisation of the taking of bodily samples for forensic testing, that the senior Garda officer in question have reasonable grounds for suspecting the person's involvement in the offence for which he is in custody and for believing that his fingerprints will tend to confirm or disprove his involvement.[34] Nor does the section expressly require that the authorisation be tendered in writing.[35]

---

31 This is also the position in relation to the taking of non-intimate bodily samples for the purpose of forensic testing. However, consent is required for the taking of intimate bodily samples. *See* Criminal Justice (Forensic Evidence) Act 1990, s.2(4)(b), discussed in chap.7 *infra*.

32 *See* discussion of *People v. Walsh* [1980] I.R. 294; *People (DPP) v. Cleary* [2005] 2 I.R. 189, *infra*.

33 *See* s.6(2). *See also* s.5 of the Criminal Justice (Drug Trafficking) Act 1996.

34 *See* ss. 2(4)(a) and 2(5) of the Criminal Justice (Forensic Evidence) Act 1990. The Law Reform Commission has recommended the removal of this requirement. *See* LRC Report, *op.cit.*, para.2.41 whereas the Irish Human Rights Commission has called for more rigorous safeguards. *See* Human Rights Commission, *Observations on the Scheme of the Criminal Justice Bill 2003* (January 14, 2004), p.33.

35 Reg. 18 of the Custody Regulations, below n.49, requires that the name and rank

The 1984 Act leaves open the question whether the Gardaí are entitled to use force in the exercise of their power to take fingerprints and, if so, the circumstances in which force may be justified and the degree of force that may be employed. The Act opts instead to criminalise conduct which frustrates the Gardaí's efforts. Specifically, any person who obstructs or attempts to obstruct the Gardaí in exercising the power to fingerprint shall be guilty of an offence and liable on summary conviction to a fine not exceeding €3,000 and/or imprisonment for a term not exceeding 12 months.[36] One view holds that the right of the Gardaí to use reasonable force is implicit in the statutory power and, indeed, that this is the only plausible reading of the provision.[37] An alternative view is that an interference of this kind with an individual's personal rights and freedoms must be explicitly prescribed by law.[38] It is perhaps with this consideration in mind that the original Scheme of the Criminal Justice Bill 2004 contained a proposal to authorise explicitly the use of reasonable force on the part of the Gardaí in the taking of fingerprints.[39] This proposal did not find its way into the Bill as published or enacted, however, and the existing position thus remains subject to doubt. A separate but related panacea in this context would be legislative or ministerial action on long

---

of the officer giving the authorisation be entered into the suspect's custody record. *See also People (DPP) v. Casey,* unreported, Court of Criminal Appeal, December 14, 2004, discussed *infra*.

36 *See* s. 6(4) of the 1984 Act; s.5 of the Criminal Justice (Drug Trafficking) Act 1996. *See also* s.28(4) of the 1984 Act. Section 13(a) and (c) of the Criminal Justice Act 2006 increased the maximum fine to €3,000 from €1,270.

37 *See, e.g.*, LRC, *Consultation Paper, op.cit.* at para.4.05 citing Boyle and Lawless (1984) I.C.L.S.A. 84/22-01 at para.22.15.

38 *See, e.g.,* Irish Human Rights Commission, *Observations on the Scheme of the Criminal Justice Bill 2003, op.cit.*, p.34 (citing the United Nations Code of Conduct for Law Enforcement Officials and the United Nations Basic Principles on the Use of Force and Firearms by Law Enforcement Officials); LRC Report, *op. cit.,* para.2.35 (recommending that any such power to use reasonable force should be explicitly prescribed and delineated in legislation).

39 The Bill has now been enacted as the Criminal Justice Act 2006, *see* n.23 *supra.* The proposal, which may be traced to the *Leahy Report, op.cit.*, p.40, also provided for the reasonable use of force in relation to the taking of photographs and palm prints under the 1984 Act (and equivalent statutes) and non-intimate samples under the Criminal Justice (Forensic Evidence) Act 1990.

standing calls for the mandatory video-recording of Garda interviews of custodial detainees.[40]

A further legislative safeguard is the inclusion of provisions governing the destruction of fingerprints and fingerprint records. The 1984 Act makes provision in section 8 for destruction of fingerprints or palm prints, and copies and records thereof, taken in pursuance of the powers conferred by section 6. Where proceedings for a section 4 offence are not instituted against the person within 12 months of the taking of the fingerprints, the prints shall be destroyed at that time.[41] The Criminal Justice Act 2006 extended the period from six to twelve months,[42] presumably to allow the Gardaí additional time to investigate an offence and gather evidence.[43] In addition, where proceedings have been instituted but the person has been acquitted, the charge has been dismissed or the proceedings have been discontinued, destruction shall take place 21 days after the acquittal, dismissal or discontinuance, respectively.[44] The person concerned, his solicitor or some other person authorised in writing to act on his behalf, shall be entitled, on request, to witness the destruction.[45] Fingerprints may be preserved, however, in certain specified circumstances: where a person is on probation;[46] where a print is required in connection with civil proceedings;[47] and where a district judge authorises its preservation on the application of the Director of Public Prosecutions.[48]

---

40 *See, e.g., People (DPP) v. Connolly* [2003] 2 I.R. 1 (*per* Hardiman J.); Leahy Report, *op.cit.*, p.54.

41 *See* s. 8(2). Provided that the failure to institute proceedings within that period is not due to the fact that the person has absconded or cannot be found.

42 *See* s.13(b)(i).

43 A view expressed in the LRC Consultation Paper, *op.cit.,* para. 4.55.

44 *See* s.8(3), as submitted by s.13(b)(ii) of the Criminal Justice Act 2006.

45 *See* s.8(5).

46 In relation to a person on probation, s. 8(4) states that the destruction shall be carried out three years after the making of an order provided that the person has not been charged with an offence during that period.

47 *See* s. 8(6). This proviso comes into play where civil proceedings are instituted before the fingerprint is required to be destroyed under the Act. Where a party to the civil proceedings serves notice on the Garda Commissioner, the fingerprint shall be preserved until 6 months from the conclusion of the proceedings or until the conclusion of any proceedings on appeal, whichever is later.

48 *See* s.8(7). The district judge may authorise the preservation of the fingerprint for a period not exceeding 12 months on being satisfied that it may be required

Regulations

The 1984 Act was supplemented by the introduction in 1987 of regulations governing the treatment of persons in custody in Garda stations.[49] In relation to fingerprints, Regulation 18 provides that the voluntary submission of fingerprints must be accompanied by written consent,[50] signed and recorded in the custody record or a separate document. The Regulation also states that the fact that fingerprints have been taken from a person in custody shall be recorded together with the name and rank of the member of the Gardaí giving the necessary authorisation. Albeit modest, these safeguards are beneficial and important, although, their legal import is curtailed by the express caveat in section 7(3) of the Act that a failure on the part of any member of the Gardaí to observe any provision of the regulations shall not of itself affect *inter alia* the lawfulness of the person's detention. Approaching the matter from an alternative perspective, a breach of the regulations might be classified as "unlawful" conduct (as opposed to "unconstitutional" conduct) which, by virtue of the principles famously set down by the Supreme Court in *People (AG) v. O'Brien,* would vest in the trial judge a discretion to exclude evidence obtained as a result of the breach.[51]

The provisions governing the taking of bodily samples for purposes of forensic testing contained in the Criminal Justice (Forensic Evidence) Act 1990 have been supplemented by regulations which represent a beneficial reinforcement of certain safeguards contained in the parent Act but add little substantive flesh to the bones of the legislation.[52] Section 14(c) of the Criminal Justice Act 2006 extended the list of matters in

---

for the purpose of proceedings or further proceedings in relation to the offence. As amended by s.13(b)(iii) of the Criminal Justice Act 2006.

[49] Criminal Justice Act 1984 (Treatment of Persons in Custody in Garda Síochána Stations) Regulations 1987 (S.I. No.119 of 1987). The regulations were made by the Minister for Justice under s.7 of the 1984 Act.

[50] Or, in the case of a person under the age of 17 years, the written consent of an appropriate adult.

[51] [1965] I.R. 142. On the legal effect of a breach of the regulations *see DPP v. Spratt* [1995] 2 I.L.R.M. 117 (HC); and *People (DPP) v. Darcy*, unreported, Court of Criminal Appeal, July 29, 1997; *People (DPP) v. Diver* [2005] 3 I.R. 270.

[52] Criminal Justice (Forensic Evidence) Act 1990 Regulations 1992, S.I. No.130 of 1992.

relation to which the Minister for Justice may make regulations under the 1990 Act. Whereas this is a limited but welcome step within the confines of the 1990 regime, the Oireachtas might do better to heed to call of the Irish Human Rights Commission for the adoption of a formal set of guidelines whether housed in legislation, a schedule thereto or regulations.[53] The 1990 Act embodies a more detailed, comprehensive regime than the statutory provisions governing fingerprinting which is understandable given the heightened degree of sensitivity and intrusion occasioned by the taking of bodily samples. In both contexts, there is ample room to enhance the existing safeguards and this might be best achieved through the introduction of a single, consolidated code. There is a strong case for bringing all forensic procedures under a single regulatory umbrella[54] and ensuring that robust principles, adequate procedures and effective safeguards are respected across the board.

The Recording of Fingerprints at Common Law

Although the authority of the Gardaí to investigate crime is delineated by statute for the most part, certain powers, and corresponding intrusions on the rights of the individual, traditionally existed (and in some instances continue to co-exist) at common law. A Garda officer had the power, for example, to arrest a person whom he reasonable suspected of having committed a felony and, incidental to arrest, to search the person arrested and take any property that he reasonably believed was connected with the offence charged. The underlying policy was that any interference with the individual's right to physical integrity, dignity and self respect were outweighed by the need to apprehend and disarm a suspected offender and to discover evidence.

The weight of authority in the common law world is that custodial fingerprinting is a similarly legitimate investigative practice.[55] In *United*

---

[53] Irish Human Rights Commission, *Observations on the Criminal Justice Bill 2004* (November 3, 2004). In support, *see* LRC Report, *op.cit.*, para. 2.31.

[54] *See id.*, para. 2.48.

[55] *See e.g. People (AG) v. McGrath* (1965) 99 I.L.T.R. 69; *Adair v. M'Garry* [1933] S.L.T. 482; *Callis v. Gunn* [1963] 3 All E.R. 677 at 681; *R v. Beare* [1988] 2 S.C.R. 387.

States v. Kelly, Hand J. encapsulated the traditional view that the power to fingerprint consequent to lawful arrest is necessary, reasonable and proportionate:

> "It is no more humiliating than other means of identification that have been universally held to infringe neither constitutional nor common-law rights. Finger printing is used in numerous branches of business and of civil service, and is not in itself a badge of crime. As a physical invasion it amounts to almost nothing, and as a humiliation it can never amount to as much as that caused by the publicity attending a sensational indictment to which innocent men may have to submit."[56]

As La Forest J. surmised in *R v. Beare,* having conducted a comparative review of the authorities, "the common law experience strongly supports the view that subjecting a person to being fingerprinted [upon lawful arrest] does not violate fundamental justice."[57] These sentiments have not received universal, resounding judicial endorsement, however.[58] Moreover, in Ireland, the common law position in relation to the powers of arrest, including incidental powers such as the taking of fingerprints, has been eclipsed by statute, as discussed above. The prevailing view is that the recording of fingerprints must be taken either with the suspect's consent or pursuant to statutory authority.[59]

---

[56] 55 F.2d 67 (2d Cir. 1932) at 70.

[57] [1988] S.C.R. 387, para.38. The authorities in the United States appear to support a more extensive common law power than their counterparts in other countries. There is support in the U.S. for the view that the power extends to arrest on reasonable suspicion of the commission of misdemeanors (as well as indictable offences) and that in certain circumstances it may be exercised even in the absence of arrest. *See e.g. Hayes v. Florida*, 470 U.S. 811 (1985).

[58] *See e,g. Dumbell v. Roberts* [1944] 1 All E.R. 326 (*per* Scott L.J.); *R . v. A.N.* (1978) 2 C.R. (3d) 55 (B.C.C.A.) (*per* Branca J.A.).

[59] Walsh, *op.cit.,* p.340; LRC Consultation Paper, *op.cit.,* para. 4.03.

Traditional Case Law

Our contemporary system of criminal justice is predicated on the twin assumptions that in investigating crime on behalf of the State the Gardaí will resort to exclusively lawful means and that the evidentiary fruits of any unlawful action on their part will be inadmissible at trial.[60] Traditionally, the contrary position prevailed at common law. As Lord Goddard famously declared in *Kuruma v. R.*, "the test to be applied in considering whether evidence is admissible is whether it is relevant to the matters at issue. If it is, it is admissible and the Court is not concerned with how the evidence was obtained."[61] The traditional principle was endorsed by the High Court in *People (AG) v. McGrath* which concerned the admissibility of fingerprint evidence.[62] The accused was charged with breaking and entering the offices of the Institute of Chartered Accountants and stealing money from the premises. The only evidence against him was expert evidence to the effect that his fingerprints matched those found on the cash box from which the money was taken. The accused's fingerprints had been taken while he was on remand in custody prior to the district court hearing. No warrant was sought for the taking of the fingerprints, his consent was not sought, nor was he advised of his right to withhold his consent. The district justice dismissed the charges but stated a case for the opinion of the High Court.

The issue, in the view of Davitt P., was whether the fingerprint

---

60 In relation to fingerprints, the most serious accusation that can be levelled against law enforcement officers is that the evidence was fabricated or planted. D. Campbell, "Fingerprints: A Review" [1985] Crim. L. Rev. 195 at p.200, writing in 1985, noted the inherent difficulty in pressing home such an allegation: "There has never been a case in the United Kingdom where satisfactory evidence of a fingerprint having been 'planted' has been proved. The technical difficulties in carrying out such an exercise are enormous and would require the active support of a fingerprint technician of great skill. The possibility of such planting being undetectable is considered to be very small indeed, even if it were capable of achievement." Nevertheless, a fingerprint tampering scandal was exposed in New York in 1995. *See* P.C. Giannelli and E.J. Imwinkelried, *Scientific Evidence*, 3rd ed. (Lexis Law Publishing, Charlottesville, Virginia, 1999), p.752. Moreover, errors by fingerprint examiners have been disclosed both in England and the United States. *Id.*, pp.740-41.

61 [1955] A.C. 197.

62 (1965) 99 I.L.T.R. 59.

evidence, though clearly relevant, should be excluded "on the ground of principle or authority".[63] Citing with approval the judgment of the Court of Appeal in *Kuruma*, he held that the manner in which evidence is obtained is not the concern of the court. Relevant evidence should not be excluded merely because it was obtained by illegal means.[64] Whereas confession evidence came within a well recognised exclusionary exception, the same could not be said of fingerprint evidence:

> "In my opinion, the taking of a prisoner's finger prints is not to be considered in the same way as an interrogation eliciting a confession. It is something completely different. Such an interrogation acts upon the mind and will of the person questioned and necessarily involves the co-operation, which may or may not in fact be fully voluntary, of both to the extent of answering some at least of the questions and of making the confession. Taking finger prints is a purely mechanical process which is quite independent of the mind of the person concerned, and does not necessarily involve any co-operation on his part. Nothing remotely resembling an answer or a confession can result. An answer to a confession may or may not be true. The finger prints can be impressions left by the person's finger tips and nothing else."[65]

In conclusion, assuming that the taking of the accused's fingerprints had

---

[63] [1960] 99 I.L.T.R. 59 at 70.

[64] Moreover, whereas the Court of Appeal in *Kuruma* had recognised a discretion on the part of the trial judge to exclude evidence where its admissibility would operate unfairly against an accused, Davitt P. took the position that such a discretion was confined to similar fact evidence. *Id.,* p.74. For a contemporary view on the existence of such a discretion, *see People (DPP) v. Meleady (No.3)* [2001] 4 I.R. 16 at 31 (CCA *per* Geoghegan J.).

[65] (1965) 99 I.L.T.R. 59 at 70. Nor was Davitt P. persuaded by the argument of counsel for the respondent that submission to fingerprinting was akin to submission to a sobriety test: "The person who submits to having his finger prints taken undergoes no test and brings no evidence into being. The evidence already exists upon his finger tips. There is nothing subjective involved, the process is purely mechanical, and his reactions are immaterial and cannot affect the matter in any way." *Id.,* p.73.

been irregular in the instant case, this was no bar to the admissibility of the evidence.[66]

The terrain was visited a few years later by the English High Court in *Callis v. Gunn.*[67] Echoing the judgment of Davitt P. in *McGrath*, Lord Parker C.J. drew a distinction between fingerprint evidence, which was governed by the general inclusionary rule, and confession evidence to which "a much stricter rule applies."[68] A confession by an accused was admissible only where the prosecution can show that it was voluntary and not coerced by oppressive police conduct. This fundamental common law principle was buttressed by the rule of practice encapsulated in the Judges' Rules, that the questioning of a custodial detainee as a prelude to the taking of a statement must be preceded by the giving of a formal caution. The taking of fingerprints was subject to no such requirement.[69]

Notwithstanding the stridency of such judicial pronouncements, the admissibility of improperly obtained evidence was to undergo a *volte face* in this jurisdiction. The traditional assumption that relevant evidence is admissible, however obtained, has since been replaced by a rule of general exclusion which obliges the prosecution to demonstrate the propriety of the means by which its evidence is gathered. The catalyst was the landmark decision of the Supreme Court in *People (AG) v. O'Brien*[70] which, together with the Court's refinement in the 1990 case of *People (DPP) v. Kenny*,[71] stands for a threefold proposition: first, that evidence obtained in deliberate and conscious breach of an accused's constitutional rights is inadmissible at trial; second, that the existence of extraordinary circumstances excusing the unconstitutional action may

---

66 In his concurring judgment, McLoughlin J. characterised fingerprint evidence in the following terms: "[A] person submitting to having his finger prints taken no more creates evidence than a person who submits to his arrest when apprehended by a police officer. The state of his finger prints is an unalterable static fact just the same as is his height when standing or sitting, or the colour of his eyes or hair, and is incapable of being rendered true or false by the act of his submitting to the taking of print impressions from his fingers. The taking of finger print impressions might be likened to the making of an unchallengeably true copy of a document." *Id.*, pp.75-76.

67 [1964] 1 Q.B. 495.

68 *Id.*

69 *Id.*, at 502.

70 [1965] I.R. 142.

71 [1990] 2 I.R. 110; [1990] 1 I.L.R.M. 569.

render the evidence admissible at the discretion of the trial judge; and, third, that the trial judge enjoys a similar discretion to admit or exclude evidence obtained through illegal as opposed to unconstitutional means.[72]

The application of these evolving principles to fingerprint evidence was discussed by a divided Supreme Court in *People v. Walsh.*[73] The appellant was convicted in the Central Criminal Court of assault with intent to rob contrary to s.23(1)(a) of the Larceny Act 1916 on the basis that his fingerprints had been found on an object used in the assault. O'Higgins C.J., speaking for the majority, rejected the first ground of appeal, namely, that the fingerprint evidence ought to have been excluded because the appellant was not in lawful custody at the time the prints were taken. The alternative challenge to the admissibility of the fingerprint evidence lay in the failure of the Gardaí to caution the appellant or to inform him that he was not obliged to submit to having his fingerprints taken. This contention was rooted in the common law privilege against self incrimination and its related premise that, before being asked to do something that may incriminate him, a person should be warned that he is under no obligation to do so.[74] However, the notion that a caution was required so that the appellant would know that he was entitled to refuse to give his fingerprints was roundly rejected by O'Higgins C.J.:

> "The purpose of a caution in relation to a confession or statement is to ensure that what is said or written is said or written voluntarily. An involuntary confession or statement, given out of fear or induced by hope, is tainted evidence of a quality not acceptable in our Courts. It is not so with a fingerprint. A fingerprint does not change. Whether the person concerned submits voluntarily to having his print taken or whether he fiercely objects and resists makes no difference

---

72 The vindication of constitutional rights provides the primary justification for the contemporary approach; the exclusion of the tainted evidence at trial is a remedial consequence flowing from a breach of such rights. *See* n.2 and *see also* D. McGrath, "The Exclusionary Rule in Respect of Unconstitutionally Obtained Evidence" (2004) 26 D.U.L.J. 108.

73 [1980] I.R. 294.

74 A point noted by Walsh J. *id.* at 320 but not expressly addressed by the Chief Justice.

> to the probative value of the evidence obtained. His fingerprint remains the same and indicates always the same association or disassociation with the crime under investigation, irrespective of the circumstances under which it is obtained. Therefore, I cannot see why the administering of a caution, or anything resembling a caution, should be a necessary preliminary to the admissibility of fingerprint evidence."[75]

In a trenchant dissent, Walsh J. rejected the majority's distinction between confession evidence and fingerprint evidence. Quoting from the landmark decision of the Court of Criminal Appeal in *People v. Madden,*[76] Walsh J. drew an analogy between the exclusion of a voluntary statement obtained in deliberate and conscious violation of the constitutional right to liberty and the exclusion of fingerprints voluntarily given.[77]

(a) Recent Case Law

The entry into force of the Criminal Justice Act 1984 marked a watershed in the law relating to custodial detention. The Act strengthened the investigative powers of the Gardaí, principally by facilitating the practice of custodial interrogation, and put in place a miscellany of related procedures and safeguards, including the provisions pertaining to the taking of fingerprints, discussed above. As a corollary, the parameters of the inquiry into the lawfulness of the taking of evidence during custodial detention were reset. Whereas the statutory regime has generated a large body of case law and jurisprudence, the powers of the Gardaí in relation

---

75 [1980] I.R. 294 at 309. The sole question for a court in circumstances such as those presented by the instant case was whether the evidence sought to be admitted was taken by illegal means, an eventuality which would permit the trial judge to exclude the evidence at his discretion. In the view of O'Higgins C.J., no question of illegality arose in this case and the fingerprint evidence was properly admitted by the trial judge in the circumstances. For a contemporary view on the distinction between confession and forensic evidence, *see People (DPP) v. Boyce*, unreported, Court of Criminal Appeal, December 21, 2005.

76 [1977] I.R. 336.

77 [1980] I.R. 294 at 317-18 and 320.

to the taking and preservation of fingerprints have received relatively little attention.

In *People (DPP) v. Casey*,[78] the applicant, together with another man, was convicted of murder by a jury in the Central Criminal Court and sentenced to life imprisonment. The victim, a barman, had been attacked in a laneway and subjected to multiple blows to the head. At trial, the prosecution presented evidence that a palm print marked in blood on a wall in the laneway matched that of the applicant. In seeking leave to appeal, the applicant submitted that the evidence should have been excluded because the matching palm print had been taken from him without lawful authority. Shortly after his arrest and detention under section 4 of the 1984 Act, the applicant consented in writing to the submission of his fingerprints. He subsequently objected to the giving of a further set of prints and alleged that this second set was taken unlawfully against his will. Although the taking of the second set of prints had been authorised by a senior Garda officer, as required by section 6 of the 1984 Act, the supporting documentation submitted in evidence revealed a clerical error.[79] The issue at trial, and later on appeal, was whether this error tainted the authorisation itself. The trial judge spoke of the need to ensure that the Gardaí did not regard the statutory requirement as a mere empty formula but concluded that the error was harmless because there was sufficient additional evidence that the authorisation had been given. The Court of Criminal Appeal endorsed this reasoning and affirmed that the fingerprints had been lawfully obtained.

The case highlights the modest nature of the statutory limits on the authority of the Gardaí to fingerprint. The judgment contains a welcome statement of the principle that the statutory safeguards must be met in substance and not merely in form. However, the application of that principle to the facts of the case demonstrates its very limits in the context

---

[78] Unreported, Court of Criminal Appeal, December 14, 2004 (McGuinness, Herbert and Peart JJ.). The judgment of the Court was delivered by McGuinness J.. A conviction for the offence of refusing to allow one's fingerprints to be taken under s.6(4) of the 1984 Act has been held not to be the proper subject of an application for an order of *certiorari* by way of judicial review: *Devereaux v. District Justice Kotsonouris* [1992] I.L.R.M. 140 (HC).

[79] The nature of this error is not specified in the judgment of the Court of Criminal Appeal.

of fingerprint evidence. Very little is required of the Gardaí, it seems, in order to satisfy the statutory provisions.

The essentially compulsory character of the power to take fingerprints was reinforced by the recent decision of the Court of Criminal Appeal in *People (DPP) v. Cleary.*[80] The applicant was convicted by a jury in the Circuit Criminal Court on two counts relating to drug offences and sentenced to concurrent terms of one and three years' imprisonment. The drugs in question were retrieved by Gardaí from a first aid box inside a holdall bag which had been concealed in some bushes behind a derelict shop. It was the prosecution's contention at trial that a fingerprint found inside the lid of first-aid box matched a fingerprint of the applicant which had been taken by Gardaí subsequent to his arrest and while he was held in custody under section 4 of the 1984 Act. The Garda evidence was that the applicant had consented to the taking of his fingerprints and that he had signed the relevant consent form. In seeking leave to appeal, the applicant submitted that the fingerprint evidence should have been excluded on three grounds: first, that the prosecution had not produced the consent form; second, that the applicant's consent had not been informed because he had not been cautioned that his prints might be used in evidence; and, third, that the taking of the prints had not been authorised pursuant to section 6.

McGuinness J. disposed of the last of these grounds first, noting that the authorisation of a senior Garda officer is required only in relation to the *involuntary* taking of fingerprints. The Act requires that fingerprints be taken either by consent or by means of the proper authority but not both. Thus, in this instance, the applicant's written consent obviated the need for an authorisation pursuant to section 6. Had the applicant refused to give his consent, it would have been open to the attending Garda officer to have sought such an authorisation for the involuntary taking of the prints.[81]

The question of whether a suspect should be cautioned as a matter of principle before his fingerprints are taken was left open by the Court of Appeal. McGuinness J. noted that the caution given upon arrest is not on

80 [2005] 2 I.R. 189. The Court allowed the appeal against the applicant's conviction and sentence on one of the counts in the indictment on a separate ground relating to the burden of proof.

81 [2005] 2 I.R. 189 at 204.

all fours with the giving of fingerprints because it refers to anything the suspect may "say". Whereas the learned judge considered it desirable that a suspect be informed both of the purpose for the taking of the prints and of his entitlement to refuse in the first instance, she did not recognise an obligation on the part of the Gardaí to administer a specific caution in these terms. In instant case, McGuinness J. was confident that the applicant had been aware of the purpose for which his fingerprints were being taken and that his consent had been freely given. Consequently, the need for a special caution had not been established.[82]

On the issue of the failure of the prosecution to produce the consent form at trial, the Court of Criminal Appeal adopted an analogous stance to its position in *Casey.* The fact that the applicant had signed the form was undisputed and the evidentiary import of the form was consequently negligible.[83] Thus, in both *Casey* and *Cleary*, the totality of the evidence suggested that the substantive requirements of the 1984 Act had been met and that the failure of the Gardaí to observe certain statutory formalities did not affect the admissibility of the fingerprint evidence. The desire of the Court of Criminal Appeal to avoid the exclusion of evidence through slavish adherence to statutory technicality is understandable. Nevertheless, the holdings in *Casey* and *Cleary* should be read in their factual contexts and not interpreted as licence to sidestep the letter of the statute and supporting regulations. As McGuinness J. observed in *Cleary*, the absence of the consent form and the failure to specifically caution the applicant were weaknesses in the prosecution's case. Though such weaknesses were not fatal to the admissibility of the fingerprint evidence in that case, by implication they might be in the circumstances of another case.

The Voluntary Submission of Fingerprints

The judgment of the Court of Criminal Appeal in *Cleary* sheds some secondary light on a significant lacuna in the law relating to the taking of fingerprints. At trial, the attending Garda testified that he had told the applicant that he intended to take his fingerprints and then went on to ask

---

82 *Id.* at 205.
83 *Id.*

the applicant to volunteer to have his prints taken. The Garda testified that the applicant said that he had "no problem" with that and the applicant subsequently signed a consent form. Far from being unusual, the taking of fingerprints, as well as other forensic samples, in this manner, by asking the suspect to volunteer to undergo the relevant procedure, is said to constitute traditional Garda practice.[84] Whereas the authority conferred by the 1984 Act relates *de facto* to the involuntary taking of fingerprints, it has no application to situations such as this in which the suspect consents. The informality of the practice means that it is essentially unregulated and not conditioned by the safeguards contained in the Act and supporting regulations. The practice has been criticised by the Circuit Criminal Court[85] and has prompted the Law Reform Commission to recommend that the taking of all forms of forensic samples should be governed by legislation.[86] This would constitute a welcome development and would ensure that the taking of fingerprints, whether voluntary or involuntary, would be subject to a uniform set of procedures.

Reform Possibilities

The publication of the Law Reform Commission's *Report on the Establishment of a DNA Database*, against the backdrop of parliamentary consideration of the Criminal Justice Bill 2004, emphasised the need for renewed debate on the regulation of forensic procedures. The law relating to the taking of forensic samples, broadly defined, is currently dispersed across several distinct statutes and statutory instruments. Aside from the fragmented regime governing the recording of fingerprints, the taking of intimate and non-intimate bodily samples is the subject of entirely separate legislation,[87] as is the taking of specimens of breath, blood or urine in

---

84 LRC Consultation Paper, *op.cit.,* para.4.10.

85 *People (DPP) v. Carroll,* Circuit Criminal Court (McMahon J.), February 24, 2004 (fingerprint evidence excluded) cited in LRC Consultation Paper, *op. cit.,* para. 4.10. The Court of Criminal Appeal recently confirmed the legality of the practice in relation to DNA evidence. *People (DPP) v. Boyce*, unreported, Court of Criminal Appeal, December 21, 2005.

86 LRC Report, *op.cit.,* para. 2.211; LRC Consultation Paper, *op.cit.,* para. 4.12.

87 Notably, the Criminal Justice (Forensic Evidence) Act 1990 and the Criminal Justice (Forensic Evidence) Act Regulations 1992, (S.I. No.130 of 1992).

connection with the investigation of road traffic offences.[88] The Criminal Justice Act 2006 has continued this trend by amending individual provisions within the various statutes. Given the complexity of forensic testing and the profound implications for the protection of human rights, serious consideration should be given to the Law Reform Commission's call for a "complete review of the statutory procedures for sampling with a view to consolidation."[89] The taking of fingerprints, whether voluntary or involuntary, should be included in any such consolidated legislation. Moreover, the legislative scheme should contain a uniform, comprehensive set of safeguards.[90]

---

88 *See* ss. 12-18 of the Road Traffic Act 1994.
89 LRC Report, *op.cit.,* para. 2.48.
90 See n.53 *supra.*

Chapter 5

Fingerprint Evidence

The issues relating to the recording of fingerprints discussed in chapter 4 by no means exhaust the realm of potential legal challenges to fingerprint evidence. This chapter touches briefly on certain other matters, notably, the duty on the part of the Gardaí to seek out and preserve fingerprint evidence and the presentation of fingerprint evidence at trial.

The Preservation of Fingerprint Evidence

The obligation resting on the Gardaí to gather and preserve evidence for possible use by the defence at trial has been the subject of a vibrant discourse in the Supreme Court in recent years. The general principle was stated by Hardiman J. in *Braddish v. DPP:*

> "It is the duty of the Gardaí, arising from their unique investigative role, to seek out and preserve all evidence having a bearing or potential bearing on the issue of guilt or innocence. This is so whether the prosecution proposes to rely on the evidence or not, and regardless of whether it assists the case the prosecution is advancing or not."[1]

Although much of the discussion, including *Braddish* and its subsequent refinement in *Dunne v. DPP*,[2] has unfolded against the backdrop of video tape evidence, the duty to preserve fingerprint evidence has also featured in the case law. The issue has tended to surface in the context of judicial review proceedings before the High Court and the first of several judicial

---

1 [2002] 1 I.L.R.M. 151 at 157. *See generally* G. Birmingham, "The Obligation to Seek Out and Preserve Evidence" (2004) 9 *Bar Rev.* 86.

2 [2002] 2 I.R. 307, [2002] 2 I.L.R.M. 241. *See also Scully v. DPP* [2005] 2 I.L.R.M. 219.

pronouncements on point was delivered by Lynch J. in *Murphy v. DPP.*[3]

The applicant was charged in April 1987 with offences relating to the driving of a stolen car which was wrecked in the incident giving rise to the charges. On May 12, his legal advisors sought the results of any Garda forensic examination and, in particular, fingerprint tests, carried out on the car. They were told by the Gardaí that no such tests had been conducted because the prosecution intended to rely solely on visual identification evidence at trial. Two days later, the applicant's solicitor requested access to the vehicle for examination by the applicant's own fingerprint expert. On or about May 20, the solicitor was informed that the car was available for inspection. However, when the solicitor contacted the Gardaí on June 11 to arrange a time and place for the examination, he learned that the car had been handed over to an insurance company by the Gardaí for purposes of valuation. The applicant sought an injunction to restrain the Director of Public Prosecutions from proceeding with the prosecution on the grounds, *inter alia,* that the disposal of the car before any forensic examination had taken place prejudiced his defence by destroying potentially exculpatory evidence. Lynch J. granted the injunction applying the established principle that "evidence relevant to guilt or innocence must so far as is necessary and practicable be kept until the conclusion of the trial". This duty to preserve extended to "articles which may give rise to the reasonable possibility of securing relevant evidence". In the instant case, the Gardaí ought not to have parted with the car without examining it forensically or, alternatively, notifying the applicant's legal advisers of their intention to hand it over to the owner/insurance company. The Gardaí's actions amounted to a breach of fair procedures because they deprived the applicant of the reasonable opportunity of rebutting the prosecution's visual identification evidence with possible corroborative evidence supporting his denial that he was driving the car.

Murphy was distinguished in the subsequent case of *Rogers v. DPP*[4] which also arose out of an incident in which the applicant was alleged to

---

3 [1989] I.L.R.M. 71. For a discussion of fingerprint evidence as a newly discovered fact to support an application for the quashing of a conviction and the granting of a certificate acknowledging a miscarriage of justice under the ss.2 & 9 of the Criminal Procedure Act 1993, *see Re s.9 of the Criminal Procedure Act 1993: People (DPP) v. Meleady (No.3)* [2001] 4 I.R. 16 (CCA).

4 Unreported, High Court, March 2, 1992.

have been driving a stolen car. The applicant was charged on August 11, 1991 and brought before the district court on September 9. On or about October 25, the applicant's solicitor sought access to the car for purposes of examination by the applicant's engineer but was informed by the Gardaí that the car had been returned to the owner shortly after the incident. O'Hanlon J. held that there had been no breach of fair procedures such as would justify the court in halting the pending prosecution. This conclusion rested in part on two points of distinction between *Murphy* and the instant case. The first was the fact that the applicant's solicitor had waited two and a half months before informing the Gardaí that the car was required for forensic examination. It is interesting to note in this respect O'Hanlon J.'s concern relating to the potentially negative effect of the preservation of evidence on third parties:

> "I think that some consideration has to be given to the owner of the motor car which has been stolen or unlawfully taken; similarly in relation to other property the subject of criminal charges where deprivation of possession thereof will seriously prejudice or inconvenience the innocent owner thereof. In relation to such property, I would hold that any forensic examination, whether by the Gardaí or on behalf of an accused person, should be sought and should take place within a reasonable time, having regard to all the circumstances of the case, so that the property can then be returned as expeditiously as possible to its true owner."

The second distinguishing feature of the case, although noted without comment by O'Hanlon J., would seem of greater doctrinal significance. In the instant case, the car had been forensically examined by a Garda expert on the day after the incident and had been searched for fingerprints with negative results.[5] This action on the part of the Gardaí would seem

---

[5] O'Hanlon J. concluded that the application for judicial review had been brought in the mistaken belief that no forensic examination had taken place. It is not clear from the facts detailed in the judgment whether the applicant's solicitor had asked the Gardaí whether a forensic examination had been carried out or requested access to the results of any such examination. The doctrinal issue of the extent of any duty on the party of the Gardaí to provide an accused with such information and access is not addressed in the judgment.

to satisfy the duty to preserve as defined by Lynch J. in *Murphy*, namely, the duty to forensically examine or, alternatively, make available for forensic examination.

Several years later, O'Hanlon J.'s cautionary approach to enjoining criminal proceedings on grounds of beach of fair procedures was firmly endorsed by the Supreme Court in *Dutton v. DPP*.[6] The posture of the application for judicial review was far less favourable to the accused than it had been in *Murphy* or *Rogers*. The Gardaí had conducted a forensic examination of the allegedly stolen car at the centre of the proceedings but no fingerprints had been found and the prosecution did not intend to use the car in evidence. Moreover, the accused had not sought access to the car for examination until some two years after the incident when the trial was about to begin. The Supreme Court dismissed an appeal from the High Court's refusal to grant an injunction and used the occasion to emphasise that whether evidence should be admitted and whether an accused is prejudiced are matters for the trial judge and are not the proper subject of proceedings for judicial review. Nevertheless, applications for injunctive relief based on alleged breaches of the duty to preserve evidence have continued to feature on the High Court docket.

DPP v. Judge Cyril Kelly[7] is one such case in which the High Court determined that the non-availability of expert evidence had the potential of prejudicing the accused by materially affecting his ability to defend himself, in this instance against charges of sexual assault. The evidence in question was not fingerprint evidence but rather the expert opinion of a doctor who had examined the victim at the behest of the prosecution and whose statement was included in the book of evidence. Once it became apparent that the doctor would not be available to testify on the date of trial (and, in particular, be available for cross-examination by the defence) the trial judge directed the jury to acquit the accused. Applying the principle enunciated in *Murphy,* Laffoy J. refused the DPP's application for an order of *certiorari* quashing the trial judge's order. She noted that the doctor's evidence would be "singularly compelling" in corroborating either the complainant's or the accused's version of events. If the trial were to proceed in the doctor's absence, the accused would be deprived

---

6 Unreported, Supreme Court, July 14, 1998.

7 [1997] 1 I.L.R.M. 497.

of the reasonable possibility of rebutting the evidence proffered against him.

In relation to fingerprints, the outcome of cases involving the non-availability of fingerprint evidence, short of loss or destruction on the part of the Gardaí, have been more difficult to predict. *Braddish* and the subsequent decision of the Supreme Court in *Dunne* stand for the proposition that rendering available potentially exculpatory evidence may rise to the level of a constitutional requirement. However, in order to secure injunctive relief, an applicant must establish that there is a real risk that his trial will be unfair and, consequently, involve a violation of Article 38.1. A reading of the recent case law indicates that the proper focus on the judicial inquiry is not the conduct or misconduct of the Gardaí *per se* but rather the likely impact of the evidentiary omission on the accused's case at trial. However, these cases also reveal that this test is not as straightforward as it may seem. There may be circumstances, in particular, in which the actions of the Gardaí have a direct bearing on the probative potential of the evidence.

The basic fact pattern of *Murphy* and *Rogers* was replicated in *Bowes v. DPP*[8] which reached the Supreme Court by way of an appeal from the High Court's refusal to grant an injunction restraining the applicant's trial on a charge of possession of heroin for purposes of sale or supply. Here again was a situation in which the Gardaí had allegedly parted with possession of an item of evidence before the applicant had an opportunity to examine it. The item in question was the car the applicant was driving when stopped by Gardaí on April 3, 2000 and in the boot of which the Gardaí had found the heroin. The Garda technical bureau carried out a forensic examination during which they found fingerprints in the boot and a single fingerprint inside the car which they believed belonged to the applicant. The car was then stored in Blanchardstown Garda station and on November 16, 2001, a few days before the date fixed for trial, the applicant's solicitors were informed by the Gardaí that it had been scrapped. On the same day, the applicant's solicitors sought from the DPP's Office the results of the forensic examination and information pertaining to the chain of custody of the car and its destruction. The Supreme Court accepted the DPP's submission that the duty to preserve evidence is not an absolute one and that an applicant is not entitled to

---

[8] [2003] 2 I.R. 25.

restrain a criminal prosecution simply by reason of the fact that the Gardaí were at some stage in possession of articles that might have been of evidential value but have since parted with such possession. Hardiman J. recalled his statement in *Braddish*:

> "But in cases where the evidence is not of such direct and manifest relevance, the duty to preserve and disclose has to be interpreted in a fair and reasonable manner. It must be recalled that, in the words of Lynch J. in *Murphy v. Director of Public Prosecutions* [1989] I.L.R.M. 71 the duty to preserve evidence is to do so 'so far as is necessary and practicable'. A duty so qualified cannot be precisely or exhaustively defined in words of general application. Certainly, it cannot be interpreted as requiring the Gardaí to engage in disproportionate commitment of man power or resources in an exhaustive search for every conceivable kind of evidence. The duty must be interpreted realistically on the facts of each case."[9]

These sentiments were echoed in *Dunne*:

> "The emphasis, which is quite explicit in *Braddish v. Director of Public Prosecutions* [2001] 3 I.R. 127 and in this judgment, on the need for the obligation to seek out, and indeed to preserve, evidence to be reasonably interpreted requires, I hope, that no remote, theoretical or fanciful possibility will lead to the prohibition of a trial … The exercise of [this] jurisdiction must be careful and realistic. There is also a responsibility on a defendant's advisers, with their special knowledge and information, to request material thought by them to be relevant."[10]

In relation to the criteria for restraining prosecution of a criminal case, Hardiman J. cited with approval dicta of Finlay C.J. in *Z v. DPP*:

---

9 *Braddish v. DPP* [2001] 3 I.R. 127 at 135.

10 *Dunne v. Director of Public Prosecutions* [2002] 2 I.R. 305 at 323-24.

> "[The] onus of proof which is on the accused person who seeks an order prohibiting his trial on the ground that circumstances have occurred which would render it unfair is that he should establish that there is a real risk that by reason of those circumstances … he could not obtain a fair trial.
>
> …
>
> An onus to establish a real risk of an unfair trial … necessarily and inevitably means an unfair trial which cannot be avoided by appropriate rulings and directions on the part of the trial judge. The risk is a real one but the unfairness of trial must be an unavoidable unfairness of trial."[11]

Hardiman J. stressed that "the focus in any such application must be on the fairness of the eventual trial, and not on the discovery of shortcomings in the investigative process except insofar as they impact on the prospects of a fair trial".[12] He acknowledged, at the same time, that where evidence has been lost to a defendant, one can only speculate about what its contents might have been, and that "[i]t is extremely difficult, perhaps impossible, to devise a basis on which this entirely speculative element can be incorporated, fairly to both sides, in a trial based on existing evidence".[13] Applying these principles to the facts of *Bowes*, Hardiman J. concluded that the applicant had failed to establish a real risk of an unfair trial. The applicant had not raised the issue of a technical examination until virtually the eve of trial and the Gardaí had not parted possession with the car until a year after the applicant's arrest. Moreover, such examination would offer no more than a negligible possibility of rebutting the prosecution's case; that case did not turn on the car itself, nor the manner of its driving, but on the proposition that drugs were found in its boot immediately after the applicant had been driving it.[14]

---

11 [1994] 2 I.R. 476 at 506-07.

12 [2003] 2 I.R. 25 at 35.

13 *Id.*

14 *Id.*, pp.30-31 and 38-39. The applicant did not dispute that he had been travelling in the car and was situated in the car at the time of his arrest. The facts of the applicant's case contrasted in material ways with those of a second applicant (McGrath) whose appeal, based on the same principal submissions, was allowed by the Supreme Court. In the case of the second applicant, the possibility of a technical examination of the item of evidence, a motorcycle, was raised by the

The Supreme Court returned to the duty to preserve evidence just two months later in *McKeown v. Judges of the Dublin District Court.*[15] The case arose out of an attempt by the Gardaí to recover a motor car allegedly stolen by the applicant and another man during which the applicant allegedly hit a Garda officer on the head with a petrol can. The applicant sought to prevent his prosecution on charges of assault and the unauthorised use of the vehicle on the ground that his right to fair trial had been violated by the actions of the Gardaí in returning the car and petrol can to the owner the day after the incident. Characterising as part of the foundation of our system of justice the notion that the Gardaí are independent of both the DPP and the accused, Geoghegan J. stated: "I have no doubt that there is an obligation on the Gardaí to disclose to both the prosecution and the defence all matters which might be of assistance either to the prosecution or to the defence". Having reviewed the now substantial body of case law on point, Geoghegan J. opined that the principles relating to the duty to preserve evidence must be tempered by the concept of reasonableness; there are limits to the lengths to which the Gardaí must go either in seeking out or preserving evidence and each case must be judged on its own facts. The question in the present case was whether the evidence could be of assistance to the defence. Geoghegan J. continued:

> "If a person is accused of driving a stolen motor car, quite clearly that car is often a vital piece of evidence. If the car could provide potential evidence favourable to the defence it should certainly be made available to the accused person or his advisors where reasonably practicable before being returned to the owner. Regard must be had to the practicalities, and in particular to the rights of the unfortunate owner of a stolen car who obviously is entitled to have it returned to

defence on the date when the summons was first returnable and formally requested within days of the service of the book of evidence. The Gardaí parted with possession of the motorcycle some two and a half months before proceedings were instituted against the second applicant. Finally, the case of dangerous driving causing death against the second applicant related directly to the manner of her driving in connection with the collision between her vehicle and the motorcycle. [2003] 2 I.R. 25 at 30-32.

15 Unreported, Supreme Court, April 9, 2003.

> him as quickly as possible. These practicalities must be judged on the facts of each case. ...[T]he proper procedure would seem to be that if evidence of this nature is to be returned to its true owner, where practicable that should only be done after notice has been given to the accused person or his legal advisors of the intention to return the evidence and a reasonable time given for an accused or his advisors either to examine the evidence or dispense with the examination."

The actions of the accused person and his legal advisors are also relevant because [j]ust as there is an obligation on the Gardaí to make evidence available to an accused, there is also an obligation on the accused to seek such evidence". In the present case, the Gardaí had not observed the proper procedure outlined by Geoghegan J. but the applicant and his legal advisors had for their part waited for some ten months before making the relevant request. The test, of course, was whether the applicant had been deprived of a real opportunity to rebut the case against him. Crucial to the outcome of the application was Geoghegan J.'s determination that even if the Gardaí had retained custody of the car for some ten months after the incident, it was "highly improbable that any real evidence to the applicant would have emerged".

The bounty of recent case law on the duty to preserve evidence has ironed out several doctrinal wrinkles while at the same time adding one or two fresh creases. *McKeown* is a case in point. Here the Gardaí parted possession with the items of evidence in question (the car and the petrol can) the day after the incident, having neither conducted a forensic examination nor notified the applicant of their intended action. Geoghegan J. emphasised that "[w]hether there has been fault on the part of the Gardaí or not, the only basis for this application must be that the applicant had been prejudiced in his right to a fair trial". However, in concluding that it was "highly improbable" that any real evidence of benefit to the applicant would have emerged even if the Gardaí had retained custody of the items until the applicant made his request some ten months later, Geoghegan J. stated:

> "Certainly, there could have been no such evidence available after the car had been used by its owner during that period. Similar comments must apply to the petrol can. These, unlike

> the video tapes which were the subject matter of several of the cases, would require a forensic examination to be carried out within a short time of the alleged crime if any useful evidence is to be obtained."

There is surely a point at which improper conduct on the part of the Gardaí has some bearing on the question whether the applicant has been prejudiced in his right to a fair trial. Indeed, Geoghegan J.'s observations about the likelihood of the contamination of the evidence following its return to the owner the day after the incident merely underscore the direct link between the Gardaí's actions and the availability of potential evidence. Certainly, this case should not be interpreted as ruling out entirely the relevance of the conduct of the Gardaí. Arguably, one might go so far as to say that a breach of proper procedure on the part of the Gardaí, as occurred in this case, is presumptively a *factor* to be considered in determining the likelihood of prejudice.

As it turns out, the dilatoriness of the applicant and his advisors in *McKeown* in seeking out this potential evidence provided Geoghegan J. with a clear basis on which to resolve the case. Given the inherent difficulty involved in speculating about the possible defence and the evidence tendered in support thereof, the action or inaction of the applicant and his advisors was relevant to the issue of likely prejudice. Picking up a thread sown by Hardiman J. in *Bowes,* Geoghegan J. pointed out that "if the applicant's advisors had felt that an independent examination for fingerprints was required, they would presumably have requested it". Instead, they waited some ten months before making such a request. In proceedings for judicial review, the onus clearly rests on the applicant to establish a real risk of an unfair trial. A timely request on the part of an accused for an opportunity to examine an item of potential evidence it seems is a virtual precondition to such proceedings.

The degree of expeditiousness required is not clear from the case law and obviously will vary depending on the circumstances of the case. But it is interesting to consider how the issue in *McKeown* would have been resolved had the applicant requested access to the car and petrol can a few days, a few weeks or even a few months after the incident. That these issues are usually resolved by the application of the concepts of "reasonableness" and "practicability" was illustrated by the recent decision of the High Court in *Connolly v. DPP*.[16] An application to prevent the applicant's trial on charges relating to a stolen car was refused where the applicant had requested a forensic examination two months after the incident in question. The car had not been damaged in the incident and the owner, who had no other means of transport, was anxious to secure its return. In the circumstances, Finlay Geoghegan J. did not consider it practicable for the Gardaí to keep the car in their possession for a period of two months.[17] As to whether the Gardaí were under a duty to seek out and preserve fingerprint evidence before returning the car to the owner, Finlay Geoghegan J. cautioned that any such duty must be interpreted "realistically on the facts of each case".[18] She continued:

> "If the facts of the case were that the Gardaí had arrested the applicant whilst actually in the car then I do not think it could be suggested that the Gardaí were under any duty to seek fingerprint evidence from the car before returning it to the owner. At the other end of the scale, if Gardaí, having received a report of the stolen car, found the car, did not see any person actually in the car and arrested and charged a youth who happened to be nearby and immediately stated he was not in the car then they probably would be under a duty to seek fingerprint evidence."[19]

This present case fell between these two extremes. Nevertheless, the court concluded that the Gardaí were not under such a duty on the facts presented: they had arrested and charged a person whom they alleged to have seen in a stolen car; he had given no indication that he was not the person in the car; and the owner was seeking the immediate return of the car.[20]

---

16 [2003] 4 I.R. 121.
17 *Id.* at 131.
18 *Id.* at 130.
19 *Id.* at 131.
20 *See also People (DPP) v. McKeever* [1994] 2 I.L.R.M. 186 in which the Court of Criminal Appeal held that there was no obligation on the Gardaí to take fingerprints from a gun which was taken from the accused. O'Flaherty J. explained: "[The Gardaí] took the view – correctly we think – that since they had arrested the applicant with a gun in his possession and in view of his confessions

The Supreme Court recently returned to this territory in *McFarlane v. DPP*[21] The case involved an appeal from the decision of Ó'Caoimh J. to grant an injunction restraining the DPP from prosecuting the applicant on charges relating to the kidnapping of Don Tiddey in circumstances where the Gardaí had lost fingerprint evidence which had been held in their custody for several years.[22] The fingerprints had been visualised on a milk carton, a plastic container and a cooking pot and then photographed. The items, but not the photographs, had been lost due to a lack of care at a time when the premises in which the evidence was being stored were being renovated. Notwithstanding that there had been a forensic examination when the Gardaí took possession of the items, Ó'Caoimh J. concluded that the failure of the Gardaí to retain them had resulted in the loss of vital evidence. In his view, the case was on all fours with *Braddish* in which the Supreme Court held that the loss of a videotape by the Gardaí justified restraining the applicant's trial even though photographic stills had been taken from the video and the applicant had signed a statement admitting his guilt. The Supreme Court allowed the appeal and overturned the grant of the injunction taking issue with the High Court's "over-rigid" application of the principle in *Braddish.* Hardiman J. began by criticising the Gardaí's failure to preserve the evidence:

> "The Court wishes to emphasise that this want of care is a very grave matter and requires the urgent attention of the

---

no further proof was required. The only real effect of the omission to have the gun fingerprinted was to deprive the prosecution of possible additional corroborative evidence if in fact the applicant's fingerprints had appeared on the gun whereas if they did not appear on the gun, whilst it would be a factor the applicant might rely upon, it would really be a neutral factor as it would not establish that he had not been in contact with the gun." The issue of the duty of the police to seek out and preserve evidence has also been litigated in the United States under the rubric of an accused's constitutional due process rights. *See e.g. Ely v. State*, 288 Md. 548, 419 A.2d 384 (1980). However, it has been held that the defence must lay an evidentiary foundation before arguing in closing statements that a jury should infer that fingerprint evidence could have been obtained and would have been exculpatory. *United States v. Hoffman*, 964 F.2d 21 (Dist. Col. Ct. App. 1992).

21 Unreported, Supreme Court, March 7, 2006.

22 Unreported, High Court, July 18, 2003.

> Garda authorities. Most unfortunately this is by no means the first case to come before the Court in which items of real evidence transpire to be missing when they are looked for trial purposes or in the course of judicial review proceedings such as these .. [T]he Court has previously drawn attention to the need for great care in the matter of the storage of evidence …"[23]

In determining the consequences that flowed from this want of care, Hardiman J. distinguished *Bowes* on the basis that meaningful comparison of fingerprints was feasible in the instant case. The *results* of forensic analysis had been preserved in the form of the photographs which facilitated the necessary independent comparison. The applicant had failed to engage in any meaningful way the issue whether the absence of the original fingerprint evidence created a real risk that he would be deprived of a fair trial given the existence of the photographic evidence. The present case was also factually distinguishable from *Dunne* and *Braddish* because in those cases the real evidence had been lost entirely: "[a] closer analogy to the facts of the present case would be if the contents of the video tape had been recorded onto another tape and the originals then lost or disposed of."[24] Recognising that the law "is not so unrealistic as to consider that the loss of an original document or item of real evidence is fatal to any litigation based upon it,"[25] Hardiman J. concluded that there was ample provision in the law for proof of the fingerprint by way of a duly authenticated photograph.[26]

Presenting Fingerprint Evidence

The opinion of a fingerprint expert must comply with the rules and procedures relating to the admission of expert evidence as means of proof in a court of law discussed in chapter 1. The reliability of expert opinion is a particularly testing issue and the governing standards are difficult to discern from the case law. The courts have tended to focus on two

---

23 Unreported, Supreme Court, March 7, 2003 at p.7.
24 *Id.*, p.9.
25 *Id.*, p.10.
26 Kearns J. dissenting.

safeguards by which the finder of fact may gauge the veracity of the expert's conclusions and, ultimately, the weight of his opinion: first, the expert's qualifications and experience[27] and, second, the expert's methodology.[28] The paucity of case law in the appellate courts suggests that judicial scrutiny has been relatively benign and uncontroversial. Certainly, the Irish courts have not yet engaged in the qualitative assessment of the predicate science itself – is the expert tendering "good" or "bad" science — which has become almost routine practice in the United States.[29] Irish law has nothing akin to the "general acceptance"[30] or "scientific validation"[31] tests which precondition admissibility in that jurisdiction.[32] The point is an important one when considered against

---

27 *R v. Silverlock* [1894] 2 Q.B. 766 (solicitor's evidence admissible as handwriting expert); *R v. Robb* (1991) 93 Cr. App. R. 161 (voice identification); *United States v. George,* 256 F.3d 774 (7th Cir. 2004) (evidence of FBI fingerprint examiner admissible).

28 *People (DPP) v. Allen* [2003] 4 I.R. 295; *State (D & D) v. Groake* [1990] 1 I.R. 305.

29 *See* chap.2 *supra. See also* e.g. *United States v. Plaza,* 188 F. Supp.2d 549 (E.D. Pa., 2002); *United States v. Haavard,* 260 F.3d 597 (7th Cir., 2001); *United States v. Crisp,* 324 F.3d 261 (4th Cir. 2003).

30 *Frye v. United States*, 293 F. 1013 (D.C. Cir. 1923).

31 *Daubert v. Merrell Dow Pharmaceuticals, Inc.*, 509 U.S. 579, 113 S.Ct. 2786 (1993).

32 Several of the US Courts of Appeals have held that fingerprint evidence is sufficiently reliable to justify its admission under the standards of Federal Rule of Evidence 702 and *Daubert. See e.g. United States v. Abreu*, 406 F.3d 1304 (11th Cir. 2005); *United States v. Janis*, 387 F.3d 682 (8th Cir. 2004); *United States v. Crisp*, 324 F.3d 261 (4th Cir. 2003); *United States v. Havvard*, 260 F.3d 597 (7th Cir. 2001). In *United States v. Sanchez-Birruetta*, (9th Cir. March 19, 2005), the Court of Appeals for the 9th Circuit ruled that a comparison of two sets of rolled prints (as opposed to a set of rolled and a set of latent prints) is particularly reliable. On the U.S. approach to measuring the reliability of expert evidence *see generally* E.J. Imwinkelried, "'Junk Science' in the Courtroom: Will the Changes in the American Law of Expert Testimony Influence the Irish Courts?" (2004) 26 D.U.L.J. 83. On the possible introduction of a reliability-based rule in English law *see* M. Redmayne, *Expert Evidence and Criminal Justice* (Oxford University Press, Oxford, 2001), chap.5; P. Roberts, "Tyres With a 'Y': An English Perspective on *Kumho Tire* and its Implications for the Admissibility of Expert Evidence" (1999) *Int'l Comm. on Evidence* (posted at www.law.qub.ac.uk/ice); P. Alldridge, "Recognising Novel Scientific Techniques: DNA as a Test Case" [1992] Crim. L. R. 687.

the backdrop of the Constitution and the European Convention on Human Rights which would presumptively require a judge to exclude demonstrably unreliable scientific evidence in order to safeguard the fairness of a trial.[33] Such evidence might also be excluded at the judge's discretion on the basis that its probative value is outweighed by its prejudicial effect.[34]

The early common law cases discussed in chapter 3 illustrate the long standing acceptance by the courts of fingerprint evidence as a means of proof at trial. These cases stand for the proposition that dactyloscopy is a science outside the ken of the average juror and, consequently, an appropriate subject for expert testimony. Indeed, courts throughout the common law world have generally accepted expert opinion on the subject with little or no inquiry into the reliability of the predicate science.[35] The dissenting judgment of Walsh J. in *People v. Walsh*[36] provides a passing insight into the deference which lawyers and judges have accorded fingerprint experts and the confidence with which they have accepted the prevailing methodology. In reviewing the trial transcript, Walsh J. concluded that there was ample evidence on which a jury could find that a fingerprint located at the crime scene belonged to the appellant. The evidence, he noted, was established "using the usual points of comparison" between a fingerprint obtained from the appellant and the fingerprint found at the crime scene.[37]

Fingerprint comparison has been the subject of more critical judicial scrutiny in recent times. Whereas the predicate scientific methodology has not been the subject of reported Irish cases, a comprehensive analysis of the use of numerical standards was undertaken by the English Court of

---

33 Art. 38.1 of the Constitution and art. 6 of the European Convention on Human Rights. In the United Kingdom, prosecution evidence may be excluded under s.78 of the Police and Criminal Evidence Act 1984, as amended, where it would have an adverse effect on fairness of the trial. Redmayne, *op. cit.*, p.97-98 (citing cases).

34 *R v. Sang* [1980] A.C. 402.

35 *See e.g.* T. Kiely, *Forensic Evidence: Science and the Criminal Law,* 2nd ed. (CRC Press, Baton Rouge, Florida, 2006), p.342; P. C. Giannelli and E.J. Imwinkelried, *Scientific Evidence*, 3rd ed. (Lexis Law Publishing, Charlottesville, Virginia, 1999), p.740.

36 [1980] I.R. 294.

37 *Id.*, pp.310-11.

Appeal in *R v. Buckley*.[38] In response to inconsistencies among the trial courts in determining the admissibility of fingerprint evidence, the Court of Appeal availed of the opportunity presented by this case to offer some guidance as to the number of similar ridge characteristics required to support an expert opinion. Rose L.J., speaking for the Court, began his analysis with a brief history of fingerprint standards, charting the emergence of a numerical standard of 12 similar ridge characteristics as the basis for a match, a requirement which was later extended to 16 such characteristics. With the passage of time, and developments in knowledge and expertise, a consensus emerged among experts that fewer than 16 ridge characteristics would establish a match beyond doubt. As the Rose L.J. explained:

> "Some experts suggested that eight would provide a complete safeguard. Others maintained that there should be no numerical standard at all. We are told, and accept, that other countries admit identifications of 12, 10 or eight similar ridge characteristics and, in some other countries, the numerical system has been abandoned altogether. In 1983 there was a conference which recognised that all fingerprint experts accepted that a fingerprint identification is certain with less than the current standard of 16 points of agreement. It was also recognised that all experts agreed that there should be a nationally accepted standard, which should be adhered to in all but the most exceptional cases. The Conference recognised that there would be rare occasions where an identification fell below the standard, but the print was of such crucial importance in the case that the evidence about it should be placed before the Court. Therefore the Conference advised that, in extremely rare cases, the evidence of comparison should be given only by an expert of long experience and high standing."

These developments prompted some trial judges to admit fingerprint

[38] April 30, 1999, [1999] E.W.C.A. Crim. 1191 (Rose L.J., McKinnon and Collins JJ.). *See* M.N. Howard, ed., *Phipson on Evidence,* 15th ed. (Sweet & Maxwell, London, 2000), para.14.31.

evidence where there were less than 16 similar ridge characteristics; they also led to commissioning of a study and the setting up of a series of committees at the behest of the Home Office and the Association of Chief Police Officers to explore the question of fingerprint standards. A Fingerprint Evidence Project Board was later established and recommended the introduction of a non-numerical system.

That system has since been formally adopted in England. In contrast, Irish practice continues to be governed by a numerical standard of 12 points with the consequence that the decision of the Court of Appeal in *Buckley* has continuing relevance in this jurisdiction.[39]

Turning to the legal position, the Court of Appeal observed that a tender of fingerprint evidence by the prosecution necessitates the resolution of two questions: first, a question of fact, as to whether the print taken from the accused has ridge characteristics and, if so how many, similar to those of the print found at the crime scene; and, second, a question of expert opinion, as to whether the print found at the crime scene was made by the accused, based on the number of similar ridge characteristics in the context of other findings. Based on the present state of knowledge and expertise in relation to fingerprints, the Court of Appeal proffered the following guidance:

> "If there are fewer than eight similar ridge characteristics, it is highly unlikely that a judge will exercise his discretion to admit such evidence and, save in wholly exceptional circumstances, the prosecution should not seek to adduce such evidence. If there are eight or more similar ridge characteristics, a judge may or may not exercise his or her discretion in favour of admitting the evidence. How the discretion is exercised will depend on all the circumstances of the case, including in particular:
> (i) the experience and expertise of the witness;
> (ii) the number of similar ridge characteristics;
> (iii) whether there are dissimilar ridge characteristics;
> (iv) the size of the print relied on, in that the same number of

---

39 *See* chap. 3 *supra*. The non-numerical standard was introduced in England in 2001. *See* M. Armer, "Fingerprint Evidence" (2001) 151 N.L.J. 1660.

similar ridge characteristics may be more compelling in a fragment of print than in an entire print; and

(v) the quality and clarity of the print on the item relied on, which may involve, for example, consideration of possible injury to the person who left the print, as well as factors such as smearing or contamination."

The Court of Appeal concluding by stating that in every case where fingerprint evidence is admitted, it will generally be necessary for the judge to warn the jury that it is evidence of opinion only and that determining whether guilt has been proved remains the task of the jury in light of all of the evidence.[40]

In the Irish context, a rare challenge to the conduct of a fingerprint expert was raised in *DPP v. Kelly*.[41] The applicant was convicted of counts of possession of a controlled drug and possession for the purpose of supply contrary to sections 3 and 15 of the Misuse of Drugs Act 1977. The prosecution established at trial that the applicant had received a plastic bag containing 1kg of cocaine from a man whom he had met at the airport arriving from England. In refusing the application for leave to appeal against conviction, the Court of Criminal Appeal rejected the applicant's contention that he had been deprived of fair procedures by the failure of the prosecution's expert to demonstrate that the characteristics of fingerprints found on the plastic bag were not those of the applicant. The expert's evidence was that he had found no more than smudges on the plastic bag from which fingerprint characteristics could not be discerned. The Court was satisfied that the smudges could not have assisted either the prosecution or the defence and, consequently, that the applicant had not been deprived of any material evidence.

---

[40] A recent decision of the U.S. Court of Appeals for the 10th Circuit suggests that fingerprint equipment or technology (as opposed to a fingerprint methodology) may not necessarily be subject to the *Daubert* standard of reliability. The Court rejected a challenge to the "live skin" method of recording fingerprints whereby digital equipment captures fingerprints (in much the same way as a machine duplicates paper copies) and prints them onto a fingerprint card. The system is used in some jurisdictions in lieu of the traditional process of inking the rolled fingerprints of a suspect. *United States v. Lauder* 409 F.3d 1254 (10th Cir. 2005).

[41] Unreported, Court of Criminal Appeal, March 4, 1996.

The science of fingerprinting was also called into question in *People (DPP) v. Casey*.[42] At issue in the application for leave to appeal was the admissibility of evidence pertaining to a palm print found in blood at the crime scene. The Court of Criminal Appeal rejected the applicant's submission that the evidence ought to have been excluded because no scientific or other evidence existed to establish that the substance in question was blood. The Garda scene of the crime examiner had testified that the palm print was in blood above a blood spattered border and the State Pathologist had given evidence of having seen the palm mark on the wall. In addition, photographic evidence of the palm print had been furnished to the court at trial. The Court noted that the purpose of the evidence was to establish that the palm print was that of the applicant and that the jury had before it all the necessary evidence.[43]

The Probative Value of Fingerprint Evidence

Cases such as *Kelly* and *Casey* focus on procedural and mechanical aspects of expert fingerprint evidence.[44] The broader and intriguing question of the sufficiency of fingerprint evidence as proof of guilt has yet to be fully explored in this jurisdiction. The issue is by no means novel. In *Re Castleton*,[45] one of the first reported cases in which the English Court of Appeal upheld the admissibility of fingerprint evidence, counsel for the appellant submitted that a conviction for burglary could not stand where the only evidence against his client had been that of fingerprints upon a candle left at the scene. Even supposing that the fingerprints were those of the appellant, the evidence was not sufficiently weighty not least

---

[42] Unreported, Court of Criminal Appeal, December 14, 2004. *See* chap.4 *supra*.

[43] Looking to the future, it is interesting to note that automated fingerprint systems have been challenged in the American courts. *See e.g. United States v. Patterson,* 277 F.3d 709 (4th Cir. 2002).

[44] The alleged deprivation of an opportunity for the defence to present its own fingerprint expert was raised in *State (Royle) v. Kelly* [1974] I.R. 259. The Supreme Court held that the alleged irregularity was not sufficient to ground an order of habeas corpus (which was the relief sought in the case) without determining whether it rendered the trial unsatisfactory (which would have been the issue on appeal).

[45] [1909] Cr. App. R. 74.

because the fingerprints may have been left by a criminal associate. The Lord Chief Justice disposed of the appeal in a few short sentences:

> "We are clearly of the opinion that this application must be dismissed. The suggestion has been made that these fingerprints may have been put there by someone else, but that suggestion was disposed of by the jury, who decided upon the evidence before them. Our attention has been drawn to the photographs of the impressions of the finger-prints. Looking at the middle finger particularly, as well as to the index finger of the right hand, we agree with the evidence of the expert at the trial."[46]

Some 50 years later, the Court of Appeal was much more circumspect in its assessment of the probative effect of fingerprint evidence. *Re Court*[47] involved an appeal from a conviction for receiving a stolen motor car secured solely on evidence that a fingerprint made by the appellant's left forefinger had been found on the back of the driving mirror. The prosecution's case was that the location of the fingerprint proved that the appellant had been the driver (as opposed to a passenger) and that, accordingly, he was in control and, therefore, in possession of the car. Donovan J. was not persuaded, however, that the mere fact that the appellant's left forefinger print was on the back of the driving mirror could be stretched into evidence of possession. The prosecution had not proved that the car was a right-hand drive; nor could it be ruled out that the fingerprint had been left by someone leaning over from behind the driver to adjust the mirror. The argument for possession based on the single fingerprint alone was "altogether too rarefied to be accepted" and the court should have accepted the submission of the defence that there was no evidence sufficiently satisfactory to be left to the jury.[48]

The permissible inferences that can be drawn from fingerprint evidence was considered by the Supreme Court of Canada in *R v. Lepage*.[49] The accused was charged with *inter alia* possession of LSD for the purpose

---

[46] *Id.*
[47] [1960] Cr. App. R. 242.
[48] *Id.,* at 244.
[49] [1995] 1 S.C.R. 654.

of trafficking. In a search of the house which the accused was renting, the police found the LSD on blotting paper in a clear plastic zip-lock bag under the sofa in the living room where the accused and his girlfriend had been sitting. The only identifiable fingerprints on the bag were those of the accused. LSD blotting paper of similar design was found in an upstairs room occupied by a subtenant, together with a vial of hash oil and a wallet containing 10 hits of LSD. The subtenant confessed to ownership of the drugs contained in the plastic bag but subsequently recanted his statement. He was tried separately to the accused and acquitted and later testified on behalf of the Crown at the accused's trial. The accused was convicted but his conviction was overturned by the Ontario Court of Appeal. In a majority judgment, the Supreme Court of Canada allowed the appeal and restored the conviction.

The relevant issue was whether the trial judge had erred in drawing the inference of possession of the LSD from the presence of the accused's fingerprints on the plastic bag or any other evidence. Sopinka J. characterised the question as one of fact, not subject to a hard and fast rule but rather dependent on all the circumstances of the case and all the evidence adduced. He noted that once the trial judge had proved a *prima facie* case, the trial judge would have been entitled to draw such an inference from the accused's failure to offer any explanation for the presence of his fingerprints. This was the point at which "the absence of defence evidence, including the failure of the accused to testify, justifies the conclusion that no foundation for a reasonable doubt could be found on the evidence". He continued: "It is no so much that the failure to testify justifies an inference of guilt; it is rather that it fails to provide any basis to conclude otherwise."[50] Sopinka J. took issue with a distinction drawn by the Court of Appeal between fingerprints found on a plastic bag, which could have been handled in a variety of innocent ways prior to the LSD paper being placed in it, and fingerprints found on the paper itself. The distinction was just another factor to be taken into account in deciding whether or not to draw the inference and, clearly, the fact that the accused's fingerprints were on the plastic bag containing the LSD was highly probative of possession.

Cory and Major JJ. dissented on the basis that the accused had been deprived of the fundamental protections embodied in the presumption of

---

50 *Id.,* at para.XXIX.

innocence and the right to silence. In a judgment delivered by Major J., the dissenters' endorsed the majority position that the drawing of the inference of possession was not subject to any hard and fast rule but concluded that it had been improperly drawn on the facts of this case:

> "In my view, there was a foundation in law for reasonable doubt in this case given that all three tenants of the house had access to the kitchen drawers where plastic bags similar to that containing the LSD were kept. It was thus possible that the respondent had innocently handled the bag in the kitchen prior to its use as a container for the LSD. The fingerprints on the container were not sufficient, in and of themselves, to draw an inference of guilt requiring the accused to provide an explanation."[51]

The possibility that the prosecution can rest its case solely or substantially on fingerprint evidence has also been recognised in the United States. However, some courts have attached the proviso that the prosecution must also establish that the fingerprints were left at the crime scene at a time contemporaneous with the commission of the crime.[52] To put it another way, expert testimony of a fingerprint match combined with evidence from which a jury could infer that the fingerprints could only have been impressed at the time the crime was committed, is a sufficient basis on which a case may be put to a jury.[53] An example is *State v. Monzo*,[54] where evidence that a room in which an assault took place had been painted prior to the attack was admitted to establish that the accused's fingerprints had been left contemporaneously at the scene. This development is indicative of the ways in which the prosecution can use forensic science to mount cases based substantially, if not entirely, on circumstantial evidence.

At the other end of the spectrum, the absence of fingerprint evidence

---

[51] *Id.*, at para.LXVI.

[52] *See e.g. People v. Zizzo,* 301 Ill.App.3d 481, 703 N.E.2d 546 (1998); *State v. Mongomery*, 341 N.C. 553, 461 S.E.2d 732 (1995); *People v. Campbell*, 146 Ill.2d 363, 586 N.E.2d 1261 (1992).

[53] Kiely, *op. cit.,* pp. 357-365.

[54] 1998 Ohio App. Lexis 616 (Feb. 17, 1998).

may exceptionally assist the defence. As we have seen, arguments to the effect that the Gardaí have failed in their duty to seek out and preserve fingerprint evidence of likely probative value to the accused have in exceptional circumstances met with some success in this jurisdiction. Some accused persons in the United States have raised another line of inquiry, namely, whether the failure of the prosecution to adduce fingerprint evidence can support an exculpatory inference that the accused was not present at crime scene. This issue was considered by the Court of Appeals for the 7th Circuit in *United States v. Sutton*.[55] The police collected fingerprints from the scene of a robbery, which matched the fingerprints of none of the accused. The accuseds sought to admit reports containing the expert conclusions and opinions of the State laboratory technician in relation to the discovered fingerprints in order to demonstrate that they were not responsible for the robbery. The trial judge excluded the evidence because the defence had not called an expert witness to explain the relevance of the reports. On appeal, the 7th Circuit affirmed the decision to exclude but not without noting that the reports were relevant, self-authenticating documents that came within the public records exception to the rule against hearsay. Their exclusion was nevertheless justified in light of the substantial probability that, without the explanation and context provided by an expert opinion, the jury would rely unduly on the reports.[56]

---

[55] 337 F.3d 792 (7th Cir. 2003).

[56] *See also People v. Towns,* 174 Ill.2d 453, 675 N.E.2d 614 (1996); *Hooker v. State,* 716 So.2d 1104 (Miss. Sp. Ct. 1998).

CHAPTER 6

DNA

INTRODUCTION

"Deoxyribonucleic acid" or "DNA" is a molecule stored inside the nucleus of virtually all living cells, whether plant or animal.[1] The DNA molecule carries genetic information in the form of a code which determines an individual's physical characteristics, the so-called "blueprint"[2] or

---

[1] This brief and general discussion represents a legal academic's attempt to grapple with the science underpinning DNA evidence. It does not purport to constitute an authoritative scientific account and should not be construed as such. Readers should consult the forensic scientific authorities cited herein and similar sources elsewhere. The discussion drawa on the following sources: F.R. Bieber, "Science and Technology of Forensic DNA Profiling: Current Use and Future Directions" in D. Lazer, ed., *DNA and the Criminal Justice System: The Technology of Justice* (MIT Press, Cambridge, Mass., 2004) 23; G.T. Duncan, M.l. Tracey and E.Stauffer, "Techniques of DNA Analysis" in S.H. James and J.J. Nordby, *Forensic Science: An Introduction to Scientific and Investigative Techniques* (CRC Press, Boca Raton, Florida, 2003) 221; P.C. Giannelli and E.J. Imwinkelried, *Scientific Evidence*, 3rd ed. (LexisNexis, Charlottesville, Virginia, 1999, & 2002 Supp.), chap.28; P. Gill, "Recent Progress in Forensic DNA Profiling – A Review: 2001 to 2004" Interpol 14th International Forensic Science Symposium Review Papers (2004) 137; D.H. Kaye, "The Admissibility of DNA Testing" (1991) 13 Cardozo L. Rev. 353; K.F. Kelly *et al.*, "Method and Applications of DNA Fingerprinting: A Guide for the Non-Scientist" [1987] Crim. L.R. 105; T. Kiely, *Forensic Evidence: Science and the Criminal Law*, 2nd ed. (CRC Press, Boca Raton, Florida, 2006), chap.10; Law Reform Commission, *Consultation Paper on the Establishment of a DNA Database* (LRC CP 29-2004), chap.1; E. Leahy, "Genetic Profiling and the Reasonable Doubt" (1995) 1 M.L.J.I. 66; B. Robertson and G.A. Vignaux, *Interpreting Evidence: Evaluating Forensic Science in the Courtroom* (Wiley & Sons, Chichester, West Sussex, 1995); R. Saferstein, *Criminalistics: An Introduction to Forensic Science*, 7th ed. (Prentice-Hall, Upper Saddle River, New Jersey, 2000), chap.14; W. Wall, *Genetics and DNA Technology: Legal Aspects* (Cavendish Publishing, London, 2002) chaps.1, 3 & 4; R.M. White, and J.J.D. Greenwood, "DNA Fingerprinting and the Law" (1988) 51 M.L.R. 145.

[2] Kelly *et al., op. cit.*, p.105.

"building block of life."[3] The discovery that the material basis of inheritance is particulate and variable was made by Gregor Mendel as early as 1865,[4] although it was only through the work of researchers James Watson and Francis Crick in the 1950s that the structure of DNA was fully comprehended.[5] These developments have revolutionised our understanding of heredity and transformed the fields of genetics and molecular biology, paving the way for cutting-edge research in areas such as medical diagnostics (including prenatal diagnostics) and, more controversially, genetic engineering. Its contribution to the forensic sciences has been no less revolutionary and its rise as a method of criminal identification has been remarkably rapid and widely accepted.

The technique of DNA profiling[6] involves the comparison of a biological sample found at a crime scene with a sample taken from a suspect or victim in order to link the suspect to the crime scene or, alternatively, eliminate him from the investigation.[7] Its development is generally attributed to British geneticist, Professor Alec Jeffreys, who pioneered the technique of multilocus probing in the early 1980s.[8] DNA profiling was first presented as a means of proof in English and American courts as recently as the late 1980s[9] and has remained a constant feature of criminal trials ever since. The science of DNA, no less than its forensic

---

3 Giannelli and Imwinkelried, *op. cit.,* §18.2; Robertson and Vignaux, *op. cit.*, p.158; N. O'Connor, *Cracking Crime: Jim Donovan–Forensic Detective* (O'Brien Press, Dublin, 2001), p.97.

4 Mendel's findings, based on his experiments on heredity in the garden pea, were rediscovered in 1900. Prior to that time, heredity materials were thought to be fluid and when mixed, incapable of separation. Mendel demonstrated that the inheritance of characteristics is controlled by genes which are particulate rather than fluid and which remain intact from one generation to the next. Duncan *et al.*, *op. cit.,* pp.221-22.

5 *Id.,* pp.226-27; Saferstein, *op. cit.,* pp.353-54.

6 Also known as DNA fingerprinting or DNA typing.

7 White and Greenwood, *op. cit.*, at p.147: "Its chief advantage is that it provides essentially positive identification, whereas previous methods can only be used to eliminate possibilities."

8 Royal Commission on Criminal Justice, *The Ability to Challenge DNA Evidence* (Research Study No.9, 1993), p.3.

9 *See e.g.* Colin Pitchfork case, discussed in Duncan *et al.*, *op. cit.,* pp.226-27; *Andrews v. Florida*, 533 So. 2d 842 (Fla. Dist. Ct. App. 1988); *State v. Searles*, 246 Kan. 567 (1990).

application, has evolved with breathtaking speed during the intervening years and the several methods of DNA profiling that now exist are the subject of ongoing refinement. No longer dependent upon samples of blood and urine, DNA analysts can now use biological material gleaned from such disparate, discrete sources as cigarette butts, dandruff and charred remains.[10]

Equally remarkable has been the willingness of courts to embrace this forensic technique and to vouchsafe its evidentiary reliability. DNA was heralded as a uniquely probative evidentiary tool with an unparalleled capacity for accuracy and precision and, initially, proffers of DNA evidence in court went virtually unchallenged.[11] As trial practice has evolved, however, lawyers have gained an appreciation of the complexities surrounding DNA profiling and the subsequent presentation of the predicate statistical evidence in court. Challenges to proffers of DNA evidence have thus increased and courts have responded by approaching issues of evidentiary admissibility and courtroom presentation with a more discerning lens.[12] Nevertheless, as recently as 2004, Lazer offered a telling remark about the use of DNA technology in criminal prosecution in the United States: "What is striking is that the dominant controversies about DNA technology now revolve around the competence of the criminal justice system rather than the reliability of the technology itself."[13] Thus, there is a continuing need for lawyers to gain familiarity with the science of DNA and to scrutinise DNA profiling techniques as the foundation for evidence in court.

Although the present discussion is concerned with the forensic application of DNA, it is interesting to note the diverse purposes to which DNA technology has been put in contemporary society. DNA can be extracted from samples taken from human remains and, when compared with the DNA of close relatives, assist in the identification of missing

---

[10] *See e.g. R v. Lashley,* Court of Appeal, February 8, 2000 (DNA evidence obtained from a half smoked cigarette left at the crime scene); *People v. Buss,* 187 Ill.2d 144, 718 N.E.2d 1 (1999) (DNA extracted from an inhaler).

[11] N. Ebisike, *An Appraisal of Forensic Science Evidence in Criminal Proceedings* (Greenway Publishers, London, 2000), p.119.

[12] *See* e.g. *R v. Doheny and Adams* [1997] 1 Cr. App. R. 369 (CA).

[13] D. Lazer, "Introduction: DNA and the Criminal Justice System" in D. Lazer, ed., *DNA and the Criminal Justice System: The Technology of Justice* (MIT Press, Cambridge, Mass., 2004) 3 at p.4.

persons. In theatres of armed conflict, DNA testing has been used to identify victims of war crimes as well as unknown soldiers. Similarly, DNA technology has contributed to the identification of missing persons in the wake of humanitarian disasters, such as the Asian tsunami of December 2004, and terrorist atrocities, such as the attacks on New York's Twin Towers on September 11, 2001.[14] In the context of civil litigation, DNA has become an increasingly prevalent form of evidence in proceedings relating to paternity, probate and immigration.[15] DNA testing was even used in the attempted impeachment of U.S. President Bill Clinton.[16]

Blood Grouping

DNA is by no means the first forensic scientific technique used to identify the perpetrators of crime. As we have seen, fingerprinting has a long and illustrious history and continues to occupy an important place in criminal investigation.[17] An alternative method of identification, and a more direct forerunner of DNA profiling, was blood grouping, a constituent of the field of serology.[18] The discovery in the early 20th century of distinct human blood types, determined by genetic variation in red blood cell surface antigens, was initially used for medical purposes such as matching patients to suitable donations for blood transfusions.[19] The potential application of blood grouping to litigation was soon realised and it has been associated, in particular, with the resolution of paternity disputes, and cases involving the mistaken identification of infants in maternity hospitals.

In the criminal domain, blood grouping has enjoyed wide success as a method of eliminating suspects from inquiries. This might occur, for

---

[14] Bieber, *op. cit.*, p.28.

[15] *See e.g.* Wall, *op. cit.,* chap.5.

[16] Giannelli and Imwinkelried, *op. cit.,* §18-2; Saferstein, *op. cit.,* pp.363-64; Robertson and Vignaux, *op. cit.,* pp.158-160.

[17] *See* chapters 2 and 3.

[18] *See generally* Saferstein, *op. cit.,* p.361; Wall, *op. cit.,* pp.12-14 and chap.3; O' Connor, *op. cit.*, pp.124-125 and pp.259-61. *See also People (DPP) v. Boyce*, unreported, Court of Criminal Appeal, December 21, 2005.

[19] Bieber, *op.cit.,* pp.24-25.

example, in a murder inquiry, where blood not belonging to the victim is located at the crime scene but is found not to match the suspect's blood type. When compared to DNA testing, the simpler and less sensitive technique of blood grouping, it is a far more rudimentary and imprecise methodology for positively identifying a suspect as the culprit of an alleged crime. Thus, the utility of blood grouping as a form of criminal identification is far more limited than that of DNA analysis.[20]

DNA Defined

The human body is made up of trillions of cells and each cell that has a nucleus contains genetic material in the form of chromosomes. A human person has 22 pairs of non-sex chromosomes and two sex chromosomes; half the chromosomes come from the father's sperm and half from the mother's ovum.[21] Each chromosome is composed of a DNA module surrounded by other material, principally proteins. Thus, half of the DNA that is inherited at conception is maternal and half is paternal. In addition to this genetic material, some forms of DNA are inherited only from fathers (such as DNA on the human Y chromosome which is passed from fathers to sons) and some only from mothers (such as mitochondrial DNA which is passed from mothers to sons and daughters).[22]

Each DNA module comprises a series of units, known as nucleotides, which are strung together in two DNA strands.[23] The backbone of each strand is composed of sugar molecules and phosphate groups and projecting from the backbone are four bases: adenine (A), guanine (G), thymine (T) and cytosine (C).[24] The two strands are coiled together to

---

[20] Robertson and Vignaux, *op.cit.*, p.158; Wall, *op. cit.*, p.45; White and Greenwood, *op.cit.*, p.146 ("[T]he traditional blood tests used in forensic science tell us about only a tiny fraction of the genetic variation. Because of this they can only eliminate certain possibilities rather than provide proof of identity").

[21] Giannelli and Imwinkelried, *op.cit.,* §18.2.; Kelly *et al., op.cit.*, p.106; LRC Consultation Paper, *op.cit.,* pp.13-14.

[22] Bieber, *op.cit.*, p.25.

[23] White and Greenwood, *op.cit.*, p.146.

[24] Saferstein, *op.cit.*, p.354; LRC Consultation Paper, *op.cit.*, p.14.

form a double helix, not unlike a spiral staircase[25] or two twisted wires.[26] That configuration is made possible by the alignment of the bases in the respective strands, a concept known as "base pairing" whereby A always attaches to T and G always attaches to C. It is the sequencing of the base pairs along the helix that determines an individual's genetic makeup.[27] A sequence or series of sequences constitutes a "gene" or unit of inheritance and may account for a particular physical trait, such as hair or eye colour, or a particular disease in a human being.[28] The term "human genome" is used to refer to the totality of a person's DNA or genetic material.

As Saferstein explains, there are no restrictions on the sequencing of the millions of base pairs located within each of the 46 chromosomes:

> "Any base can follow another on a DNA strand, which means that the possible number of different sequence combinations is staggering! Consider that the average human chromosome has DNA containing 100 million base pairs. All the human chromosomes taken together contain about 3 billion base pairs. From these numbers we can begin to appreciate the diversity of DNA and hence the diversity of living organisms. DNA is like a book of instructions. The alphabet used to create the book is simple enough: A, T, G, and C. The order in which these letters are arranged defines the role and function of a DNA molecule."[29]

In fact, the sequencing of base pairs is virtually the same in all human beings. The number of sequences that vary from one person to the next has been estimated to be less than one percent[30] although the degree of

---

25 Giannelli and Imwinkelried, *op.cit.*, §18.2; Robertson and Vignaux, *op.cit.*, pp.160-161.

26 Saferstein, *op.cit.*, pp.354-55; Duncan *et al*, *op.cit.*, p.232.

27 Giannelli and Imwinkelried, *op.cit.*, §18.2.

28 The totality of a person's DNA or complete set of genetic material is sometimes referred to as the "human genome".

29 *Op.cit.*, at pp.355-56.

30 Giannelli and Imwinkelried, *op.cit.*, §18.2. Bieber, *op.cit.*, p.26, offers a slightly higher figure: "Geneticists have documented that 98 percent of the human genome shows little, if any, sequence variation within the population. That is, only 2

variation in those small number of sequences may be substantial.[31] It is in this variation that the uniqueness of each person's genetic code resides; with the exception of identical twins (or triplets *etc.*), no two persons are genetically alike. As Kaye explains: "Because 99.9% of the DNA sequence in any two people is identical, the technical challenge is to detect the relatively rare stretches of DNA, sometimes called alleles, that vary among individuals."[32]

The ability of DNA to determine genetic traits is linked to its role in the production of proteins. Comprised of combinations of amino acids, proteins are complex molecules which play a crucial role in the structure and functioning of all aspects of human life. DNA essentially stores the genetic information that determines the amino acid sequence for every protein manufactured in the human body.[33] Differences in amino acid coding from one person to the next explain the prevalence or absence of particular physical attributes and genetic disorders. Hence DNA is often said to contain the instructions, in the form of genes, necessary to produce human characteristics.[34] Those areas of the DNA molecule housing genes and, consequently, issuing instructions for the production of proteins are known as "coding regions". There is very little variation in the coding regions from person to person and for this reason forensic scientists place increasing importance on the "non-coding regions" of the DNA molecule. These regions are substantial, lack the biological function of their coding counterparts, and contain a high degree of variation.[35]

---

percent of the genome has sufficient variation in DNA sequence to be useful for forensic distinctions."

31 LRC Consultation Paper, *op.cit.*, p.16.

32 Kaye, *op.cit.*, p.354.

33 Saferstein, *op.cit.*, p.356.

34 See *e.g.* Duncan *et al.*, *op.cit.*, p.222 ("We inherit the information required to produce all our characteristics in the form of DNA. We do not inherit the characteristics – only the information to produce them").

35 LRC Consultation Paper, *op.cit.,* pp.17-18 (citing Human Genone Management Information System, *The Human Genome Project and Beyond – A Primer* (March 2003), 3, available at *http://www.ornl.gov/hgmis/publicat/primer/*; Bieber, *op.cit.*, p.26; Kiely, *op.cit.*, p.433.

DNA Profiling: Forensic Techniques

First developed in the 1980s, the forensic application of DNA technology has gained widespread acceptance as a routine facet of criminal investigation. DNA analysis has proved a powerful means of linking suspects to serious crimes, such as murder and rape, and thereby securing convictions. But it has also served the fundamental purpose of exonerating the innocent, whether suspected or convicted of offences. In the United States, an estimated 140 convicted persons, some resident on death row, have had their convictions set aside on the basis of results of post-conviction DNA testing.[36] Given the dramatic implications of this relatively new area of forensic science for criminal justice, it is not surprising that DNA analysis has spawned a veritable industry. Several distinct DNA profiling techniques have been developed and more are likely to follow. The flourishing science and its application in practice are now also the subject of a burgeoning literature.[37]

It is important to note that no single DNA profiling technique may work in each and every circumstance. A laboratory that has a preference for a particular DNA profiling system may nevertheless use alternatives in exceptional cases or employ a combination of different techniques.[38] Factors informing decisions about which of the various DNA profiling methods to use include the nature of the investigation, the likelihood that the sample to be tested contains a DNA mixture (the DNA of more than one person), and the level of degradation in the sample.[39]

---

[36] Bieber, *op.cit.*, p.22; Kiely, *op.cit.*, pp.451-454.

[37] *See e.g.* Giannelli and Imwinkelried, *op.cit..*, §18.3 ns.33 & 34 (listing citations); Kiely, *op.cit.* p. 462, n.4.

[38] *See e.g. People v. Buss*, 187 Ill. 2d 144, 718 N.E.2d 1 (1999). DNA analysis played a significant role in the trial of O.J. Simpson for the murder of his wife Nicole Brown Simpson and Ronald Goldman. At the crime scene, blood drops were found leading away from the bodies and bloodstains on the rear gate to the premises. The samples were tested using two DNA techniques, PCR and RFLP. *See* Saferstein, *op.cit.*, p.376; Ebiske, *op.cit.*, pp.130-32.

[39] Bieber, *op.cit.*, p.33. On the problems posed by DNA mixtures *see* Kiely, *op.cit.*, pp.441-43; Gill, Interpol Review Papers, *op.cit.*, p.138. A further, super-sensitive emergent technique called "low copy number (LCN)" may permit the extraction of DNA from samples which would otherwise be insufficient for purposes of DNA testing. See Gill, Interpol Review Papers, *op.cit.*, pp.140-42; LRC

(a) Restriction fragment length polymorphisms (RFLPs)

As noted above, the first DNA profiling technique applied in the criminal justice system was developed by Professor Alex Jeffreys at the University of Leicester in the mid-1980s. The technique focuses on length variations in DNA strands, known as restriction fragment length polymorphisms (RFLPs).[40] It involves the use of restriction enzymes which cut DNA molecules like a "biological scissors" at specific, recognised base sequences.[41] The length of the resulting DNA fragments is then measured in each of the two samples being compared. The technique combines several distinct processes: separating the fragments by electrophoresis, transferring the fragments on to a nylon membrane by a method called "Southern Transfer", visualising the separated RFLPs by hybridisation and autoradiography.[42] The RFLPs are manifest as a series of bands on the autoradiograph; these bands embody in effect the DNA profile.[43] A comparison by the DNA analyst of the length and position of the bands on the autoradiographs from the respective samples, establishes the likelihood of a match.[44] With this technique, "the key to declaring a match is finding that the same sized fragments are in the same position on both autorads."[45]

In addition to being time consuming,[46] one of the drawbacks of

---

Consultation Paper, *op.cit.*, p.34 (citing the webpage of the UK Forensic ScienceService, *http://www.forensic.gov.uk/forensic/foi/foi_docs// 36L_DNA_LCN.pdf.*

40 For judicial description and assessment of the technique *see R v. Deen* [1994] T.L.R. 11 at 12 (approved in *R v. Gordon* [1995] 1 Cr. App. R. 290); *R v. Doheny and Adams* [1997] 1 Cr. App. R. 369; *United States v. Porter,* 618 A.2d 629 (D.C.App. 1992); *State v. Cauthron,* 120 Wash.2d 879, 846 P.2d 502 (1993); *State v. Armstead,* 342 Md. 38, 673 A.2d 221 (1996); *People v. Miller,* 173 Ill.2d 167, 670 N.E.2d 721 (1996).

41 Giannelli and Imwinkelried, *op.cit.,* §18.3(A); Kaye, *op.cit.,* pp.355-56; Kelly *et al., op.cit.*, p.107; Robertson and Vignaux, *op.cit.*, p.161.

42 Saferstein, *op.cit.*, p.362; Giannelli and Imwinkelried, *op.cit.,* §18.3(A); Wall, *op.cit.,* pp.59-60; Robertson and Vignaux, *op.cit.*, p.162.

43 Kiely, *op.cit.,* p.433. For a judicial description of the technique *see People v. Miller*, 173 Ill.2d 167, 670 N.E.2d 721 (1996).

44 M. Redmayne, "Doubts and Burdens: DNA Evidence, Probability and the Courts" [1995] Crim. L.R. 464, p.465.

45 Giannelli and Imwinkelried, *op.cit.,* §18.3(A).

46 See *e.g.* Robertson and Vignaux, *op.cit.,* p.162 (noting that the development of

Jeffreys's technique is that the large number of bands generated by multilocus probing can complicate the interpretation of the autoradiograph. The advent of single locus RFLP overcame this difficulty by providing a test that produces far fewer bands on the autoradiograph. In order to generate sufficient data to formulate high match probabilities, several tests are run, each one testing a locus on a different chromosome.[47] The multiple use of single probes on different chromosomes increases the likelihood that each probe will garner independent information; one of the criticisms of the multilocus technique was that the location of several probes on the same chromosome compromised the independence of each result.[48]

RFLP was a revolutionary technique in its day and, at one time, single locus probing was the DNA profiling method of choice. It has since been overtaken in contemporary forensic practice by more modern technologies and its significance is increasingly historical.

(b) Polymerase chain reaction

The dominant DNA profiling technique is short tandem repeat analysis (STR). There are variants on the STR theme and the particular technique used in Ireland and most of Europe is known as SGM Plus™[49] Polymerase chain reaction (PCR) technology capitalises on the ability of DNA strands to naturally replicate within a cell through the functioning of an enzyme known as "DNA polymerase."[50] At its essence, PCR facilitates the repeated duplication or amplification of a DNA strand.[51] The process has the merit of flexibility in that even trace amounts of DNA can be amplified. Thus, in contrast to RFLP, only a small biological sample is

---

an autoradiograph formerly took about 5 days but that luminescent chemicals now permit immediate visualisation).

47 Wall, *op.cit.*, pp.60-61.

48 Giannelli and Imwinkelried, *op. cit.* §18.3(A) and (B). In the United States, the National Research Council in its 1992 report recommended the use of single locus probes instead of multilocus probes for these very reasons. National Research Council Committee on DNA Technology in Forensic Science, *DNA Technology in Forensic Science* (1992).

49 LRC Consultation Paper, *op.cit.*, p.26.

50 Duncan *et al.*, *op.cit.*, p.233; Kaye, *op.cit.*, p.354-55.

51 Saferstein, *op.cit.*, p.365; Wall, *op.cit.*, p.65.

required (e.g. blood, semen, hair or saliva) and even degraded samples may suffice.[52] PCR enables the analyst to target specific regions (short sequences) of DNA in a sample for amplification and it potentially makes available for analysis millions of duplicates of the original DNA source.[53]

The significance of PCR also lies in its embodiment of the highly sensitive, precise and discriminatory capacities of DNA technology. Summarising the virtues of modern scientific advances, Bieber explains:

> "Scientists interested in genetic variation at the DNA level in animal and plant populations employ a number of methods for study of biological samples. First, chemical and physical extraction methods are capable of removing intact DNA molecules from various tissues, even those compromised by environmental or storage conditions. The chemical methods use detergents to remove other cellular or chemical components of the tissue or fluid sample, whereas the physical methods utilize special synthetic membranes to physically bind to the membrane DNA molecules from individual samples. Second, PCR allows amplification of trace amounts of extracted DNA into a quantity sufficient for analysis. Third, automated methods for direct determination of the base-pair sequence of DNA are now available, and a variety of laboratory methods allow detection and comparison of length differences in certain defined regions of the genoMe that are know to exhibit stable inherited variation. Finally, in cases involving human DNA specifically, computerized digital storage of the resulting DNA profile (*i.e.*, the specific length or sequence of DNA identified at one or more loci) allows rapid comparison of sample profiles from evidence or from individuals whose profiles have been stored in a central database."[54]

---

[52] Kiely, *op.cit.*, p.436 (discussing *People v. Davis*, 185 Ill.2d 317, 706 N.E.2d 437 (1999)).

[53] Bieber, *op.cit.*, p.29; Saferstein, *op.cit.*, p.365.

[54] Bieber, *op.cit.*, p.29 (internal citations omitted).

(c) Single nucleotide polymorphisms (SNP)

Single nucleotide polymorphisms ("SNPs", pronounced "Snips") are variations in the individual DNA base pair which occur throughout the genome, in active genes and non-active areas.[55] The objective of SNP analysis is to "target a single base out of the entire genome of 3,000,000,000 bases and see how it varies between individuals."[56] A relatively new technology, SNP analysis has been touted as a potential successor to STR in the construction of DNA databases.[57] Various techniques may be used to detect SNPs including PCR analysis, microchip technology, and automated systems.[58] Although a single SNP analysis is relatively uninformative standing alone, vast numbers of these analyses can be combined to generate forensically significant results.[59]

(d) Mitochondrial DNA

The discussion thus far has focused on "nuclear DNA," *i.e.* the DNA found within the nucleus of a cell. A second form of DNA, known as "mitochondrial DNA (mtDNA)" resides in small structures outside the nucleus of the cell and, unlike nuclear DNA, is inherited solely from the mother.[60] MtDNA is used in situations where nuclear DNA is unavailable or its quality is poor. Where human tissue is unavailable, MtDNA may potentially be extracted from human hair, teeth, and bones.[61]

---

55 Wall, *op.cit.,* p.71; LRC Consultation Paper, *op.cit.*, p.34.

56 Wall, *op.cit.,* p.71 . Wall observes, *id.*, at p.72, that "SNP analysis is really a shorthand version of the ultimate method of detecting DNA variation, which is sequencing the whole genome."

57 Wall, *op.cit.*, p.71. Gill, Interpol Review Papers, *op.cit.*, p.143, reports a "consensus view that this is unlikely to occur in the short to medium term." *See also* P. Gill, "An Assessment of the Utility of Single Nucleotide Polymorphisms (SNPs) for Forensic Purposes" (2001) 114 Int. J. Leg. Med. 204.

58 Bieber, *op.cit.*, p.30; Duncan *et al, op.cit.*, p.240.

59 Wall, *op.cit.*, p.72.

60 Saferstein, *op.cit.*, p.373; Duncan *et al, op.cit.,* pp.241-43; Giannelli and Imwinkelried, 2002 supp., *op.cit.,* §18.3(D); Robertson and Vignaux, *op.cit.*, p.164; LRC Consultation Paper, *op.cit.*, p.32. The maternal inheritance of mtDNA may render it particularly useful for kinship analysis or victim identification. Bieber, *op.cit.*, p.33. For a detailed discussion of the maternal inheritance of mtDNA, *see* Wall, *op.cit.,* pp.73-74.

61 Gill, Interpol Review Papers, *op.cit.,* p.138; Kiely, *op.cit.*, p.444. On mtDNA

The abundance of mtDNA is a boon to forensic scientists: each cell contains hundreds if not thousands of mitochondria, each of which in turn contains several loops of DNA.[62] The downside of mtDNA analysis is its low discriminatory capability. It is also "more rigorous, time consuming, and costly when compared to nuclear DNA profiling."[63] Nevertheless, within its limited sphere of application, the utility of mtDNA analysis has been noted[64] and, in the United States, several courts have recognised the probative value of the technology.[65]

Processing of DNA Samples

A step-by-step examination of the PCR technique provides a useful general guide to DNA analysis.[66] The process of examining DNA samples is detailed, time-consuming and costly which explains the fact that it is used only in relation to serious crimes such as murder and rape.[67]

(a) The taking of crime scene samples

First, criminal investigators locate evidence at the crime scene[68] from which biological material and, potentially, a DNA profile may be

---

and hair analysis, see *id.*, pp.106-119.

62 Saferstein, *op.cit.*, p.373; Bieber, *op.cit.*, p.32.

63 Saferstein, *op. cit.*, p.375.

64 *See e.g.* "DNA Report", 14th Interpol International Forensic Science Symposium (2004), pp.138-39.

65 *See e.g. State v. Pappas*, 256 Conn. 854, 776A.2d 1091 (2001); *United States v. Beverely*, 369 F.3d 516 (6th Cir. 2004); *Wagner v. State*, 160 Md.App. 531, 864 A.2d 1037 (Md. App. 2005); Saferstein, *op.cit.*, p.375 (discussing *Tennessee v. Ware* (1996)). One of the notable applications of mtDNA analysis involved the posthumous identification of Anastasia, daughter of Russian Czar Nicholas II, of the Romanov family, discussed in Wall, *op.cit.*, pp.75-76; N. O'Connor, *Cracking Crime: Jim Donovan–Forensic Detective* (O'Brien Press, Dublin, 2001), pp.138-42.

66 *See generally* Ebiske, *op.cit.*, pp.32-36; Robertson and Vignaux, *op.cit.*, pp.161-163.

67 *Id.*, p.161.

68 *See* J. Donovan, "The Obtaining, Examining, Analysis and Retaining of Forensic Samples in Criminal Investigation" (2001) 7 M.L.J.I. 25 p.25; P. Moore, *The Forensics Handbook* (Eye Books, London, 2004), pp.25-31.

generated. Typical biological sources of DNA include blood, semen, vaginal secretions, saliva and the roots of strands of hair. But in some instances DNA may also be extracted from less obvious biological material such as skin, nasal secretions, vomit, urine and faeces.[69] The crime scene evidence that will typically be examined in the laboratory for the presence of biological material will vary depending upon the crime under investigation. For example, in a murder investigation, samples of blood stains found on floors and walls or on weapons or clothing might be taken and preserved for examination. Items such as chewing gum, cigarette butts, drinking glasses, cans or bottles might contain samples of saliva, and discarded tissues samples of nasal secretions. A post-mortem examination of the corpse of the deceased might also generate biological samples containing the assailant's DNA. In a sexual assault case, a vaginal swab taken from a complainant might be tested in the laboratory in the hope that it might reveal the presence of semen. Tests on items such as bedding, clothing and condoms might also yield semen, vaginal secretions or pubic hair roots. One of the advantages of DNA testing is that it is not dependent upon fresh biological material. Samples up to several days old will be adequate and, in the case of blood and semen stains that have dried quickly, samples months and even years old.[70]

The processing of a crime scene is conducted by a specialised team of Garda officers according to a designated protocol.[71] A key concern is the need to preserve the integrity of the evidence; the scene must be secured, access must be limited to investigators directly involved, and officers and visitors must wear protective clothing to avoid contaminating the scene. The search for evidence must be undertaken as soon as possible and must be thorough and comprehensive.[72] In the case of potential DNA evidence, once items likely to contain biological material have been

---

69 For a detailed graph summarizing the relevant biological sources, *see* LRC Consultation Paper, *op.cit.,* pp.24-25 (taken from Hagerman, Prevett and Murray, *DNA Handbook* (Butterworths Canada Ltd 2002), .22-23. See *also* Kiely, *op.cit.,* pp.51-52.

70 White and Greenwood, *op.cit.*, p.147. *See also* Kelly *et al., op.cit.*, p.105 noting that "[u]nder the correct circumstances DNA is remarkably stable and indeed has been extracted from Egyptian mummies."

71 See Donovan, *loc.cit.*

72 See Moore, *op.cit.,* p.25.

identified, they must be preserved and removed for transportation to the laboratory.[73] The method of collection obviously varies depending upon the nature of the material and its location. Transportable items, such as clothing, tissues or utensils are generally photographed and then placed individually in purpose-made bags or containers which are marked for purposes of identification. Substances such as blood found on surfaces at the crime scene, are also photographed and samples taken in the form of swabs which are preserved in similar fashion. Where the blood is located on a weapon or implement, it is left undisturbed and the item removed in its entirety from the crime scene for testing in the laboratory. In the case of a physical or sexual assault, the physical evidence taken from the victim's person may include swabs of the assailant's blood found on the skin, vaginal swabs of the assailant's semen, and traces of the assailant's skin found under the victim's fingernails. Once crime scene material has been received in the laboratory, it is tested for the presence of body fluids. Samples sent forward for DNA analysis undergo an initial screening to ascertain the quantity and quality of DNA and how much amplification is required.[74]

(b) Extraction

The second step in the process, known as DNA extraction, involves the isolation of the DNA. The biological material is first removed from its source, whether a swab or item such as clothing and the DNA is then separated from the other biological material. Various methods exist and the method of choice may be determined by the material being tested. One traditional method involves mixing blood with a solution containing an enzyme (which digests proteins), detergents (which breaks down membranes and lipids) and salt (which stabilises the DNA). The mixture is then purified through incubation at high temperatures. Organic solvents are then used to separate the DNA from other cellular components.[79] Ebiske describes an alternative method:

---

[73] See *id.*, pp.42-43.

[74] The taking of comparative DNA samples from suspects is discussed in chap.8 *infra*.

[75] This procedure for the extraction of DNA from blood is outlined in detail and other procedures discussed in Duncan *et al.*, *op.cit.*, pp.230-31.

> "DNA is routinely extracted using the Puregene DNA extraction kit from Gentra Systems Inc. (available from Flowgen). This is a rapid procedure based on ammonium acetate precipitation of proteins. No organic solvents are employed. The DNA obtained seems to be of high molecular weight and is readily soluble, resulting in a less viscous, more homogenous solution than that obtained using a proteinase K/SDS and phenol/chloroform protocol."[76]

Once the DNA has been extracted, the quantity and quality of the material is tested using a commercially produced kit.[77] The kit identifies the "target DNA"[78] and short sequences of DNA on either side of the region of interest which must be available in a pure form known as a "primer."[79]

(c) Amplification

The third and major step in the process involves the amplification of the DNA through the mixing together of various elements: the target DNA, the primers, the polymerase enzyme, and free nucleotides (A, T, G, C) which can be ordered to replicate the original template.[80] Saferstein explains the process in the following terms:

> "The first step in the PCR process is to heat the DNA strands to about 94°C. At this temperature, the double-stranded DNA molecules separate completely. … The second step is to add the primers to the separated strands and allow the primers to combine or hybridise with the strands by lowering the test

---

[76] *Op.cit.*, p.33. The Law Reform Commission provides the following account of DNA extraction: "[T]he biological material is removed from the clothing or swab by soaking in water or a buffered solution. The solution is spun in a centrifuge which pushes the cells to the bottom of the tube. Unwanted material such as red blood cells and protein is removed and discarded. The remaining cells are burst through hearing or chemical action, which releases the DNA from inside the cells." LRC Consultation Paper, *op. cit.* at para.1.39.

[77] Ebiske, *op.cit.*, p.33; LRC Consultation Paper, *op.cit.*, p.27.

[78] Wall, *op.cit.*, p.65.

[79] Saferstein, *op.cit.*, p.365.

[80] Wall, *op.cit.*, pp.65-66.

> tube temperatures. ... The third step is to add the DNA polymerase and a mixture of free nucleotides (G, A, T, C) to the separated strands. When the test tube is heated up to 72°C the polymerase enzyme directs the rebuilding of a double-stranded DNA molecule, extending the primers by adding the appropriate bases, one at a time, resulting in the production of two complete pairs of double-stranded DNA segments. ...This completes the first cycle of the PCR technique, and the outcome is a doubling of the number of DNA strands – that is, from one to two. The cycle of heating, cooling, and strand rebuilding is then repeated resulting again in a doubling of the DNA strands. Upon completion of the second cycle, four double-stranded DNA molecules will have been created from the original double-stranded DNA sample. Typically, 25 to 30 cycles are carried out to yield more than one million copies of the original DNA molecule."[81]

PCR thus allows the analyst to take a very small sample of DNA and to amplify it through a relatively quick and purportedly reliable and consistent procedure.[82]

(d) Short tandem repeat analysis (STRs)

Following amplification, the next stage in compiling a DNA profile consists of analysing the amplified material to generate a DNA profile. One of the first techniques used to process amplified material, known as the dot blot procedure, employs probes that test for a specific DNA sequence.[83] The procedure has the merit of simplicity (the dots colour if the sequence is present and do not colour if it is absent) but suffers from significant drawbacks. Critics point to the limited range of DNA that can be measured, the modest level of random match probabilities, and the risks of contamination.[84] A more sophisticated PCR typing kit known as

---

81 *Op.cit.*, p.367.

82 Wall, *op.cit.*, p.66.

83 Robertson and Vignaux, *op.cit.*, p.164.

84 *See* Giannelli and Imwinkelried, *op.cit..*, §18.3(C); Wall, *op.cit.*, p.66; Saferstein, *op.cit.,* pp.367-69; Duncan *et al, op.cit.*, p.236; Bieber, *op.cit.*, p.30.

Polymarker (PM) uses the dot blot technique but enables the analyst to simultaneously test five different genetic markers leading to a more precise, discriminating result.[85]

SGM Plus™, the system used in Ireland and most of Europe, employs short tandem repeat analysis (STR). As we have seen, the human genome contains abundant non-coding regions of DNA, the characteristics of which differ from one person to the next.[86] Within these regions are locations that contain repetitive short sequence elements; the repeating sequence is short (between three and six bases) as is the entire STR strand (considerably shorter than strands generated through the RFLP procedure) which renders STRs less susceptible to degradation.[87] But the true value of STRs to the DNA analyst lies in the high level of variation that exits among STRs found in the genome; "[t]he more STRs one can characterize, the smaller will be the percentage of the population from which these STRs can emanate."[88] The term "multiplexing" is used to describe the simultaneous amplification of a combination of STRs through the use of PCR technology.[89] Recent developments in STR technology include the detection of genetic variation at STR loci on the human Y chromosome, which is transmitted from fathers to sons.[90]

One of the advantages of STR profiling in other jurisdictions is that it works hand in glove with DNA databases and automated systems.[91] The

---

85 Saferstein, *op.cit.*, p.369; Giannelli and Imwinkelried, *op.cit.*, para.18.3(C); Bieber, *op.cit.*, p.30.

86 Wall, *op.cit.*, pp.67-68.; Saferstein, *op.cit.*, p.369; Giannelli and Imwinkelried, *op.cit.*, §18.3(C).

87 Saferstein, *op.cit.*, p.369.

88 Saferstein, *op.cit.*, pp.370-71; Duncan *et al, op.cit.*, pp.238-39. See *also* Bieber, *op.cit.*, at p.31: "[A]t any given locus, an individual could have inherited eleven repeats from each parent and would therefore be referred to as an 11,11 homozygote. However, his sister might have inherited 11 repeats from one parent and 14 from the other and be referred to as an 11, 14 heterozygote at that locus. At any genetic locus there can be ten or more alleles in a population, yet a single individual can have only one or two alleles, as stated in Mendel's first and second laws" (internal citations omitted).

89 Saferstein, *op. cit.*, p.371; *see also* Bieber, *op.cit.*, p.31.

90 Gill, Interpol Review Papers, *op.cit.*, p.143; Bieber, *op.cit.*, p.31; LRC Consultation Paper, *op.cit.*, p.33.

91 Duncan *et al, op.cit.*, at p.240 observe: "The future of forensic testing will follow the path of greater automation of the DNA fingerprinting process." See *also* Gill, Interpol Review Papers, *op.cit.*, p.144.

end result of the analyst's efforts is a DNA profile, recorded in digitalised format, which can be compared directly with information stored on a database.[92] For this reason, STR has also contributed to increased standardisation in DNA profiling.[93] STR is a relatively fast technique and, at the stage of matching DNA profiles, can be used to generate higher random match probabilities.[94] The SGM Plus™ method uses 11 STRs to produce a DNA profile and this seemingly small number can in turn generate very large probabilities.[95] For these reasons, the trend in favour of PCR STR-based technology is now firmly established.[96]

Interpreting DNA Results

Interpreting DNA results and, where appropriate, matching DNA profiles, represents the culmination of the analyst's efforts. It is a complicated process and, as we shall see in chapter 9, provides fertile ground for legal challenge. The underlying objective of forensic DNA analysis is to compare DNA extracted from material found during the course of a criminal investigation with the DNA of a known suspect. As we have seen, tests conducted on the samples under comparison (*i.e.* the sample collected at the crime scene and the sample taken from the suspect, respectively) lead to compilation of a DNA profile in respect of each sample. The form in which a DNA profile appears will depend upon the

---

92 Bieber, *op.cit.*, p.31.

93 Giannelli and Imwinkelried, *op.cit.*, §18.3(C). In the European Union, moves to standardise PCR testing are being coordinated by an organization called the Standardization of DNA Profiling Techniques in the European Union (STADNAP). See *http://www.stadnap.uni-mainz.de/.*

94 Giannelli and Imwinkelried, *op.cit.,* §18.3.(C).

95 Wall, *op.cit.,* pp.69-70. In the United States, standard procedures use 13 core STR loci. Kiely, *op.cit.,* p.461; Saferstein, *op.cit.*, p.371.

96 Kiely, *op.cit.*, p.436 (quoting D.J. Werrett, "DNA Evidence", Proceedings of the 12th Interpol International Forensic Science Symposium (1998), p.61). For judicial determinations on the reliability of STR *see e.g. Commonwealth v. Rosier,* 425 Mass. 807, 685 N.E.2d 739 (1997); *State v. Jackson,* 255 Neb. 68, 582 N.W.2d 317 (1998); *People v. Allen,* 72 Cal.App.4th 1093, 85 Cal.Rptr.2d 655 (Cal. Ct. App. 1999). *But see* Wall, *op. cit.*, pp.70-71 (suggesting that STR profiling will be superseded in time by new technologies). *See also* Gill, Interpol Review Papers, *op. cit.*, pp.140-42.

particular profiling technique that has been employed. RFLPs appear as a series of bands on an autoradiograph; when comparing two autoradiographs, the analyst must compare the position of the bands to determine the existence of a match. In the case of the STR technique, the DNA profile is digitally transcribed and resembles a chart or graph.

A comparison of the DNA profiles will generally lend itself to one of three interpretations: "inclusion" or a "match" where the same alleles are present in the loci tested in both samples, "exclusion" where they are not so present, and "inconclusive" where no definitive conclusion can be reached.[97] As a practical matter, the first step involves considering whether the suspect can be excluded as the source of the crime scene sample.[98] If the DNA profiles match, the suspect cannot be excluded, and the analyst must move on to assess the significance of the match or, more broadly, the value of the DNA evidence.[99] With the aid of statistical calculations, the analyst must estimate how common or rare the particular profile is the general population or, possibly, a substructure of the population.[100]

There is no one definitive method of calculating the match probability.[101] The most common technique, sometimes referred to as the "frequentist approach," is to determine the match probability — the frequency of a random DNA match – using a product or multiplication

---

[97] Giannelli and Imwinkelried, *op.cit.,* §18.4(C); Bieber, *op.cit.*, p.35.

[98] Robertson and Vignaux, *op.cit.*, at p.166 ("In a criminal case it is assumed that the sample taken from the suspect under controlled conditions will be better than the sample taken from the scene. If any bands are present in the sample from the scene which are not present in the sample from the suspect this will result in exclusion, unless it can be determined that the presence of the band is due to contamination.")

[99] *Id.*, p.166; Redmayne, *op. cit.*, p.465 (noting that because only a tiny portion of the DNA from the two sources is compared, it is possible for such a match to occur by coincidence.").

[100] *Id.*; LRC Consultation Paper, *op.cit.*, p.30; Ebiske, *op.cit.,* pp.127-29.

[101] On probabilities *see generally* Robertson and Vignaux, *op.cit.,* appendix; P. Dawid, "Probability and Proof", online appendix to T. Anderson *et al., Analysis of Evidence,* 2nd ed. (Cambridge University Press, Cambridge, 2005), s.2, posted at *www.cambridge.org/9780521673167.*

rule.[102] The Law Reform Commission has explained the operation of this approach in an Irish context:

> "The match probability is the probability that a randomly selected, unknown, unrelated person would have the same DNA profile as the suspect. The smaller the probability or the less the possibility of an adventitious match, the greater the likelihood that the two samples came from the same person. The forensic scientist requires some knowledge of the frequency within which the alleles occur within a population, and so population databases are used for this calculation. In this jurisdiction, the DNA Population Database most commonly used in criminal cases is that of the Forensic Science Laboratory. The present system involves calculating a match probability for each of the ten loci that make up a given profile. Then the match probabilities for the individual loci are multiplied together. For a DNA profile of ten loci, the combination of the individual estimates of the likelihood of each allele occurring in a population will result in a very rare event indeed. In respect of a match calculated on the basis of ten loci, the probability that a randomly selected, unknown, unrelated person would have the same DNA profile as the suspect is 1 in a billion."[103]

The traditional SGM technique was based on 6 loci of the DNA molecule and typically generated match probabilities for unrelated individuals in the range of 1 in 10 million to 1 in 100 million.[104] The more advanced profiling system, SGM Plus™, that is used by the Forensic Science Laboratory, is based on 11 loci, each located on a different chromosome.

---

[102] Robertson and Vignaux, *op.cit.,* pp.166-67; D.J. Balding and R.A. Nichols, "DNA Profile Match Probability Calculations: How to Allow for Population Stratification, Relatedness, Database Selection and Single Bands" (1994) 64 Forensic Science Int'l 125. On the use of the product rule in the U.S., *see* Kiely, *op.cit.,* p.434; Bieber, *op.cit.*, p.35. Statistical calculations differ for mtDNA and Y-STR data. *Id.*, p.36. On probabilities and odds *see* Wall, *op.cit.,* pp.81-83.

[103] LRC Consultation Paper, *op.cit.*, p.248.

[104] Evett *et al, op.cit.*, p.342.

The significance of the additional loci lies in the fact that the less common the alleles identified in a profile and the more extensive the number of loci types, the smaller the chance statistically of finding that particular DNA profile in a randomly selected individual.[105] Put simply, the SGM Plus™ technology permits match probabilities in the range of 1 in 10 billion to 1 in 100 trillion."[106] For this reason, the Forensic Science Laboratory and its UK counterpart tend to use conservative estimates of the figures involved as opposed to exact, case specific calculations.[107] As Evett *et al.* have pointed out, the notion that a particular match probability can be reduced to an exact statistic may be mythical:

> "There appears to be a fairly widespread misconception that there is a real 'statistical probability' to be assigned to a profile but this is not the case. There is an infinite range of ways of carrying out the calculation that underlies the figure given. The method chosen in the individual case must be seen to be as much a matter of opinion as one given in other areas of forensic science. The match probability is 'personal'.

---

[105] Bieber, *op.cit.*, pp.35-36. Bieber offers the following example (based on American methodology which may employ as many as 13 loci): "For example, if the DNA profile in a sample is the same as that in a particular individual at only two loci, and if the allele combination observed at each locus occurs with a frequency of one in ten individuals in the population, then the calculated combined random-match probability (*i.e.,* the expected chance of observing the same DNA profile in the sample and in a randomly selected person unrelated to the sample source) for the two independent loci would be one in one hundred. In contrast, if the calculation were based on thirteen loci, and the allele combination observed at each locus occurred with a frequency of one in ten individuals, the calculated random-match probability would be one in ten trillion. Actual estimates generated can range anywhere from one chance in ten for a single-locus profile to one chance in seven hundred quintillion or less for a sixteen-locus profile with uncommon alleles."

[106] Evett *et al., op.cit.,* pp.246-47.

[107] *Id.*, p.348 ("Experiments with SGM Plus™ data have shown that the largest match probabilities that would be expected, given the standard method of calculation, would be approximately 1 in 3 billion, whichever of the three ethnic databases is used. The policy of the FSS therefore, will be to report a general figure of 1 in one billion for all 10 locus match cases."); LRC Consultation Paper, *op.cit.*, p.248.

> It is based on what the scientist considers to be the most appropriate calculation given the circumstances of the case."[108]

Where a DNA profile is mixed, it may be necessary to use an alternative method of calculating the probability of a match.[109] The so-called "likelihood ratio" uses a simple mathematical formula to compare the probabilities of the profile under alternative explanations.[110] The Law Reform Commission explains it in the following terms:

> "This involves conducting a measure of the strength of the evidence regarding the hypothesis that the two profiles came from the same source. Here we find that the profiles of the person contributing the evidence sample and the suspect are both x. Two hypotheses are considered: (1) the source of the evidence and the suspect are the same person and (2) the source of the evidence is a randomly selected person unrelated to the suspect. The likelihood ratio is the probability under hypothesis (1) that the suspect profile and the evidence-sample profile will both be x, divided by the corresponding probability under hypothesis (2)."[111]

The presentation in court of statistical interpretations of DNA matches has been a controversial aspect of DNA evidence.[112] Sources of contention have included the forensic scientist's statistical methodology and the range

---

[108] Evett *et al., op.cit.*, at p.346.

[109] Giannelli and Imwinkelried, *op. cit.* §18.4(C).

[110] Robertson and Vignaux, *op.cit.*, p.225 ("The likelihood ratio is a number which is the ratio of two probabilities for the *same* assertion assuming *different* conditions. It is a number that can take any value above zero. It measures the weight of the assertion as evidence in distinguishing the conditions.") *See also* Giannelli and Imwinkelried, *op.cit.,* §18.4(C); Wall, *op.cit.,* pp.85-86.

[111] LRC Consultation Paper, *op.cit.*, p.249. *See also* Redmayne, *op. cit.*, p.467, n.21 ("Likelihood ratios express the probability of an event in terms of two alternative hypotheses.") There is some support in the legal and scientific literature for the use of Bayes' theorem in the presentation of DNA analysis. See chapter 9 *supra.*

[112] See *generally* Giannelli and Imwinkelried, *op.cit.,* §18.4(C). and §18.5(C).

of factors included in his calculations, the questions put by counsel during the forensic scientist's testimony, and the ability of judges and juries to comprehend complex statistical data. These and other difficulties associated with the presentation of statistical DNA evidence are discussed in chapter 9.

CHAPTER 7

The Taking of DNA Samples[1]

INTRODUCTION

The law currently makes provision for the taking of bodily samples from suspects for the purpose of forensic testing. This has enabled the Gardaí to compare biological material found at a crime scene, such as traces of blood, semen or hair, with a bodily sample taken from a suspect with a view to identifying the suspect as the possible perpetrator of the crime or, conversely, removing him from the ambit of their inquiries. In contrast to the long standing forensic technique of fingerprinting, there is no permanent collection of DNA profiles to which a profile derived from a crime scene sample can be compared and thus the use of DNA analysis is currently limited to known suspects. The Law Reform Commission has recently recommended that Ireland follow the lead of other jurisdictions[2] by enhancing the investigative strength of this forensic technique through the establishment of a limited DNA database.[3] This recommendation was published while the Oireachtas was considering certain less dramatic changes to the current law under the terms of the Criminal Justice Bill 2004,[4] an omnibus measure, since signed into law, which contains other

---

1 This chapter is a version of "The Taking of Forensic Samples: A Review of Proposed Reforms" (2006) 16 I.C.L.J. 2. The author is grateful to Thomson Round Hall for permission to use the material in this context.

2 Such as the United Kingdom, the United States, Canada and New Zealand.

3 The Commission had been requested by the Attorney General to examine the issue. Its recommendation is contained in its *Report on the Establishment of a DNA Database* (LRC 78-2005) which followed the publication of a *Consultation Paper on the Establishment of a DNA Database* (LRC CP 29-2004). The Attorney General welcomed the publication of the Commission's Report but indicated that the Government would seek to introduce a less restricted database than the model proposed. C. Coulter, "Attorney General Welcomes Report on DNA Database" *Irish Times*, Nov. 11, 2005, at p.7. *See* Chap.8 *infra.*

4 S.I. No. 34 of 2004. The Criminal Justice Act 2006 was signed by the President on July 16, 2006. Commencement orders have yet to be issued. The origins of

disparate and controversial changes, such as increased powers of detention under the Criminal Justice Act 1984,[5] and the admissibility in court of pre-trial witness statements.[6] One of the matters touched upon both by the Commission and in the new Act is the power of the Gardaí to take forensic samples.

The Criminal Justice (Forensic Evidence) Act 1990

The Gardaí lack any general power to take bodily samples and may do so only with the consent of the person concerned or pursuant to some specific statutory authority.[7] The Oireachtas has conferred such authority on the Gardaí under a number of statutes, the most pertinent of which is the Criminal Justice (Forensic Evidence) Act 1990.[8] The Act is styled "an act to amend and extend the law to authorise the taking of bodily samples for forensic testing from persons suspected of certain criminal offences".[9] The power to take forensic samples, which is conferred on the Gardaí by

---

several of the changes can be traced to the *Report of the Steering Group on the Efficiency and Effectiveness of the Garda Síochána* (the Garda SMI Report) (Nov. 1997), sec.4 (Legal Framework) and the *Report of the Expert Group Appointed to Consider Changes in the Criminal Law Which Were Recommended in the Garda SMI Report* (Leahy Report) (1998).

5 S.9. *See, e.g.*, Y.M. Daly, "The Criminal Justice Bill, 2004: No Step Forward, Two Steps Back" (2004) 14 I.C.L.J. 2.

6 Pt.3. *See, e.g.*, J. Healy, "Proposed Reform of Evidence Law in Ireland and England: Times They are a 'Changin'?" (2004) 9 Bar Rev. 195.

7 *See generally People (DPP) v. Boyce*, unreported, Court of Criminal Appeal, December 21, 2005; D. Walsh, *Criminal Procedure* (Thomson Round Hall, 2002), pp.345-50; LRC Consultation Paper, *op.cit.*, pp.83-106. On the implications of sampling under the ECHR, *see X v. Netherlands*, App. No. 5239/78, 16 D&R 184; *Peters v. Netherlands*, App. No. 21132/93, 77–A D&R 75; *X v. Germany*, App. No. 8334/78, 24 D&R 103.

8 S. 6 of the 1990 Act repealed s.6(1)(e) of the Criminal Justice Act 1984 and s.7(1)(e) which provided for the taking of hair and swabs from skin to test for the presence of firearm or explosive residue. By virtue of s.2(11), the 1990 Act otherwise leaves intact other statutory Garda powers such as the taking of fingerprints and palm prints pursuant to s.6 of the Criminal Justice Act 1984 and the taking of specimens of an arrested person's breath, blood or urine pursuant to ss.12-18 of the Road Traffic Act 1994.

9 Long Title. *See* E. Leahy, "Genetic Profiling and the Reasonable Doubt" (1995) 1 M.L.J.I. 66, pp.67-68.

section 2, is limited in three important respects.

First, section 2(1) specifies the range of persons from whom samples may be taken, namely, persons in Garda custody pursuant to section 30 of the Offences Against the State Act 1939, section 4 of the Criminal Justice Act 1984 or section 2 of the Criminal Justice (Drug Trafficking) Act 1996.[10] The legislative intent was to facilitate the taking of forensic samples from persons suspected of serious offences; detention under the cited statutory provisions relates for the most part to offences attracting severe penalties[11] although it may apply exceptionally to offences subject to minor penalties.[12] Confining forensic sampling to serious offences is a justifiably proportionate restriction given the inherently intrusive nature of most of the procedures at issue. It is also consistent with general international practice[13] although legislation in England and Wales has bucked this trend.[14] There have been calls in this jurisdiction for the retention of a strict limit on the taking of forensic samples to persons suspected of serious offences.[15] Although this would not involve any

---

[10] S.2(1) of the 1990 Act as amended by the s.3 Criminal Justice (Drug Trafficking) Act 1996.

[11] Such as imprisonment for a term of five years or a more severe penalty. S.4 of the 1984 Act.

[12] Such as some offences under the Offences Against the State Act 1939 and the Criminal Justice (Drug Trafficking) Act 1996. *See* P.O'Connor, (1990) I.C.L.S.A. 90-34.04; LRC Consultation Paper, *op.cit.,* p.87.

[13] *Id.,* pp.118-119.

[14] S.62(2)(a) of the Police and Criminal Evidence Act 1984, as amended, permits the taking of samples from persons suspected of "recordable" offences. This represents a liberalisation of the sampling regime from the original statutory remit of persons suspected of "serious arrestable" offences.

[15] On the issue of a sampling threshold, the Law Reform Commission did not recommend any amendment to the present position under s.2(1) of the 1990 Act. LRC Report, *op.cit.,* para. 2.47. *See also* the views of the Irish Council for Civil Liberties, *Human Rights Compatibility of the Establishment of a DNA Database* (ICCL Position Paper, October 2003), p.11. The Human Rights Commission responded to publication of the initial Scheme of the Criminal Justice Bill 2003 with an expression of concern that the proposed wide-ranging powers in relation to the taking of samples from *all* persons arrested on suspicion of having committed an arrestable offence is not necessary in a democratic society or proportionate to the aims of preventing crime and protecting the rights of others. Irish Human Rights Commission, *Observations on the Scheme of the Criminal Justice Bill 2003* (January 14, 2004), pp.32-33.

substantive change in the law, a reformed legislative scheme might benefit from a more explicit statement of this underlying principle.

Bodily samples may also be taken where the suspect is in prison.[16] The legislation provides that the samples must be sought in relation to the investigation of an offence to which the stated provisions of the 1939, 1984 or 1996 Act, respectively, applies[17] and that the offence must be neither the offence for which the person is in prison nor a related offence.[18] The legislative intent, it seems, was to bring within the scope of the Act persons who would be liable to arrest and detention under the 1939, 1984 or 1996 Act if they were not in prison.[19]

Turning to the second limitation on the power of the Gardaí, section 2(1) of the Act, as amended by section 14 of the Criminal Justice Act 2006, contains an exhaustive list of the forensic samples that may be taken:

> "(a) a sample of —-
> (i) blood,
> (ii) pubic hair,
> (iii) urine,
> (iv) saliva,
> (v) hair other than pubic hair,
> (vi) a nail,
> (vii) any material found under a nail,
> (b) a swab from any part of the body including the mouth but not from any other body orifice or a genital region,
> (c) a swab from a body orifice, other than the mouth, or a genital region,
> (d) a dental impression,
> (e) a footprint or similar impression of any part of the person's body other than a part of his hand."

---

16 S.2(2).

17 S.2(3)(b) as amended by s.3 of the Criminal Justice (Drug Trafficking) Act 1996.

18 S.2(3)(a). A related offence in this context is specifically an offence arising out of the same indictment as the offence for which the person is serving his sentence.

19 O'Connor, *op.cit.* at 90-34.05, argues, however, that the statutory phrase "person in prison" is sufficiently broad to cover persons on remand. For an extended discussion of the interpretation of the subsection *see also* Walsh, *op.cit.*, p.346; and LRC Consultation Paper, *op.cit.*, pp.85-86.

The Gardaí "may take or cause to be taken" from a suspect "all or any" of the listed samples and, by implication, the taking of any bodily samples other than those listed is unlawful in the absence of the suspect's consent. The terms "sample" and "swab" are not defined.

The third limitation on the forensic sampling power is the stated purpose for which the samples may be taken under section 2(1), namely, "for the purpose of forensic testing". Although the term is not statutorily defined, a commonsense interpretation would exclude the taking and use of samples for purposes unconnected with the investigation of crime, such as an immigration procedure or a paternity dispute. Implicit in such an interpretation is the further refinement that the forensic testing should relate to the investigation of the offence for which the suspect was arrested or, in the case of a person in prison, for which he could otherwise have been arrested. Within the realm of forensic investigation, the statutory power to take bodily samples clearly includes but is not limited to the taking of samples for purposes of DNA analysis. Indeed, the statutory language is sufficiently broad to permit the use of a sample for more than one forensic purpose. For example, a sample of blood might be used not only for DNA testing but also for toxicology screening.

Preconditions to the Taking of Samples

In addition to the aforesaid limitations, the 1990 Act specifies three preconditions which the Gardaí must satisfy before taking samples or causing samples to be taken: (a) securing the necessary authorisation, (b) obtaining an appropriate consent, and (c) cautioning the suspect. The extent of the duty resting on the Gardaí in relation to each of these matters varies depending upon the nature of the sample to be taken and the age of the suspect.

(a) Authorisation

First, the need for authorisation applies across the board in relation to the taking of any of the stated bodily samples from any suspect within the terms of the 1990 Act. The authorisation must be given by a member of the Gardaí not below the rank of superintendent[20] who in turn must have

---

[20] S.2(4)(a).

reasonable grounds for suspecting the person's involvement in the offence for which he is in custody[21] and for believing that the sample will tend to confirm or disprove his involvement.[22] The statutory language indicates the need for a tangible evidential basis for authorising the exercise of the sampling power and, as such, "prevents the police from engaging in fishing expeditions."[23] It comprises two limbs, the second of which speaks to the relationship between the proposed forensic test and the criminal investigation. Something more is required than a suspicion on the part of the senior Garda officer, however well-founded, that the suspect committed the offence in question; a general suspicion of this kind is already covered by the first limb. Presumably, however, the second limb would be satisfied by the retrieval at the crime scene of any physical material that might be used to connect the suspect with the offence. For example, if the senior Garda officer has reasonable grounds for suspecting that the suspect committed a rape, the discovery of semen on the victim or at the crime scene might provide grounds for believing that the taking of a bodily sample from the suspect would tend to confirm or disprove his involvement. The two limbs of the test are interrelated, however, and thus the discovery of the semen could not in itself justify an authorisation to take a bodily sample. The senior Garda officer would need some reasonable grounds, independent of the discovery of the semen, for suspecting the person's involvement in the offence.

The inclusion of the term "reasonable grounds" arguably adds a further commonsensical gloss on the statutory test. Not every form of physical material found at a crime scene could reasonably support any authorisation to take a bodily sample from any suspect. Obviously, the discovery of semen at the crime scene could potentially confirm only the involvement

---

[21] S.2(5)(a)(i). Where the person is in prison, s.2(5)(a)(ii) provides that the member giving the authorisation must have reasonable grounds for suspecting the person's involvement in an offence to which the relevant provision of the Offences Against the State Act 1939, Criminal Justice Act 1984 or the Criminal Justice (Drug Trafficking) Act 1996 applies.

[22] S.2(5)(b). O'Connor, *op.cit.,* 90-34.05, argues that "reasonable grounds" is synonymous with "reasonable cause" citing *Lister v. Perryman* (1870) L.R. 14 H.L. 521 ("There must be reasonable cause – such as would operate in the mind of the discreet man, and there must be probable cause – such as would operate in the mind of the reasonable man").

[23] O'Connor, *op.cit.,* 90-34.05.

of a male suspect within a certain age bracket. Similarly, the discovery of a very large footprint at the crime scene could hardly justify the taking of a footprint sample from a suspect with very small feet. Moreover, even where physical crime scene material could be compared to material taken from the suspect, there should be a direct correlation between the nature of that material and the type of bodily sample specified in the authorisation. For example, the discovery of semen would bear no obvious or direct relation to the taking of a footprint or similar impression.

In recommending the establishment of a limited DNA database, the Law Reform Commission has proposed that authorising the taking of forensic samples should no longer depend upon the potential relevance of the samples to the underlying investigation. In other words, the Commission would remove the second limb of the statutory test.[24] This would place the practice of authorising the taking of bodily samples on a par with the taking of photographs and the collection of fingerprint and palm print impressions. The purported justification for the liberalisation of the existing requirement is the proposed wider use of sampling in conjunction with database collection and storage. The Commission considers that "the pragmatic principles of collection" applied to fingerprints and photographs should be transferred to the DNA sampling of suspects and that this would be in line with the establishment and use of a DNA database.[25]

In contrast, the Human Rights Commission has expressed concern at the broadening of Garda powers in relation to forensic sampling in general and the authorising of sampling without consent in particular. As we shall see below, the consent of the suspect is not required for the taking of non-intimate samples. Thus, in relation to these bodily samples, the precondition of authorisation on the part of a Garda not below the rank of superintendent assumes particular importance. The HRC has recommended that the legislation explicitly condition the circumstances in which such authorisation may be given. Specifically, the senior Garda officer in question should be satisfied that the carrying out of the forensic procedure without consent "is justified in all the circumstances" based on a balancing of the potentially conflicting public interests in obtaining evidence and upholding the physical integrity and private life of the

---

[24] LRC Report, *op.cit.*, para. 2.41.

[25] *Id.*, paras. 2.39 & 2.40.

suspect.[26] In making this assessment, the HRC considers that the law should require the Garda officer to have regard to the following factors:

> "(i) The seriousness of the circumstances surrounding the commission of the relevant offence and the gravity of the relevant offence;
> (ii) the degree of the suspect's alleged participation in the commission of the relevant offence;
> (iii) the age, physical and mental health, cultural background and religious beliefs of the suspect, to the extent that they are known;
> (iv) whether there is a less intrusive but reasonably practical way of obtaining evidence tending to confirm or disprove that the suspect committed the relevant offence;
> (v) if the suspect gives reasons for refusing to consent – the reasons for refusing."[27]

The current legislation contains no such contextual elucidation of the authorising power. In addition, the requirement is watered down by the statutory concession that the authorisation may be oral and, if so, confirmed in writing "as soon as is practicable."[28]

(b) Consent

The need for appropriate consent as a precondition to the taking of certain bodily samples constitutes a more robust safeguard, at least at first glance. The taking of so-called "intimate" bodily samples (blood, pubic hair, urine, a swab from a body orifice or a genital region, or a dental impression) involves a substantial interference with the rights to privacy and bodily integrity and must be sanctioned by consent in writing by or on behalf of the suspect.[29] In contrast, no such consent is required for the taking of non-intimate samples (hair other than pubic hair, a nail, any material found under a nail, saliva, a swab from any part of the body

---

26 HRC, *Observations on the Scheme of the Criminal Justice Bill 2003, op.cit.*, p.33.
27 *Id.*, pp.33-34.
28 S.2(7).
29 S.2(4)(b).

other than a body orifice or a genital region, a footprint or similar impression of any part of the person's body other than a part of his hand). The Act itself does not expressly embrace the distinction between "intimate" and "non-intimate" samples nor does it employ these actual, or indeed similar, terms; the provision in question merely identifies from the statutory list those bodily samples for which consent is required.[30]

One effect of this approach is that it eases the future transfer of specified samples from the category requiring consent to the category for which no consent is required. The Criminal Justice Act 2006 effected such a change by providing that mouth swabs and saliva become samples that may be taken without consent.[31] The importance of this reclassification lies in the fact that current technology permits a complete DNA profile to be established from saliva.[32] Thus, the change effectively permits the taking of a DNA sample without consent. As discussed below, it might also allow the use of reasonable force by the Gardaí when a suspects refuses to cooperate, and render the suspect open to prosecution for obstruction.[33]

Within the realm of so-called intimate bodily samples, the Act specifies that only a registered medical practitioner may take samples of blood or pubic hair and swabs from a body orifice or a genital region.[34] Similarly, only a registered dentist or a registered medical practitioner may take a dental impression.[35] Any of the other samples covered by the Act may presumptively be taken by the Gardaí.[36]

Where a suspect has attained the age of 17 years, he may himself give

---

30 The practical effect is essentially the same although questions may arise at the margins as to whether, for example, a urine sample is an intimate sample and consequently properly designated as subject to appropriate consent.

31 S. 13(a). *See* N. O'Connor, *Cracking Crime: Jim Donovan–Forensic Detective* (O'Brien Press, Dublin, 2001), p.301 (noting that this is the general international practice).

32 Leahy Report, *op.cit.*, p.41.

33 *Id.* The Leahy Report preferred this proposal to the more dramatic recommendation of making it an offence to refuse to permit the taking of samples.

34 S.2(8).

35 *Id.*

36 S.14(a)(vi) of the Criminal Justice Act 2006 inserted a subs. 8(A) into s.2 of the 1990 Act in relation to the taking of samples of hair other than pubic hair. The sample may be taken either by cutting hairs or by plucking hairs singly with their roots. Where hairs are plucked, no more can be plucked than the person taking

the appropriate consent.[37] The consent of a parent or guardian is required for the taking of intimate samples from a suspect below the age of 14 years[38] and, for suspects between 14 and 16 years, both the suspect and his parent or guardian must give their consent.[39] The Act also requires the Gardaí to caution the suspect before seeking his consent or taking a sample. Specifically, the suspect must be informed of the nature of the offence under investigation, that the necessary authorisation has been given, and that the results of any tests on the sample may be given in evidence in any proceedings.[40] No provision is included, however, for the cautioning of a parent or guardian in equivalent terms before seeking his consent in relation to a suspect under the age of 17 years. And in relation to a suspect of any age, the Act imposes no requirement that the validity of consent depends upon the person having received legal advice.[41]

In the case of suspects aged 17 years or over – the vast majority of suspects to whom the Act applies — the significance of consent is seriously undermined by the negative consequences that may flow from a suspect's refusal to consent. Specifically, a court may draw "such inferences, if any, from the refusal as appear proper" when determining whether a charge should be dismissed against the suspect, whether there is a case to answer or, ultimately, whether the suspect is guilty of the offence charged (or of any other offence of which he could lawfully be convicted on that charge).[42] In addition, the court may treat a refusal to consent as corroboration of any evidence in relation to which the refusal is material. Thus, for example, a refusal to consent to the taking of an intimate bodily sample might corroborate material aspects of a suspect's confession, incidentally obviating the need for the judge to caution the jury about the dangers of convicting on the confession standing alone.[43]

---

the sample reasonably considers to be necessary to constitute a sufficient sample for the purpose of forensic testing.

37 S.2(10)(a).

38 S.2(10)(c).

39 S.2(10)(b). P. O'Connor, *op.cit.* at 90-34.05, notes that the legal implications of a conflict between parents over the question of consent is not addressed.

40 S.2(6).

41 P. O'Connor, *op.cit.* at 90-34.05.

42 S.3(1)(a) & (b).

43 S.10 of the Criminal Procedure Act 1999; *People (DPP) v. Connolly* [2003] 2 I.R. 1.

An inference drawn from a refusal, however, is not in itself sufficient to support a conviction.[44] In any event, the possibility of a court drawing inferences from a refusal to consent arises only where the suspect was cautioned by the Gardaí in ordinary language of the need for his consent and of the possible effect of refusal.[45]

It is also worthy of note that these statutorily prescribed negative consequences do not accompany every refusal to consent to the taking of an intimate bodily sample but only a refusal "without cause." The Act neither defines this term nor hints at the circumstances in which a suspect might be justified in refusing to consent. The provisions of the 1990 Act are drafted in almost identical terms to provisions contained in the Criminal Justice Act 1984 which permit a court to draw inferences from the failure or refusal of a suspect to account for an object, substance or mark found on his person or in his possession,[46] or for his whereabouts at a particular location.[47]

The constitutionality of these provisions was upheld by the Supreme Court in *Rock v. Ireland*[48] against challenges based on the presumption of innocence and the privilege against self incrimination. The statutory regimes are not strictly comparable, however, insofar as the 1990 Act contemplates a far greater degree of interference with the personal rights of the suspect. The compatibility of the provisions of the 1990 Act with the Constitution and the European Convention on Human Rights turns in large measure on the proportionality of the legislative response to the societal aims of preventing crime and protecting the rights of others. And in assessing proportionality, a court might well focus on the exception for refusal "with cause" as a matter of substance and not merely of form.

In the absence of guiding principles, the concept of justifiable refusal to consent will be determined, if at all, by *ad hoc* retrospective judicial determination. We may speculate that, for example, a failure on the part of the Gardaí to properly caution the suspect or to abide by the letter of the statute and regulations would constitute cause to refuse. Similarly, a suspect would presumably be justified in refusing consent on valid medical

---

[44] S.3(1).
[45] S.3(3).
[46] S.18.
[47] S.19.
[48] [1997] 3 I.R. 484, [1998] 2 I.L.R.M. 35.

grounds, such as haemophilia in the case of a blood sample. Beyond this, however, the definitional waters grow murky. For example, a refusal to consent in advance of consultation with a solicitor might seem defensible but the existing case law in this jurisdiction on the taking of samples in relation to road traffic offences points in the other direction.[49]

Again, it is worth emphasising that consent is not required for the taking of non-intimate samples, *i.e.* hair other than pubic hair, a nail, any material found under a nail, saliva, a swab from any part of the body other than a body orifice or a genital region, a footprint or similar impression of any part of the person's body other than a part of his hand. In relation to any of these samples, the Garda officer need only secure the necessary authorisation from a member not below the rank of superintendent, and caution the suspect before taking the sample or causing it to be taken.

Finally, it should be noted that the 1990 Act leaves open the question whether the Gardaí are entitled to use force in the exercise of their power to take bodily samples and, if so, the circumstances in which force may be justified and the degree of force that may be employed. The Act opts instead to criminalise conduct which frustrates the Garda objective. Specifically, any person, whether a suspect or another person, who obstructs or attempts to obstruct the Gardaí in the exercise of their power to take samples shall be guilty of an offence and liable on summary conviction to a fine not exceeding €3,000 and/or imprisonment for a term not exceeding 12 months.[50] The view has been expressed that implicit in the statutory power to take non-intimate samples without consent is the right of the Gardaí to use reasonable force.[51] An alternative view is that an interference of this kind with an individual's personal rights and

---

[49] *See, e.g., Walsh v. O'Buachalla* [1991] 1 I.R. 56; *DPP v. Spratt* [1995] 2 I.L.R.M. 117. *But see Condron v. United Kingdom* [2001] E.H.R.R. 1. Similarly, the status of a refusal based on religious grounds might be the subject of debate. *See, e.g., North Western Health Board v. H.W.* [2001] 3 I.R. 622.

[50] S.2(9), as amended by s.14(a)(vii) of the Criminal Justice Act 2006. In this context, O'Connor, *op.cit.* at 90-34.05 cites Lord Goddard in *Bastable v. Little* [1955] 3 All E.R. 406 for the loose definition of obstruction as that which makes it more difficult for the police to carry out their duties.

[51] LRC Consultation Paper, *op.cit.,* para. 4.45 (quoting the Dáil Debates in support); LRC Report at para. 2.35; Leahy Report, *op.cit.,* p.40; O'Connor, *op.cit.,* 90-34.05.

freedoms must be explicitly prescribed by law. The use of force is questionable in any custodial context[52] but would be particularly problematic in relation to the taking of forensic samples. It is perhaps with these considerations in mind that the original Scheme of the Criminal Justice Bill contained a proposal to authorise explicitly the use of reasonable force on the part of the Gardaí in the taking of non-intimate samples under the 1990 Act.[53] This proposal was not included in the legislation as adopted, however, and the existing position thus remains uncertain.[54] A separate but related issue is the need for legislative or ministerial action on long standing calls for the mandatory video-recording of Garda interviews of custodial detainees.[55]

The issue of consent was addressed by the Court of Criminal Appeal in its recent decision in *People (DPP) v. Costigan*.[56] The applicant for leave to appeal was convicted of murder primarily on the basis of the prosecution's DNA evidence. His challenge to his conviction was based in part on the contention that the sample of his blood used in the forensic analysis had been taken from him unlawfully during custodial detention with the consequence that the DNA evidence should have been excluded at trial. The court roundly rejected the applicant's first submission on point, namely, that the gardaí had obtained the consent of the applicant's father (in his capacity as guardian) to the giving of the sample through the ruse of an assurance that the applicant was not a suspect in the murder investigation. On a reading of the trial transcript, the court was satisfied

---

52 *See, e.g.*, Irish Human Rights Commission, *Observations on the Scheme of the Criminal Justice Bill 200, op.cit.*, p.34 (citing the United Nations Code of Conduct for Law Enforcement Officials and the United Nations Basic Principles on the Use of Force and Firearms by Law Enforcement Officials). *See generally Ribitsch v. Austria* [1995] 21 E.H.R.R. 573; *Raminen v. Finland* [1997] 26 E.H.R.R. 563.

53 Head 10 of the Scheme of the Criminal Justice Bill 2003. The proposal, which may be traced to the Leahy Report, *op.cit.,* p.40, also provided for the use of reasonable force in relation to the taking of photographs, fingerprints and palm prints under the Criminal Justice Act 1984.

54 *See* LRC Consultation Paper, *op.cit.,* para. 2.35 (expressing the view that any such power to use reasonable force should be explicitly prescribed and delineated in legislation).

55 *People (DPP) v. Connolly* [2003] 2 I.R. 1 *(per* Hardiman J.); Leahy Report, *op.cit.,* p.54.

56 Unreported, Court of Criminal Appeal, April 28, 2006.

that no such assurance had been given.[57] The applicant's second submission, namely, that the prosecution had failed to adduce evidence of valid, informed consent, was also unsuccessful. Macken J. distinguished between "a consent in the form of an admission, or to be considered as a type of confession" and "a consent to the giving of a blood sample, *simpliciter*" which is "simply a consent to a medical procedure" albeit one that necessitates a valid consent.[58] In her view, the signing by the appellant's father of a standard consent form constituted *prima facie* evidence of consent:

> "The contention by the Applicant is that a valid consent did not exist because there was no evidence that his father had read the form or had its contents read to him before signing it. The Court is not satisfied that, when asked to sign a form consenting to the taking of a blood sample, no consent can be implied from the fact of such signing unless the prosecution has also established that the form was read by the party signing it, or that it had been read over to him. Unless there is evidence of some exceptional circumstance, such as evidence of an inability to read, for example, which would require the form to be read over to a signatory in advance, the signing of the form by the party concerned is *prima facie* evidence that the party both understands fully and agrees to its contents".[59]

(c) Caution

The final precondition that must be satisfied before samples are taken under the Act is the cautioning of the suspect. Before a Garda officer takes any sample or causes any sample to be taken, he must inform the suspect of the nature of the offence under investigation, of that fact that the necessary authorisation for the taking of the sample has been given, and of the possibility that the results of any tests of the sample may be

---

57 *Id.* p.7.
58 *Id.*, p.7.
59 *Id.* p.8.

given in evidence in any proceedings.[60] As noted above, where the taking of the sample is subject to an appropriate written consent, the suspect must also be told in ordinary language that the sample is required for forensic testing and that the suspect's consent is required and further cautioned as to the effect of a refusal to consent.[61] These safeguards, though immensely important, have less of a resonance than the cautions that customarily precede the questioning of a suspect and the recording of any inculpatory statement. The forensic process is a step removed from the suspect and the information tendered by the Gardaí has no direct bearing on the accuracy or reliability of the evidence ultimately proffered.[62]

In its recent decision in *People (DPP) v. Costigan,*[63] the Court of Criminal Appeal espoused a flexible approach to the giving of cautions as a precondition to the taking of samples. There was evidence that a caution had been administered to the applicant for leave to appeal and to his father who had given the necessary consent. However, the caution had not been specifically addressed to the applicant's father in his capacity as guardian. The court concluded that is was permissible for the trial judge to have inferred from the overall evidence that the consent of the applicant's father had been given both in his own capacity and in his capacity as guardian.[64]

In *Costigan*, the Court of Criminal Appeal distinguished forensic evidence from confession evidence for the purposes of consent and caution.[65] The self same distinction underpinned the court's decision in another recent case involving DNA evidence, *People (DPP) v. Boyce.*[66] In that case, the admissibility of the taking of a blood sample from the applicant for leave to appeal had been tried on a *voir dire* in the absence of the jury. One of the several arguments put before the court was that the trial judge had erred in refusing to allow the issue of whether a caution

---

60 S.2(6).
61 S.3(3).
62 O'Connor, *op.cit.,* 90-34.05.
63 Unreported, Court of Criminal Appeal, April 28, 2006.
64 *Id.* pp.9-10.
65 *Id.* p.7.
66 Unreported, Court of Criminal Appeal, December 21, 2005. *See also Brown v. Stott* [2001] 2 All E.R. 97; *R v. Stillman* [1997] 1 S.C.R. 607.

had been given to be considered by the jury as a question of fact.[67] The Court of Criminal Appeal held that the admissibility of the evidence relating to the taking of the blood sample is a question of law to be decided by the trial judge. However, unlike confession evidence, evidence relating to the taking of a sample does not subsequently go before the jury. As Murray C.J. explained, forensic evidence falls into a different category because it does not implicate the right to silence and the right against self incrimination in the manner of confession evidence:

> "Generally speaking forensic samples such as samples of blood, hair or a nail involve the obtaining of objective evidence, that is to say, evidence of a forensic nature, including what emerges from a subsequent forensic analysis, the validity of which is not usually susceptible to being affected by transient factors. ... Thus, a person's blood group, or indeed DNA analysis, based on the inherent characteristics of the blood, will always be the same whenever the sample is taken and analysed. For those types of analyses, an arrested person or an accused will always have available to him a means of verifying, should he or she feel the need to do so, such forensic analysis. That is not to say that such samples can be obtained otherwise than in accordance with law but they give rise to different legal considerations than that which arises under the law relating to the right to silence or protection against self-incrimination. The law may make it compulsory or a serious offence not to provide a forensic sample, such as fingerprints or a blood sample, to an extent which may not be permissible with regard to the making of oral statements contrary to a person's right to silence. Such matters as forensic samples and indeed documents and other property of an accused which may be obtained in the course of the gathering of evidence for the purposes of a criminal prosecution exist independently of the will of the accused and their objective evidential value is not dependent on a

---

[67] Specifically, in the course of the trial before the jury, the trial judge refused to permit counsel for the applicant to cross-examine the relevant witnesses as to whether the caution had in fact been given. *Id.* p.20-21.

> self-incriminating statement or communication by the accused."[68]

In the instant case, the admissibility of the taking of the blood sample was a matter of law to be determined by the trial judge. The findings of fact which the trial judge made in the course of his rule on admissibility were inextricable linked to that question of law. Consequently, the trial judge was correct in not permitting the jury to revisit the issue, already determined by him, as to whether the caution had been administered.[69]

Additional Safeguards

Section 5 of the 1990 Act empowers the Minister for Justice to make regulations relating to the taking of samples for the purposes of the Act. To date this power has been exercised on one occasion in the form of the Criminal Justice (Forensic Evidence) Act 1990 Regulations 1992.[70] Whereas the bulk of this short, modest set of regulations relate to specific aspects of the taking of forensic samples, Regulation 3, the first of the substantive regulations, articulates a general, guiding principle:

> "In carrying out their functions under these Regulations members or other persons concerned shall act with due respect for the personal rights of persons in custody and their dignity as human persons, and shall have regard for the special needs of any of them who have not attained the age of 17 years or who may be under a physical or mental disability."

Regulations 4 to 7 concern the recording "as soon as practicable" in the custody record[71] or prison record of details pertaining to the taking of

---

68 *Id.*, p.21 (citing *Saunders v. United Kingdom* [1997] 23 E.H.R.R. 313 in support.)

69 *Id.* p.24.

70 S.I. No. 130 of 1992. *See also* Regulation 18 of the Criminal Justice Act 1984 (Detention of Persons in Custody in Garda Síochána Stations) Regulations 1987, S.I. No.119 of 1987 ("Custody Regulations").

71 On the custody record, *see* reg.6 of the Custody Regulations.

forensic samples: the giving of the authorisation,[72] the cautioning of the suspect,[73] the consent or refusal to consent,[74] and particulars pertaining to the actual taking of the sample.[75] The relevant forms for these various purposes appear as appendices to the regulations. Regulation 8 incorporates a safeguard in relation to the taking of samples from persons under the age of 17 years: samples shall not be taken from such a person nor his consent to the taking of samples sought other than in the presence of his parent or guardian. In summary, these regulations are a beneficial reinforcement of the safeguards in the parent Act although in substance add little flesh to the bones of the legislative provisions.

The power to make regulations under section 5 is expressed both in general and specific terms. Subsection (1) states that the minister shall make regulations and subsection (2) that those regulations shall make provision for the specific matters addressed in regulations 4 to 8. Clearly, the generality of subsection (1) leaves open the possibility of future regulations directed towards other aspects of the taking of forensic samples. Nevertheless, section 14(c) of the Criminal Justice Act 2006 has put the matter beyond doubt by specifying some such additional matters:

> "(i) the manner in which samples may be taken,
> (ii) the location and physical conditions in which samples may be taken, and
> (iii) the persons (including members of the Garda Síochána), and the number of such persons, who may be present when samples are taken."

This provision is mandatory insofar as it obliges the Minister to make regulations pertaining to the stated matters. The introduction of these safeguards would be a welcome step and it is hoped that the Minister will act expeditiously in making the envisioned regulations and laying

---

72 Reg.4.
73 Reg.5.
74 Reg.6.
75 Namely, the name of the person from whom the sample was taken, the offence in respect of which the sample was taken, the nature of the sample, the name of the person who took the sample, the date and time the sample was taken, and the manner in which it was taken. Reg.7.

them before the Oireachtas in accordance with the Act.[76] In so doing, the Minister would be wise to heed the call of the Human Rights Commission for the inclusion in such regulations of adequate and effective safeguards in relation to the taking of samples.[77] In particular, the HRC has recommended the inclusion in a set of formal guidelines of the following general safeguards:

> "(i) the taking of bodily samples should be carried out in circumstances affording reasonable privacy to the suspect;
> (ii) the taking of bodily samples should be carried out in the presence or view of a person who is of the same sex as the suspect;
> (iii) the taking of bodily samples should not be carried out in the presence or view of a person whose presence is not necessary for the purposes of the forensic procedure;
> (iv) there should be no questioning during the taking of bodily samples;
> (v) the taking of bodily samples should not involve any cruel, inhuman or degrading treatment;
> (vi) the taking of bodily samples should be carried out by specified professionals including nurses, medical practitioners, and dentists depending on the procedure;
> (vii) a child or incapable person should be entitled to have present a parent, guardian, legal practitioner or other independent person who is not a member of the Garda Síochána during the taking of bodily samples;
> (viii) the number of members of the Garda Síochána present during the taking of bodily samples must not exceed that which is reasonably necessary to ensure that the procedure is carried out effectively;
> (ix) the taking of bodily samples must be video recorded in all circumstances unless the suspect objects to the video

---

[76] S. 5(3).

[77] Irish Human Rights Commission, *Observations on the Criminal Justice Bill 2004* (November 3, 2004). The IHRC's call has been supported by the Law Reform Commission. LRC Report, *op.cit.*, para. 2.31.

recording and the suspect must be informed of the reasons for the video recording;

(x) the suspect should have the right to an interpreter where he or she does not speak English as his or her first language;

(xi) the suspect should have the right of access to legal advice of his or her choice to decide the implications of refusing to give a bodily sample."[78]

The need for detailed, comprehensive standards in relation to the taking of samples cannot be gainsaid. In pursuing the legitimate societal aim of preventing and detecting crime, the Gardaí should have at their disposal the benefits of modern science and technology. No less than in any other area of criminal investigation, however, law and practice must ensure that the human rights of the individual are adequately protected. Indeed, the inherent intrusiveness of forensic sampling coupled with the sensitivity of personal genetic data suggest the need for heightened human rights scrutiny in this area. Safeguards along the lines suggested by the HRC would serve as an essential bulwark against arbitrariness and abuse in the practical exercise of the power to take samples.

The importance of additional safeguards raises the question whether they should be housed in the legislation itself, or perhaps a schedule appended thereto, as opposed to regulations. There is merit to the HRC's recommendation that the safeguards constitute a cohesive code of practice, whether contained in codifying legislation or promulgated by ministerial order, in relation to which members of the Gardaí should receive special training.[79] However, the form in which the safeguards are adopted will also have a significant bearing on their enforcement and, in particular, the evidentiary consequences that may flow from their breach.

The point is illustrated by an analogy with the Custody Regulations adopted under the Criminal Justice Act 1984.[80] Neither the 1990 Act nor the Criminal Justice Act 2006contain a provision equivalent to s.7(3) of the 1984 Act which states that a failure on the part of the Gardaí to observe

---

[78] IHRC, *Observations on the Criminal Justice Bill 2004*, *op.cit.*, pp.4-5.

[79] *Id.*, p.5.

[80] *See* n.70 *supra*.

any provision of the regulations shall not of itself affect the admissibility in evidence of any statement made by the detained person.[81] The courts have recognised that whereas non-compliance with one or more of the Custody Regulations may not result in the automatic exclusion of the detainee's inculpatory statement,[82] it may constitute a factor in the court's constitutionally mandated assessment of whether the statement was voluntary and the product of fair procedures in all the circumstances of the case.[83] Approaching the issue from an alternative perspective, a breach of the Custody Regulations might be classified as "unlawful" conduct (as opposed to "unconstitutional" conduct) which, by virtue of the principles famously set down by the Supreme Court in *People (AG) v. O'Brien*,[84] would vest in the trial judge a discretion to exclude any confession obtained as a result of the breach.[85]

The effect of a breach of the Forensic Evidence Regulations is open to debate. Notwithstanding the absence of an express limitation along the lines of section 7(3) of the 1984 Act, one may hazard a guess that the courts would adopt a similar stance when faced with breaches of the Forensic Evidence Regulations. Much might depend upon the nature of the regulation at issue. With the possible exception of regulation 8 (concerning the taking of samples from persons under the age of 17 years), a breach of any of the existing, modest regulations would be a slim reed on which to hang an argument in favour of the exclusion of the forensic evidence. It might, however, combine with other factors to bear upon the exercise of the trial court's discretion to exclude. In contrast, looking to the future, a breach of the more robust safeguards contained in the IHRC's suggested guidelines might have more direct bearing on admissibility. Thus, the importance of any future safeguards will lie not only in the

---

[81] S.7(3) also states that such a failure shall of itself render the member of the Gardaí in question liable to any criminal or civil proceedings or affect the lawfulness of the custody of the detained person.

[82] *DPP v. Spratt* [1995] 2 I.L.R.M. 117; *People (DPP) v. Darcy*, unreported, Court of Criminal Appeal, July 29, 1997.

[83] *People (DPP) v. Diver* [2005] 3 I.R. 270.

[84] [1965] I.R. 142. The principles were refined in *People (DPP) v. Kenny* [1990] 2 I.R. 110.

[85] On the causation requirement see *People (DPP) v. Healy* [1990] 2 I.R. 73; *People (DPP) v. Buck* [2002] 2 I.R. 268.

substance of the standards but also in their form and enforceability in practice.

THE TAKING OF ADDITIONAL SAMPLES

The 1990 Act makes no provision for the taking of an additional sample in the event that the sample taken is forensically unusable. The Law Reform Commission has recommended the enactment of legislation conferring on the Gardaí the power to obtain an additional sample "in the event of the first sample being insufficient or unsatisfactory, or where the first sample is contaminated, destroyed or lost."[86] The inspiration for this recommendation is legislation in England and Wales which permits the taking of a second sample where the first proves "insufficient."[87] The second sample must be taken within one month of the appropriate officer being informed of the discovered insufficiency.[88] There may be circumstances in which the taking of a second sample is necessary and desirable and indeed this may be so from the point of view of the suspect as well as the Gardaí. Nevertheless, a power to take additional samples should be narrowly defined and crafted with circumspection. Terms such as "insufficient" and "unsatisfactory" are broad and subjective and, under the English model, cover not only the loss, destruction or contamination of a sample but also less clear-cut scenarios in which forensic testing produces no results or unreliable results.[89] If the Oireachtas takes up the Commission's recommendation, it will be important to ensure that the envisioned provision neither encourages nor condones sloppy practice and lax procedures in the gathering and processing of forensic evidence.

THE POWER TO TAKE SAMPLES OUTSIDE THE 1990 ACT

As noted above, the 1990 Act is not the exclusive statutory source of the Garda authority to take forensic samples. The taking of fingerprints and

---

[86] LRC Report, *op.cit.,* para. 2.26.
[87] S.65 of the Police and Criminal Evidence Act 1984 as amended.
[88] S.63A of the Police and Criminal Evidence Act 1984 as amended.
[89] S.65 of the Police and Criminal Evidence Act 1984 as amended.

palmprints, for example, is governed by other legislation,[90] as is the taking of specimens of breath, blood or urine in connection with the investigation of road traffic offences.[91] This dispersal of legislative authority has prompted the Law Reform Commission to recommend "a complete review of the statutory procedures for sampling with a view to consolidation."[92]

A more pressing argument in favour of a comprehensive legislative foundation is the traditional Garda practice of taking forensic samples informally with a person's consent. Because the informal practice of asking a person to "volunteer" a sample operates outside the 1990 Act, it is not conditioned by the statutory and administrative safeguards outlined above.

The legality of the practice was recently upheld by the Court of Criminal Appeal in *People (DPP) v. Boyce*.[93] The court observed that prior to the coming into force of the 1990 Act, a blood sample could be lawfully taken from a person in custody provided that it was voluntary.[94] It held that the admissibility of evidence based on a forensic sample voluntarily given is not, or does not have to be, dependent on an express statutory power.[95] Nor could the court find any support in the 1990 Act for the proposition that the Oireachtas had intended to abolish the existing faculty of the Gardai to take or cause to be taken a blood sample with the consent of the custodial detainee.[96] The Act created "a distinct statutory regime fundamentally different in nature and consequences from the gathering of evidence under common-law rules or powers" which

---

90 Notably, s.6(1)(d) of the Criminal Justice Act 1984 and s.11 of the Criminal Justice (Miscellaneous Provisions) Act 1997. See chap.4 *supra*.

91 Ss. 12-18 of the Road Traffic Act 1994.

92 LRC Report, *op.cit.*, para. 2.48.

93 Unreported, Court of Criminal Appeal, December 21, 2005.

94 *Id.* p.16.

95 *Id.* p.17.

96 *Id.* p.19 (*per* Murray J.) "It would indeed be extraordinary if the Oireachtas contemplated that any forensic sample freely and voluntarily provided by a person in custody and then forensically examined by the Gardaí which was lawful before the passing of the Act should then be considered unlawful after the passing of the Act without any express provision to that effect, even though it was provided without any element of coercion and when the consequences of the refusal were nil from the point of view of an accused."

constituted "an expression of the law rather than an abrogation of the existing law."[97]

At the same time it seems anomalous that the Oireachtas should perceive a need for regulation of the inherently sensitive practice of forensic testing but that the promulgated legislative regime should then be sidestepped in practice. In criticising the *status quo*, the Law Reform Commission observed that doubts have been cast over the legality of the analogous Garda practice of obtaining fingerprints through the voluntary submission of the suspect[98] and concluded that "the practice of obtaining a bodily sample outside the legislative framework is objectionable in principle and creates significant evidential risks."[99] Serious consideration should be given to the Commission's recommendation on this point, namely, that the taking of forensic samples should be governed exclusively by legislation.[100]

---

97 *Id.* p.19.

98 The Commission cited the decision of the Circuit Criminal Court in *People (DPP) v. Carroll*, February 24, 2004, in which McMahon J. declared inadmissible evidence relating to fingerprints obtained voluntarily from the accused. See LRC Consultation Paper, *op.cit.*, para. 4.10.

99 LRC Report, *op.cit.*, para. 2.20. The Commission's "Draft Criminal Justice (DNA Database) Bill" appears as an appendix to the Report.

100 LRC Report, *op.cit.*, para. 2.21.

Chapter 8

A DNA Database

Introduction

A turning point in the use of fingerprinting for purposes of criminal identification was the development of an effective system of fingerprint classification.[1] The gradual application of evolving computer technology has enabled law enforcement authorities to significantly improve the efficiency and effectiveness of that process. A vital step was the introduction of automated systems which allow a fingerprint analyst to electronically search a database of recorded prints in order to identify a possible match for prints found at a crime scene.[2] An issue currently under debate in Ireland is whether the concept of a criminal identification database should be extended to DNA technology. At the present time, the benefits of DNA profiling are gleaned only where the Gardaí have already identified a suspect using traditional investigative means. A DNA database would electronically store DNA profiles which could be compared to profiles generated from biological samples found at crime scenes. The primary advantage would lie in the ability of the database to generate suspects, to link to possible crimes persons on whom suspicion might not otherwise have been cast. The database would also hold the promise of greater efficiency in excluding suspects from investigations, establishing links between separate crimes, and identifying repeat offenders of particular crimes.

These considerations prompted the Law Reform Commission to publish a report in 2005 recommending the establishment of a national DNA database[3] which would be operated by the Forensic Science

---

1 *See supra,* chap.3.

2 On the history of this development *see* S.A. Cole, "Fingerprint Identification and the Criminal Justice System: Historical Lessons for the DNA Debate" in D. Lazer, ed., *DNA and the Criminal Justice System: The Technology of Justice* (MIT Press, Cambridge, Mass., 2004) 63, pp.72-74.

3 Law Reform Commission, *Report on the Establishment of a DNA Database* (LRC

Laboratory, re-instituted as an independent statutory body called the Forensic Science Agency.[4] The Government has since signalled its intention to legislate promptly on the matter although it has indicated that it intends to introduce a less restricted form of database than that recommended by the Commission.[5] The law enforcement establishment has called for some time for Ireland to replicate the experience of countries such as the United Kingdom, Canada and New Zealand which have operated DNA databases for the past several years.[6] The initiative is, nevertheless, deceptively complex and countervailing voices have emphasised the need for caution on at least two grounds.[7]

First, the possible establishment of a DNA database raises significant, challenging human rights and public policy concerns. Fingerprints are "two-dimensional representations of the physical attributes of our fingerprints ... useful only as a form of identification."[8] In contrast, aside from their use in criminal identification, DNA samples can provide "insights into the most personal family relationships and the most intimate workings of the human body".[9] The retention and storage of DNA profiles have profound implications for the individual's constitutionally and

---

78-2005). The recommendation was made in response to a request by the Attorney General in 2003 that the Commission consider the matter. The Commission's report followed its *Consultation Paper on the Establishment of a DNA Database* (LRC CP 29-2004).

4 LRC Report, *op. cit.,* chap.4.

5 C. Coulter, "Attorney General Welcomes Report on DNA Database" *Irish Times,* Nov. 16, 2005, p.7.

6 LRC Report, *op. cit.,* para.1.15 (citing the publicly stated support of the Garda Commissioner, the Director of Public Prosecutions, and the Director of the Forensic Science Laboratory for the establishment of a DNA database). *See also* J. Donovan, "The Obtaining, Examining, Analysis and Retaining of Forensic Samples in Criminal Investigation" (2001) 7 M.L.J.I. 25, p.26 (noting the impossibility of building a database within the current legislative scheme and the beneficial crime-solving effect of such databases in other jurisdictions).

7 *See e.g.,* Irish Council for Civil Liberties, *Human Rights Compatability of the Establishment of a DNA Database* (2003).

8 B. Steinhardt, "Privacy and Forensic DNA Databanks" in D. Laser, ed., *DNA and the Criminal Justice System: The Technology of Justice* (MIT Press, Cambridge, Mass., 2004) 173, 173.

9 *Id.*

internationally protected rights, notably, the rights to privacy[10] and bodily integrity[11] and, less immediately, the rights to fair trial[12] and against self incrimination.[13] The rights of persons who are genetically connected to the individual whose DNA is sampled are also affected.[14] The establishment of a national database is not a step lightly taken and should be the subject of diverse, informed public debate. Should the Government press ahead, as seems probable, the database initiative should be placed on a firm, comprehensive legislative footing. In particular, the necessary mechanisms should be put in place to ensure that the expanded use of DNA technology is strictly limited to the purpose of criminal identification.

Second, there is considerable variation in the way in which other countries have structured DNA databases and organised their functional operation.[15] In the absence of a standard international model, important

---

[10] Art.40.3.1 of the Constitution; art.8 of the European Convention on Human Rights. *See e.g. Norris v. AG* [1984] I.R. 36; *Kane v. Governor of Mountjoy Prison* [1988] I.R. 321; *People (DPP.) v. Davis* [2001] 1 I.R. 587; *McVeigh v. U.K.* [1983] 5 E.H.R.R. 71; *Friedl v. Austria* [1995] 21 E.H.R.R. 85; *Rataru v. Romania,* App.No.28341/95, May 5, 2000.

[11] Art.40.3 of the Constitution; art.3 of the ECHR. An unenumerated personal right, it protects the individual from direct physical interference with his person, including torture and inhuman and degrading treatment, and operates *in tandem* with the guarantees of due process and fair procedures. *See e.g. State (Richardson) v. Gov. Mountjoy Prison* [1980] I.L.R.M. 82; *State (C) v. Frawley* [1976] I.R. 365; *State (Healy) v. Donoghue* [1976] I.R. 325.

[12] Art.38.1 of the Constitution; art.6 of the ECHR; *see supra,* chap.1.

[13] The right is essentially a disparate group of immunities, including the right of a suspect not to answer questions and the right of an accused not to be compelled to give evidence or make incriminating statements at his trial, and is most commonly associated with the right to fair trial (Art.38.1 of the Constitution and art.6 of the ECHR) and the freedom of expression (Art.40.6.1 of the Constitution and art.10 of the ECHR). *See e.g. R v. Director of Serious Fraud Office, ex parte Smith* [1993] A.C. 1 (*per* Lord Mustill); *Re National Irish Bank* [1999] 3 I.R. 145, [1999] 1 I.L.R.M. 321; *Heaney v. Ireland* [1994] 3 I.R. 593, [1994] 2 I.L.R.M. 420 (HC); *Heaney v. Ireland* [1996] 1 I.R. 580, [1997] 1 I.L.R.M. 117 (SC); *Funke v. France* [1993] 16 E.H.R.R. 297; *Saunders v. United Kingdom* [1996] 23 E.H.R.R. 313; *Heaney v. Ireland* [2001] 33 E.H.R.R. 1.

[14] Steinhardt, *op. cit.,* p.173.

[15] *See e.g.,* C. McCartney, *Forensic Identification and Criminal Justice* (Willan Publishing, Devon, 2006) chap. 5.

questions arise as to how best to structure a database that is tailored to the needs and policy imperatives of Irish society. For example, to what precise purposes should the database be put? Whose profiles should be stored on the database and for how long? Who should control and operate the database? And should the information stored on the database be made available to law enforcement authorities in other countries? These questions are each encapsulated in the issue of how extensive a possible database should be. As noted above, the Law Reform Commission has recommended a limited form of database whereas the Government has indicated that it will legislate for a less restricted model.[16]

It is essential to realise that a DNA profile stored on a database serves no direct evidentiary function in a court of law; specifically, it cannot be offered in court as a means of proof.[17] Where an electronic search establishes a positive match between a DNA profile generated from a crime scene sample and a profile stored on the database, the Gardaí must take a fresh sample of biological material from the suspect which is then processed in the usual way. It is the DNA profile generated from this sample and the forensic scientist's evaluation of the profile that is presented as evidence at any subsequent trial.[18] Thus the function of the proposed database would be investigative rather than evidentiary. Nevertheless, because investigative conduct and practices have a bearing on the admissibility of evidence, the database would operate as a link in the evidentiary chain. Although many of the issues surrounding the establishment of a database are outside the scope of this book, this chapter will provide a brief overview of the Commission's recommendations and some of the evidentiary implications to which they give rise.

---

[16] Revelations concerning the exclusion of possibly flawed DNA evidence in the recent trial of Wayne O'Donoghue for the murder of Cork schoolboy, Robert Holohan, have also contributed to scepticism over the use of DNA. *See Irish Times*, January 25, 2006; F. O'Toole, "New Risk in DNA Database", *Irish Times*, January 31, 2006, p.16.

[17] P. Dawid, "Probability and Proof", online appendix to T. Anderson *et al., Analysis of Evidence,* 2nd ed. (Cambridge University Press, Cambridge, 2005) posted at *www.cambridge.org/9780521673167. See also* P. Donnelly and R.D. Friedman, "DNA Database Searches and the Legal Consumption of Scientific Evidence" (1998-1999) 97 Mich. L. Rev. 931.

[18] LRC Report, *op. cit.,* para.1.11.

THE SCOPE OF THE DATABASE

The DNA database proposed by the Law Reform Commission is limited in the sense that it would house the DNA profiles of only certain categories of persons. Given that the primary permitted use of the database would be crime investigation, the Commission recommends that the database include the profiles of suspects of serious crime, convicted persons and volunteers. This recommendation represents a compromise between two opposing schools of civil libertarian thought. Proponents of comprehensive DNA databases argue that the only egalitarian and non-discriminatory answer to the issue of whose DNA should be stored is to include the DNA profiles of every person in the State. A comprehensive database would also be much more effective in exonerating the innocent and identifying the guilty and, ultimately, in solving and preventing crime.[19] Opponents tend to be sceptical of DNA databases in any form given the degree of intrusion their operation involves into fundamental personal rights. They fear that, once stored, genetic information may be put to other uses, and that even the seemingly most robust of safeguards may be rolled back by future governments.[20] The Commission concludes that a comprehensive database would involve a disproportionate interference with the privacy and bodily integrity rights of innocent citizens that would run counter to the European Convention on Human Rights.[21] It notes that even limited DNA databases have been a boon to law enforcement in other countries and concludes that no issue of discrimination would arise if the compulsory inclusion of some categories

---

19 D.H. Kaye and M.E. Smith, "DNA Databases for Law Enforcement: The Coverage Question and the Case for a Population-Wide Database" in D. Lazer, ed., *DNA and the Criminal Justice System: The Technology of Justice* (MIT Press, Cambridge, Mass., 2004) 247; Cole, *op. cit.*, pp.83-84; LRC Report, *op.cit.*, para.1.17.

20 *See e.g.* Irish Council for Civil Liberties, *loc. cit.*; Steinhardt, *op.cit.*, p.174 (noting the emergence of so-called "function creep" whereby the scope and purposes of DNA databases are gradually expanded). *See also McVeigh et al. v. United Kingdom* (1981) 5 E.H.R.R. 71; *Leander v. Sweden* (1987) 9 E.H.R.R. 433; *Rotaru v. Romania* App. No. 28341/95 (May 5, 2000); *Peck v. United Kingdom* (2003) 36 E.H.R.R. 41; Council of Europe Recommendation No. R(92) 1 (1992) (on DNA and criminal justice).

21 LRC Report, *op.cit.*, para. 1.18 (citing the ECHR standard that an interference with such rights must be necessary in a democratic society).

of persons and the exclusion of others could be justified on objective criteria such as reasonableness and proportionality.[22]

The three categories of persons recommended for inclusion in the DNA database are suspects, convicted persons and volunteers, whose profiles would be housed in a suspects' index, a convicted persons index, and a volunteers' index, respectively.[23] These are the categories of persons from whom DNA samples may be taken under current practice, whether by virtue of the Criminal Justice (Forensic Evidence) Act 1990 in the case of suspects and convicted persons, or of the unregulated Garda practice of asking persons to provide DNA samples in the case of volunteers. The broad thrust of the Commission's proposal for each of these categories of persons is to extend the consequences that attend the giving of a biological sample to the Gardaí. A DNA profile generated from the sample could be used, as now, for the immediate investigative purpose, and as evidence in a possible criminal trial, but under the Commission's proposal it would now also be stored on the DNA database. Along with the other profiles stored on the database, it could then form the basis of searches in unrelated criminal investigations.

(a) Suspects

The inclusion of suspects' profiles on the database is the most controversial aspect of this specific proposal. The Commission's provisional recommendation, contained in its Consultation Paper, was that DNA profiles obtained from individuals in custody under section 30 of the Offences Against the State Act 1939, section 4 of the Criminal Justice Act 1984 and section 2 of the Criminal Justice (Drug Trafficking) Act 1996 be retained indefinitely on the national database.[24] The Commission's logic was that storing the profiles of persons suspected of committing serious, arrestable offences would increase the number of profiles on the database and correspondingly the number of offenders

---

[22] *Id.*

[23] The database would consist of a crime scene index (containing DNA profiles obtained from crime scenes) and five comparator indexes: the three indexes noted, a missing persons index and an unidentified persons index. S.14 of the draft bill, LRC Report, *op.cit.*, appendix.

[24] LRC Consultation Paper, *op.cit.*, p.136.

likely to be detected.[25] It defended this approach as a fair and proportionate balance between the rights of the individual and the interests of society in the prevention and detection of crime.[26] The Commission's final recommendation reflects a welcome, partial change of heart: the profiles of suspects are to be stored on the database, but not indefinitely.

Neither the Consultation Paper nor the Report engage the propriety of retaining on a national database the DNA profile of a person who has not been convicted of any criminal offence as a philosophical question. At a minimum, it must be conceded that this step would encroach on the basic presumption that negative consequences do not flow from the fact that an individual has been processed within our criminal justice system (arrested, detained, charged or prosecuted) but ultimately has neither pled guilty to, nor been convicted of, an offence.[27] The Commission's decision to include a suspects' index on the database seems to have been influenced primarily by the ubiquity of the practice in other database jurisdictions. In the United Kingdom, legislation permits the indefinite retention on the national database of a profile taken from a person suspected of a recordable offence regardless of the outcome of the investigation.[28] The compatibility of this measure with the Human Rights Act 1998[29] was upheld by a unanimous House of Lords in *R(S and Marper) v. Chief Constable of South Yorkshire*.[30] Observing that Lord Steyn's majority judgment may understate the potential application of the European Convention on Human Rights to DNA databases,[31] the Commission has opted to follow the lead of the majority of European countries[32] in

---

25 LRC Report, *op.cit.,* para.2.53.

26 LRC Consultation Paper, *op.cit,* p.32.

27 This assumption is echoed in the general evidentiary rule against the admission of evidence of an accused's bad character. *See generally* D. McGrath, *Evidence* (Thomson Round Hall, Dublin, 2005), chap.9.C.

28 S.82 of the Criminal Justice and Police Act 2001 (amending s.64(1)(A) of the Criminal Justice and Police Act 1984). The police are permitted to retain any samples taken during the investigation of a recordable offence.

29 The 1998 Act incorporated the rights contained in the ECHR into U.K. law.

30 [2004] 4 All E.R. 193. This had been the view of the Court of Appeal below. [2003] 1 Cr. App. R. 16.

31 LRC Report, *op.cit.* para.260 (preferring the position stated in the concurring judgment of Baroness Hale).

32 *Id. para.*2.54 n.48 (citing a legislative survey prepared by the European Network of Forensic Science Institutes). The Commission also notes, *id.*, para.2.54, that

recommending temporary rather than indefinite retention. This is the wiser course of action. It is predicted that the inclusion of a suspects' index will bear significantly on the effectiveness of the database in detecting and preventing crime.[33] However, legislating for the deletion of the profile of a person who is no longer a suspect[34] seems a more rational and proportionate means of vindicating this societal objective.[35] Having provisionally recommended the indefinite retention of suspects' profiles, the Commission is clearly on the defensive in justifying temporary retention. This discursive posture should not obscure the fact that the recommendation, even in its more limited form, would upset traditional notions of fair procedures. The Irish courts have vindicated the principle that where an individual is arrested on a particular charge, the Gardaí may not use his custodial detention as a means of gathering evidence in relation to other offences for which he is not charged.[36] Since this is the very purpose for which the suspect's DNA profile would be added to the database, we may speculate that the courts will be asked to revisit the issue in the future should the database come into operation as envisaged.

An inherent difficulty with this category of database profiles, and one which the Commission neglects to address, is concept of a "suspect". The Commission's provisional recommendation refers to the retention of "individuals in custody" under any of the three statutes,[37] its final recommendation speaks simply of "suspects",[38] and its draft bill of "a

---

Scotland departs from U.K. practice in providing for temporary rather than indefinite retention of samples and profiles.

33 *Id*, para.2.63 (citing UK Forensic Science Service statistics for matches between crime scene profiles and profiles that would have been removed from the national database but for the introduction of indefinite retention in the 2001 Act).

34 The practical mechanics of the Commission's recommendation are as follows: after a biological sample has been taken from a suspect and a DNA profile produced, the profile would be added to the database and searched against crime scene profiles in the hope of finding a match. If the suspect is not convicted or the investigation is discontinued, the profile would then be removed from the database. LRC Report, *op.cit.* para.2.52.

35 The Commission's characterisation of its conclusion is "finely balanced" rather than "mandated by the proportionality principle". *Id.* para.2.66.

36 *See e.g. People (DPP) v. O'Loughlin* [1979] I.R. 85.

37 *Id.*, p.136.

38 LRC Report, *op.cit.* para.2.67.

suspect of a specified offence".[39] The Commission's intention, it seems, is to bring within the scope of the database, profiles generated from biological samples taken from individuals arrested and detained under the legislative provisions governing serious offences. In relation to the taking of forensic samples, we noted the definitional ambiguity caused by the absence in Irish law of a unitary, statutory concept of serious or arrestable offence.[40] The Commission's recommendation adds an interpretative wrinkle: at what point does an individual become a "suspect" for purposes of inclusion in the suspects' index of the national DNA database? Presumably, the answer lies in section 2(1) of the 1990 Act which permits the taking of forensic samples from persons in Garda custody pursuant to section 30 of the 1939 Act, section 4 of the 1984 Act or section 2 of the 1996 Act.[41] The fact that the Gardaí suspect that an individual has committed an offence for which he may be arrested under one of these Acts does not make him a "suspect" for purposes of the proposed DNA database; nor does the fact that the individual has been arrested. The individual must be "in custody" pursuant to one of the stated legislative provisions before the Garda may "take or cause to be taken" a biological sample for forensic testing and, by extension, the production of a DNA profile to be included in the database.[42] However pedantic, this criticism of the Commission's linguistic laxity underscores the inherent complexity of legislative drafting in this field and the importance of clarity and precision.

A further substantive point worth mentioning in this context is that the existence and operation of the database will provide the Gardaí with an incentive to make the taking of biological samples for DNA testing a routine aspect of custodial detention under the stated legislative provisions. The 1990 Act establishes certain limited preconditions to the taking of samples, notably, the authorisation of a senior Garda officer, the cautioning of the individual, and in relation to intimate samples, the individual's consent.[43] The Criminal Justice Act 2006 reclassified saliva as a non-intimate bodily sample for purposes of the 1990 Act. This will facilitate the taking of oral swabs from suspects without consent and

---

[39] *Id.*, appendix, s.17.

[40] *Supra* chap.7.

[41] Discussed *supra.* chap.7.

[42] The quoted language is taken from s.2 of the 1990 Act.

[43] Discussed *supra.* chap.7.

subject only to a caution and the senior officer's reasonable belief that the individual was involved in the offence and that the sample will tend to confirm or disprove that involvement.[44] Nevertheless, a factor likely to temper the frequency with which the Gardaí seek DNA tests is the cost of the procedure. Nor would it be feasible for the Gardaí to take a biological sample from a suspect during custodial detention and postpone the decision whether or not to forensically test the sample. The provisions in the 1990 Act governing the destruction of samples place temporal limits on the retention of samples.[45] More significantly, a delay on the part of the Gardaí in submitting a sample for DNA testing might be open to constitutional challenge on the basis that the infringement of the suspect's rights occasioned by the taking of the sample must be strictly limited to that immediate purpose.

(b) Convicted persons and volunteers

The other less controversial categories of persons whose profiles are recommended for inclusion on a database are convicted persons and volunteers. Under section 2(2) of the 1990 Act, a biological sample may be obtained from a "person in prison" who, but for his imprisonment, would be liable to be arrested and taken into custody under the Offences Against the State Act 1939, the Criminal Justice Act 1984 or the Criminal Justice (Drug Trafficking Act) 1996. The effect is to put persons in prison on a par with other suspects in relation to the giving of samples. With the proposed establishment of a DNA database, the Commission recommends that any person convicted of a serious offence (defined as an offence for which the detention provisions of the 1939, 1984 or 1996 Act apply) should be subject to a compulsory sampling regime regardless of whether

---

44 *But see* N. O'Connor, *Cracking Crime: Jim Donovan–Forensic Detective* (O'Brien Press, Dublin, 2001), p.126 and p.301 (noting that this is general international practice).

45 S.4(2), as amended by s.14(b)(i) of the Criminal Justice Act 2006, provides for the destruction of a sample where proceedings have not been instituted against the suspect within 12 months of the taking of the sample and the failure to proceed is not due to the fact that he has absconded or cannot be found. Where proceedings have been so instituted and the person is acquitted, the charge dismissed or the proceedings discontinued, s.4(3) as amended by s.14(b)(ii) of the 2006 Act provides for the destruction of the sample within 21 days of the acquittal, dismissal or discontinuance.

a custodial sentence is imposed.[46] It further recommends that compulsory sampling apply retrospectively to any person serving a prison sentence for such an offence at the date of the introduction of the database.[47] In relation to convicted persons, the Commission would dispense with the requirement in the 1990 Act that a senior Garda officer authorise the taking of the sample on the basis that he has reasonable grounds for suspecting the involvement of the person in an offence and for believing that the sample will tend to confirm or disprove that involvement.[48] The underlying premise of these recommendations is that the inclusion of convicted persons is central to the database objective of enhancing criminal investigation and that restrictions on the taking of samples and retention of profiles should be kept to a minimum.

One of the more problematic aspects of the present regime is the Garda practice of obtaining samples from persons other than convicted persons or formal suspects. This practice, which operates outside the governance of the 1990 Act, was recently upheld by the Court of Criminal Appeal in *People (DPP) v. Boyce*.[49] The Commission sensibly recommends that the position in relation to volunteers should be brought within a revised legislative framework. Recognising the need to safeguard the rights of persons not suspected of a criminal offence, the Commission proposes that the taking of samples from volunteers should be subject to "appropriate consent" within the meaning of the 1990 Act.[50] In an interesting *volte face,* the Commission's final position on the issue is that there are no circumstances that would justify the taking of a biological sample from a volunteer without his consent.[51]

---

[46] The Commission recommends that a profile obtained from a convicted person should be destroyed in the event that the conviction is quashed. LRC Report, *op.cit.,* para.2.74.

[47] *Id.* para.2.75 (acknowledging the significant cost implications of this recommendation).

[48] S.2(5) of the 1990 Act.

[49] Unreported, Court of Criminal Appeal, December 21, 2005.

[50] S.2(10) of the 1990 Act. *See supra* chap.7. Under the Commission's proposed scheme, failure to consent to the taking of a sample would not constitute a reasonable ground for suspecting a person's involvement in an offence so as to justify the compulsory taking of a sample under s.2 of the Act. LRC Report, *op.cit.,* para.2.83.

[51] *Id.,* para.2.85, reversing its provisional recommendation that a sample could be so taken on foot of a court order where the person is attempting to obstruct the

Issues relating to consent similarly pervade the possible retention of volunteer profiles on a DNA database. Here also, the Commission is influenced by the need for heightened protection for volunteers, recommending that retention be conditioned upon the giving of informed consent[52] and that volunteers be permitted to subsequently withdraw their consent.[53] The legislation should, in the Commission's view, provide for two distinct forms of consent: consent to the giving of a sample for use in connection with a particular investigation and consent to the storage of the profile on the database.[54] The giving of informed consent necessarily presupposes that the person has been advised of the full implications surrounding the retention of profiles on the database. Although the need for the person to be adequately cautioned in clear, ordinary language is arguably implicit, it would have been preferable had it been made explicit in the Commission's recommendation and its draft bill.

---

course of justice by refusing to give the sample and the sample is necessary for the investigation of a serious offence. LRC Consultation Paper, *op.cit.,* p.148.

52 LRC Consultation Paper, *op.cit.,* pp.148-49 ("It is therefore important that before the volunteer's profile is inserted onto the database that a full and informed consent is given to this retention and that full information is given about the implications of having the profile on the database, including its use for speculative searches".).

53 LRC Report, *op.cit.,* paras.2.91-92. The Commission recommends that persons unconnected with any particular investigation be permitted to have their profiles retained on the database. The apparent motivation of this exceptional species of volunteer would be to eliminate him from suspicion in relation to any future crime. *Id.,* paras.2.89-90. The possibility of the Gardaí conducting a mass screening is envisaged in limited circumstances. *Id.,* paras.2.93-98. For an example of a mass screening, *see* the discussion of the Colin Pitchfork case, *infra* chap.9. Individuals may volunteer for various, disparate reasons. One of the innovative aspects of the proposed regime is the establishment of a missing persons index which would contain the DNA profiles of relatives of missing persons (or, where possible, DNA derived from the personal effects of the missing person). However, the missing persons index would not be speculatively searched against the crime scene index. LRC Report, *op. cit.,* paras.2.99-102. A separate unidentified persons index would contain the profiles of unidentified human remains or of individuals so severely injured as to be unable to identify themselves. *Id.,* para.2.100.

54 LRC Report, *op.cit.,* para.2.88.

The Permitted Uses of the DNA Database

There is a second though less controversial basis for styling the Commission's proposal a "limited" DNA database. The operation of the database would be confined to three uses: crime investigation, the identification of deceased persons, and the identification of severely injured persons.[55] To safeguard against future expansion in database usage, the Commission recommends that these purposes be set out explicitly in primary legislation.[56]

The primary application of the database would be the investigation of crime, a function which the Commission concedes is potentially very broadly defined.[57] The English legislation, for example, contains the stand-alone formula "purposes related to the prevention or detection of crime, the investigation of an offence or the conduct of a prosecution."[58] The Commission sensibly recognises that legislative provision for a broad purpose such as crime investigation should be curtailed by the inclusion of a non-exhaustive list of examples:

1. To conduct forensic matching.
2. To make the information available to the person to whom the information relates.
3. To administer the DNA database system.
4. To facilitate a review of an alleged miscarriage of justice under section 2 of the Criminal Procedure Act 1993.
5. To investigate a complaint by the oversight commissioner of the database.

---

54 *Id.,* paras.2.09, 2.14 and 2.17. In the case of deceased persons, the Commission recommends that the database be used solely for purposes of identifying such persons (and not for other purposes such as paternity determination). The Commission also recommends permitting the Gardaí to apply for a court order to conduct a database search where there is a reasonable suspicion that a deceased person committed an offence. A court order would also be necessary to sanction the third stated use of the database, namely, to search for a possible match that would identify a person who is so severely injured as to be unable to identify himself.

56 *Id.,* para.2.04.

57 For example, database information might potentially be used for research purposes related to crime detection and prevention.

58 S.64(1)(A) of the Police and Criminal Evidence Act 1984 as amended.

6. To compile statistics for the oversight commissioner on the operation of the database.
7. To enable the exchange of DNA profiles between jurisdictions in accordance with relevant international obligations.
8. To identify unknown deceased persons.
9. To identify severely injured persons where the court sanctions it.
10. Or any other related purpose.[59]

The inclusion of the final proviso "or any other related purpose" unfortunately undercuts the Commission's attempt to limit the broad general purpose of criminal investigation. The purported justification for its inclusion, namely that it would "facilitate the day-to-day running of the database" is less than persuasive and the Commission's stated belief that the proviso "would be interpreted in the light of the specific examples given and would not be interpreted in any wider manner" may be called into question.[60] Given the sensitivity of genetic information and the need to ensure that the application of this technology respects human rights, great care must be taken when drafting core legislative provisions such as these.

DNA Samples

Biological samples are the raw material from which DNA profiles are extracted. It is the profiles alone that are stored on a DNA database. Whereas the discussion thus far in this chapter has concerned the potential powers of the State to store DNA profiles for criminal investigative purposes, similar questions pertain to the retention of samples, both samples taken from a crime scene and comparator samples obtained from an individual, such as a suspect, under controlled conditions. Contrary to popular perception, the DNA profile contains relatively little genetic

---

[59] LRC Consultation Paper, *op.cit.*, p.189. The proposed statement of purposes is produced in full as s.13 of a draft Criminal Justice (DNA Database) Bill 2005 contained in an appendix to the Commission's Report.

[60] LRC Report, *op.cit.,* para.2.08.

information; the loci on the genome from which the profile is compiled form "only a tiny portion of a person's DNA".[61] In contrast, the biological sample from which the profile was generated is potentially an abundant source of genetic data. Thus, the rights of the individual concerned apply with equal if not greater force in relation to the retention of samples.

The Gardaí and the prosecution are obliged by law to preserve material evidence, including crime scene samples, during an investigation and any subsequent trial.[62] In practice, crime scene samples are retained in the event that a person convicted mounts a post-conviction challenge to the DNA evidence. Recognising the importance of this safeguard, the Commission recommends that whereas crime scene profiles should be removed from the database following conviction, crime scene samples should be retained indefinitely.[63] There is an argument in favour of explicitly including in the legislation a prohibition on the use of samples for any purpose other than the composition of a DNA profile. The Commission endorses this view in relation to comparator samples[64] but is considerably more equivocal on the permissible use of crime scene samples. The issue is whether to permit the use of the samples for other forms of forensic testing:

> "In the future it could become straightforward to subject a scene of crime stain to analysis which will identify common characteristics, such as ethnicity, skin, hair and eye colour, stature, weight, age and facial characteristics. This could create a 'genetic photo-fit'. Being able to find out that the person whose DNA was left at the scene of crime may have certain physical characteristics would undoubtedly be useful intelligence in the investigation of an offence, particularly when the investigating authorities have not found other evidence to lead them to the perpetrator."[65]

---

[61] M. Redmayne, "The DNA Database: Civil Liberties and Evidentiary Issues" [1998] Crim. L. R. 437 at p.438.

[62] *See e.g. Braddish v. DPP* [2002] 1 I.L.R.M. 151; *Dunne v. DPP* [2002] 2 I.R. 307; *McFarlane v. DPP*, Supreme Court, unreported, March 7, 2006.

[63] LRC Report, *op.cit.*, para.3.06.

[64] *Id.*, para.3.26.

[65] LRC Consultation Paper, *op.cit.* p.176. *See also* G. Allen, "DNA and Human-Behaviour Genetics: Implications for the Criminal Justice System" in D. Lazer,

The Commission is anxious to facilitate analysis of the coding regions to determine non-sensitive phenotype information in respect of such common characteristics. At the same time, it recognises a potentially slippery slope "from predictions about non-sensitive phenotype information, to predictions regarding behavioural traits or medical information."[66] Its compromise is to allow expanded forensic analysis, beyond the compilation of a DNA profile, in exceptional cases subject to strict oversight.[67] An example would be the investigation of a specific crime where the only lead is the DNA sample recovered from the scene and there is no obvious link between the perpetrator and the victim. Obtaining full intelligence from the sample could assist in generating an offender profile, as opposed to a DNA profile, and would provide a useful basis upon which the Gardaí could proceed with the investigation.[68]

As noted, the Commission not surprisingly rules out the possibility that the analysis of comparator samples should stray beyond the compilation of DNA profiles.[69] Because comparator samples are taken from a known source, their use and possible retention are subjects of predictable controversy. The provisional view expressed by the Commission was that a comparator sample should be destroyed after the profile has been generated and verified and a final judicial decision reached in the particular case.[70] That conclusion was prefaced by the following explanation:

> "In considering this subject the Commission is acutely aware that the prospect of governmental organisations having the power to collect, analyse, and retain (perhaps for future analysis) an individual's genetic material may to most people be particularly unpalatable. The indefinite retention of

---

ed., *DNA and the Criminal Justice System: The Technology of Justice* (MIT Press, Cambridge, Mass., 2004) 287.

66 LRC Report, *op.cit.* para.3.19.

67 *Id.*, para.3.21. Specifically, the Commission recommends that analysis of crime scene samples should always be limited to purposes that further criminal investigation and that the results of any analysis should be kept under careful custody.

68 *Id.*, para.3.19.

69 *Id.*, para.3.26.

70 LRC Consultation Paper, *op.cit.*, p.173.

> samples could discourage people from volunteering a sample in order to help with an investigation (or for that matter consenting to a forensic procedure). It is necessary for the sample to be retained until the conclusion of the trial in order for it to be presented as an exhibit in court. However, after the trial, it should be destroyed. Destroying the comparator sample after a profile has been generated and verified would go a long way in allaying concerns about misuse and possible future analysis, as well as inspiring public confidence in DNA profiling and the establishment of a profile database."[71]

The cogency of these arguments notwithstanding, the Commission's final recommendation is that comparator samples should be retained under "strict security measures" set out in legislation.[72] It seems that this dramatic u-turn was prompted by criticisms of the provisional recommendation raised during the consultation process. The destruction of comparator samples might extinguish evidence required by a convicted person on appeal or in proceedings for miscarriage of justice.[73] There is a further technological objection to the destruction of comparator samples: "profiles are the product of current technology and may become obsolete in the event of further technological advancement in profiling."[74] The retention of the original samples would facilitate the manufacture of replacement profiles using new methodologies thereby ensuring that the database would not be "locked, by legislation, into current technology."[75]

---

71 *Id.,* at p.173.

72 LRC Report, *op.cit.,* para.3.14. If a DNA profile is removed from the database and destroyed, the Commission recommends that the corresponding sample should also be destroyed.

73 Pursuant to the Criminal Procedure Act 1993.

74 LRC Consultation Paper, *op.cit.,* at p.169.

75 LRC Report, *op.cit.,* at para.3.12. *See also id.,* at para.3.13 ("The science in this area is continually developing and improving. The law is often criticised for failing to keep up-to-date with scientific advances. The Commission is concerned that if the database is tied by legislation to the current technology, the Gardaí would be unable to take full advantage of developments in the field of forensic science until the legislation is amended. Even then, the use of the database for speculative searches could be significantly hampered until a new sample is obtained from all those on the database and a profile developed using the current technology.").

The difficulty and divisiveness of this issue is reflected in a certain ambivalence on the Commission's part; it appends to its recommendation in favour of retention the caveat that the situation be reassessed in 5 years' time.[76]

As regards security measures, the Commission recommends that all DNA samples be retained by the proposed custodian of the database, a newly created Forensic Science Agency.[77] Samples should be accommodated in secure conditions within the agency's laboratory. Rather than detail the form such measures should take, the Commission proposes that an expert study be carried out on the subject and offers the following pointers:

> "The samples should be identified by virtue of an identification code rather than a person's name. In addition, they should be stored in a room that is accessible only by a magnetic strip card and a PIN. Within the room of their storage, they should be retained within locked freezers, as is currently the situation. Electronic access to these compartments should be given to a limited number of individuals with positions of responsibility within the agency. Electronic access with varying levels of security and combinations should be required to access the samples. On each occasion in which an authorised person enters the laboratory, they should be required to enter the purpose of their visit in a log book provided for that purpose. A CCTV camera or digital equivalent within the laboratory would record all the activity within it. A supervisor would be responsible for accounting for all actions within the laboratory and investigating any suspicious behaviour."[78]

Additional Safeguards

Experience in other jurisdictions suggests that however adequate a

---

[76] *Id.,* para.3.14.
[77] *Id.,* paras.4.20-22.
[78] LRC Consultation Paper, *op.cit.,* at p.215.

legislative system of governance appears on paper, problems can and do arise in practice. The destruction of profiles and samples has created one such blot on the database landscape. Whereas a great deal of energy has been expended on *when* destruction should take place, far less attention is devoted to *how* it should be achieved. Physical destruction of samples and profiles is the most secure option but is less straightforward that might be assumed because of the inherent difficulty of tracing all remnants of samples that have been subjected to various forensic processes. There are forensic procedures short of physical destruction that achieve "de-identification" but the Commission shies away from making a recommendation, suggesting instead that the issue be taken up by yet another expert group.[79] The destruction of samples and profiles would be the responsibility of the Forensic Science Agency and subject to external oversight possibly by the Irish National Accreditation Board.[80]

In fashioning safeguards in relation to destruction, the Commission is clearly minded to avoid the situation that unfolded in the United Kingdom where a substantial backlog in material destined for destruction resulted in the improper retention of profiles on the national database. In *Attorney General's Reference No.3 of 1999*,[81] the House of Lords held that evidence obtained through the use of such profiles was not necessarily inadmissible. Adopting the position that the issue was one of statutory construction, Lord Steyn concluded that the provision in the Police and Criminal Evidence Act 1984, as amended,[82] mandating the destruction of samples and profiles merely vested in the trial judge a discretion to exclude evidence obtained in breach of its terms. This interpretation, he opined, was reinforced by the public interest in the effective investigation and prosecution of crime. Notwithstanding Lord Steyn's confident statement that the law as interpreted was "fully compatible" with the relevant rights under the European Convention on Human Rights, it is doubtful that an Irish court would follow the Lords' lead if faced with a similar case. Unfortunately, the legislative change that followed in the wake of the

---

79 LRC Report, *op.cit.*, para. 4.27.

80 *Id.*, para.4.28; LRC Consultation Paper, *op.cit.*, p.218. Australian experience points to the wisdom of programming the database system in such a way that it can remind the authorities of a pending destruction date some time in advance.

81 [2001] 1 All E.R. 575.

82 S.64(3B)(a).

judgment took the form of a retrospective licence to retain indefinitely samples and profiles that would otherwise have been destined for destruction.[83]

A further difficulty associated with DNA evidence is the risk that samples will be contaminated during its collection, transportation or analysis. The Commission's call for compliance with best international practice in crime scene management and laboratory performance should be heeded in this regard.[84]

Finally, mechanisms designed to further international co-operation have become increasingly prevalent in the field of criminal investigation. Initially limited to the sphere of strictly transnational crimes, the drive for greater sharing of information and resources now extends to the full gamut of law enforcement. In addition to the European Arrest Warrant, EU justice ministers have recently agreed to a European Evidence Warrant that will enable authorities in one member state to request evidence from other member states in relation to 32 categories of offences.[85] Steps are also underway to promote the use of DNA databases and to facilitate the sharing of data among law enforcement agencies. Interpol now operates an international DNA database containing profiles supplied from national databases which may be used by participating States.[86] The sharing of information among forensic science organisations[87] and the standardisation of DNA profiling also feature on the European agenda.[88]

The Law Reform Commission provisionally recommended that the Irish authorities should engage in the sharing of DNA profiles only with jurisdictions operating collection and retention regimes compatible with Irish law.[89] Accession to an international database should similarly be

---

83 S.82 of the Criminal Justice and Police Act 2001.

84 LRC Report, *op.cit.*, paras. 4.30-41.

85 "EU Justice Ministers Agree on Sharing Files" *Irish Times,* June 2, 2006, p.14.

86 *See www.interpol.int*. The establishment of a European DNA database under the auspices of Europol has been proposed. *See generally*, A. Puri, "An International DNA Database: Balancing Hope, Privacy and Scientific Error" (2000-2001) B.C. Int'l and Comp L. Rev. 341.

87 For example under the auspices of the European Network of Forensic Science Institutes (ENFSI). See *www.enfsi.org*.

88 Under the Standardization of DNA Profiling in the European Union project. *See www.stadnap.org*.

89 LRC Consultation Paper, *op.cit.*, p.197.

contingent on limiting Irish participation, both in the transferring and receiving of profiles, to uses permissible under Irish law.[90] Perhaps recognising the myriad of complex issues to which international co-operation give rise, the Commission has understandably eschewed any concrete recommendation in its final report, opting instead to endorse the continuation of existing bilateral co-operative arrangements until such time as appropriate framework decisions regarding the exchange of DNA samples and profiles have been agreed at EU level or otherwise.[91] The issue warrants very careful analysis and consideration in the context of the debate over the establishment of a national database.

---

[90] *Id.*, p.198.

[91] LRC Report, *op.cit.*, para.4.48.

Chapter 9

The Presentation of DNA Evidence

The Development of DNA Evidence

One of the more striking aspects of DNA profiling is the speed with which it gained acceptance among forensic scientists, investigators, judges and juries, as the ultimate means of criminal identification.[1] Whereas novel forms of evidence, including innovative scientific fields of expertise, generally have to "earn their spurs,"[2] the probative power of DNA was initially accepted almost without question. DNA profiling became the darling of forensic investigation and the existence of the technology, as much as its application in the particular instance, became a significant factor in plea bargaining.[3] The first reported proffers of prosecution DNA evidence in court were neither challenged by the defence nor rigorously scrutinised by the judges.[4] This new, convincing and, indeed, almost unassailable method of criminal identification had rapidly become entrenched within the criminal justice system.

The geneticist, Professor Alec Jeffreys of the University of Leicester, is attributed with actively applying the first widely recognised form of

---

1 T. Kiely, *Forensic Evidence: Science and the Criminal Law*, 2nd ed. (CRC Press, Boca Raton, Florida, 2005), p.425.

2 H. O'Flaherty, "The Expert Witness and the Courts" (1997) 3 M.L.J.I. 3 at p.6.

3 N. Ebiske, *An Appraisal of Forensic Science Evidence in Criminal Proceedings* (Greenway Publishers, London, 2000), p.119; G. O'Donnell, "Legal Situation of Forensic DNA Analysis in the Republic of Ireland" (1997) 88 For. Sci. Int. 63, p.65.

4 Ebiske, *op. cit.*, pp.119-120. *See also* Royal Commission on Criminal Justice, *The Ability to Challenge DNA Evidence* (Res. Study No.9) (1993) at p.3: "It is reasonable to suggest that at this point in time there may have been a feeling among many defence lawyers that frequently DNA profiling evidence was overwhelming and that it was not possible to contest the evidence in court."

DNA profiling[5] in an early, sensational case.[6] In 1986, a youth was arrested by the Leicestershire police for the rape and murder of 15-year old Dawn Ashworth and confessed to the crimes. Jeffreys compared a DNA profile produced from semen stains left on the victim with the suspect's DNA profile and concluded that the suspect could not have been the rapist. Further tests conducted on the crime scene sample and on a sample of semen stains retrieved in connection with a similar crime — the rape and murder of a local teenage girl three years earlier – suggested that the two assaults were probably carried out by the same individual. In January 1987, the police took the unprecedented step of inviting all males in the small, village community to provide a blood sample. A preliminary screening of the approximately 5,000 samples taken, using the conventional technique of blood grouping, narrowed the number of samples to be DNA tested to the still daunting figure of 500. This time-consuming and energy-intensive process was unsuccessful in that a match was not found. The police were ultimately led to the perpetrator, Colin Pitchfork, by a tip-off from a witness who had heard another man, Ian Kelly, boast that he had provided a sample on Pitchfork's behalf. Pitchfork confessed to both murders and DNA evidence subsequently confirmed that his profile matched the profiles produced by the semen stains retrieved from the respective crime scenes.[7] This pioneering case, exceptional on its facts, provided important lessons about some of the strengths and weaknesses of DNA evidence: the extraordinary exculpatory power of DNA technology, its value as a means of corroborating or refuting confessions and other forms of suspect evidence, and the potential for error or abuse in the taking and preservation of

---

5 *See* chap.6 *supra*. *See e.g.* A.J. Jeffreys *et al.*, "Individual-Specific 'Fingerprints' of Human DNA" (1985) 316 Nature 76.

6 For summaries of the case *see* R.M. White and J.J.D. Greenwood, "DNA Fingerprinting and the Law" [1988] 51 M.L.R. 145; C. Walker and I. Cram, "DNA Profiling and Police Powers" [1990] Crim. L.R. 479 at pp.480-81; W. Wall, *Genetics and DNA Technology: Legal Aspects* (Cavendish Press, London, 2002), pp.16-17; G.T. Duncan *et al.*, "Techniques of DNA Analysis" in S.H. James and J.J. Nordby, *Forensic Science: An Introduction to Scientific and Investigative Techniques* (CRC Press, Boca Raton, Florida, 2003), pp.226-27; Law Reform Commission, *Consultation Paper on the Establishment of a DNA Database* (LRC CP 29-2004), p.36.

7 Pitchfork was sentenced to life imprisonment in 1988.

forensic samples.[8]

Another early use of DNA evidence in England occurred in the 1987 prosecution of Robert Melias for the burglary and rape of a physically disabled woman. When DNA tests on a crime scene sample of semen and a sample of Melias's blood revealed a match, Melias pleaded guilty and was subsequently sentenced to eight years' imprisonment.[9] The probative import of DNA was also recognised in several rape cases in the late 1980s and, in at least one instance, a conviction was secured without the need for the victim to testify.[10] It is a truism that the general response to DNA evidence in the early years was overwhelmingly positive and that great faith was placed in its accuracy and reliability.[11]

In the United States, law enforcement authorities were quick to capitalise on the advent of DNA profiling. As early as 1986, a Pennsylvania court accepted the probity of PCR-based DNA analysis in determining the origins of two autopsy samples.[12] Two years later, a New York State trial judge famously proclaimed DNA fingerprinting to be "the single greatest advance in the 'search for truth' … since the advent of cross-examination."[13] Numerous trial courts had accepted DNA evidence by the late 1980s[14] when challenges to the technology began to surface in the appellate courts.[15]

---

[8] *See e.g.*, A.P.A. Broeders, "Of Earprints, Fingerprints, Scent Dogs, Cot Deaths and Cognitive Contamination–A Brief Look at the Present State of Play in the Forensic Arena" (2006) 159 For. Sc. Int. 148, p.152.

[9] *See* Ebiske, *op. cit.*, pp.119-120; C. Wilson, *Written in Blood: A History of Forensic Detection* (Grafton Books, London, 1989), p.223.

[10] *See* White and Greenwood, *op. cit.*, pp.148-49.

[11] *See e.g.* I.H. Dennis, "Reconstructing the Law of Criminal Evidence" (1989) 42 C.L.P. 21, pp.43-44; R.M. White and J.D. Greenwood, "DNA Fingerprinting and the Law (1988) 51 M.L.R. 145, p.145.

[12] *Commonwealth v. Pestinikas,* 617A.2d 1339 (PA Super. 1992) cited in F.R. Bieber, "Science and Technology of Forensic DNA Profiling: Current Use and Future Directions" in D. Lazer, ed., *DNA and the Criminal Justice System: The Technology of Justice* (MIT Press, Cambridge, Mass., 2004) 23, p.27.

[13] *People v. Wesley*, 140 Misc.2d 306, 533 N.Y.S.2d 643 (Albany Co. St. 1988).

[14] E.S. Lander, "DNA Fingerprinting on Trial" (1989) 339 Nature 501 (noting that DNA evidence had been used in more than 80 trials). *See also* E.S. Lander. "DNA Fingerprinting: Science, Law and the Ultimate Identifier" in D.J. Kevles and L. Hood, eds., *The Code of Codes: Scientific and Social Issues in the Human Genome Project* (Harvard U. Press, Cambridge, Mass., 1992) 191.

[15] *See e.g. People v. Wesley,* 140 Misc.2d 306, 533 N.Y.S.2d 643 (Albany County

One of the first was *Andrews v. Florida*[16] in which an intermediate appellate court held that DNA evidence was admissible under Florida's "relevancy test" and went on to state, *obiter dicta*, that DNA evidence would also meet the so-called "*Frye* test", then prevailing in the majority of the States, namely, whether the scientific technique was sufficiently well established to have garnered "general acceptance" within the forensic science community.[17] DNA profiling was soon used as a means of proof in death penalty cases including the high profile conviction of Timothy Spencer for the rape and murder of several women in Virginia.[18] Overall, the trend among American trial courts, demonstrated by these early cases, was to admit DNA evidence "as a matter of course."[19] It is also worthy of note that on those rare occasions when courts excluded DNA evidence, they did so for stated reasons other than the validity of the predicate science.[20] A factor bearing on the overwhelmingly favourable induction of DNA evidence into the American trial process was the limited number and nature of challenges mounted by the defence in these early cases.[21]

The United States also provided the context in which DNA profiling suffered its inevitable fall from grace. Growing concerns among some forensic scientists about the reliability of DNA evidence crystallised in the *Castro* case.[22] Joseph Castro was charged with the murder of Vilma Ponce and her two-year old daughter who were stabbed to death in their

---

Ct. 1988), *aff'd sub nom. People v. Bailey,* 156 A.D.2d 846, 549 N.Y.S.2d 846 (1989). The trial judge allowed the prosecution to submit DNA evidence but ordered that the statistics be adjusted downward before being presented to the jury.

16 533 So.2d 841 (Fla. Dist. Ct. App. 1988.)

17 *See also Kansas v. Searles,* 246 Kan. 567 (1990). On the *Frye* general acceptance test, *see* chap.2 *supra.*

18 *Commonwealth v. Spencer,* 393 S.E.2d 609 (VA 1990). *See also Texas v. Fuller,* 827 S.W.2d 919 (1992).

19 P. C. Giannelli and E.J. Imwinkelried, *Scientific Evidence*, 3rd ed. (Lexis, Charlottesville, VA, 1993) (& Supp. 2002) at §18.5(A).

20 *Id.*

21 *Id;* D.H. Kaye, "The Admissibility of DNA Testing" (1991) 13 Cardozo L. Rev. 353, p.357; M.J. Saks and J.J. Koehler, "What DNA 'Fingerprinting' Can Teach the Law About the Rest of Forensic Science" (1991) 13 Cardozo L. Rev. 361, p.361.

22 *People v. Castro*, 545 N.Y.S.2d 985 (N.Y. Sup. Ct., Bronx County, 1989). For summaries of the case *see* Ebiske, *op. cit.,* pp.120-21; B. Robertson and G.A. Vignaux, *Interpreting Evidence: Evaluating Forensic Science in the Courtroom*

New York apartment. A bloodstain found on Castro's watch was sent for DNA testing to a commercial laboratory, Lifecodes Corporation. Lifecodes compared the DNA retrieved from the sample with Vilma Ponce's DNA and declared a match; the frequency of the pattern in the Hispanic population was reported to be 1 in 189,200,000. The defence challenged the admissibility of the DNA evidence on various grounds and, at an admissibility hearing, presented the testimony of Dr. Eric Lander of the Massachusetts Institute of Technology.[23] Lander criticised several, fundamental aspects of Lifecodes' scientific methodology: the subjectivity of its matching criteria, the fact that it had ignored potentially exculpatory data, the absence of adequate controls to verify the accuracy of its interpretations, the use of a different, inappropriate matching rule to determine the frequency of the pattern in the population. In an unprecedented step, the prosecution and defence experts later met and issued a joint statement to the effect that the DNA data was insufficient to support the prosecution's assertion of a DNA match. The court ultimately held that Lifecodes had failed to apply generally accepted procedures and techniques[24] and that the inadequacy of the scientific foundation for the evidence rendered it inadmissible. In an ironic twist to the case, Castro later confessed to the murders and admitted that the blood found on his watch had been that of Vilma Ponce.

In *Castro*, the trial court conducted its admissibility inquiry around three questions:

> (1) "Is there a theory, which is generally accepted in the scientific community, which supports the conclusion that

---

(Wiley & Sons, Chichester, 1995), pp.168-171; C. Fennell, *Law of Evidence in Ireland*, 2nd ed. (Lexis Nexis, Dublin, 2003), pp.188-90; P. Alldridge, "Recognising Novel Scientific Techniques: DNA as a Test Case" [1992] Crim. L. R. 687, pp.691 and 693; W.C. Thomson, "Evaluating the Admissibility of New Genetic Identification Tests: Lessons from the DNA War" (1993) 84 J. Crim. L. & Criminology 22.

23 Lander's account of the case and his criticisms of the use of DNA evidence in American courts at that time were published in the leading scientific journal Nature, *supra* n.14.

24 As required by the then prevailing *Frye* test for the admissibility of scientific evidence.

DNA forensic testing can produce reliable results?

(2) Are there techniques or experiments that currently exist that are capable of producing reliable results in DNA identification and which are generally accepted in the scientific community?

(3) Did the testing laboratory perform the accepted scientific techniques in analysing the forensic samples in this particular case?"[25]

The court concluded that DNA evidence is generally reliable but that the failure of Lifecodes to use generally accepted procedures rendered it inadmissible in the present case. Subsequent courts debated the wisdom of these admissibility criteria as well as the underlying question of how best to scrutinise a proffer of DNA evidence. Challenges to DNA testing procedures soon became commonplace and the admissibility of this novel means of proof increasingly contested.[26]

By the early 1990s, controversy surrounding DNA profiling had shifted from laboratory testing procedures to the statistical analysis used to support a DNA match. In virtually all instances, the proponent of DNA evidence proffers testimony not only that the DNA profiles under comparison matched but also testimony regarding the significance of that match. The latter testimony takes the form of a "match probability," namely, a figure representing the probability that the DNA retrieved from the crime scene sample would match the DNA of a person chosen randomly from the general population or, in some instances, a specific subset of that population. Again, the initial stance of the American trial courts was one of uncritical acceptance of the multiplication or "product rule" method of calculating match probabilities. Criticisms of this

---

[25] 144 Misc.2d at 958, 545 N.Y.S.2d AA 986.

[26] *See e.g. State v. Scwartz,* 447 N.W.2d 422 (Minn. 1989); *United States v. Two Bulls*, 918 F.2d 56, 61 (8th Cir. 1990) *vacated,* 925 F.2d 1127 (8th Cir. 1991); *People v. Venegas,* 18 Cal. 4th 47, 954 P.2d 525 (1998); *United States v. Jakobetz,* 955 F.2d 786 (2d Cir. 1992). *See also* E.J. Imwinkelreid, "The Debate in the DNA Cases Over the Foundation of the Admission of Scientific Evidence: The Importance of Human Error as a Cause of Forensic Misanalysis" (1991) 69 Wash. U.L.Q. 19.

traditional approach led to a retreat,[27] with courts demonstrating a greater willingness to scrutinise and exclude such evidence[28] and to admit statistical evidence based on an alternative approach. In the past decade, the pendulum has swung back in favour of the admission of statistics computed in the traditional fashion.[29] The reverberations from these "DNA wars"[30] were felt on this side of the Atlantic; for example, in the mid-1990s, the English Court of Appeal declared certain convictions unsafe due to flawed expert evidence on DNA match probabilities.[31]

The dust has since settled on the use of DNA evidence in the U.S. courts and, although the subject remains controversial, the overall impression of such evidence on criminal justice is largely favourable. DNA profiling has been the subject of numerous studies[32] including two reports of the National Research Council[33] and several reviews by the Federal Bureau of Investigation.[34] Indeed, the level of scrutiny prompted Saks and Koehler to comment as early as 1991 that "more is known about the strengths and weaknesses of DNA fingerprinting evidence than about most of the other, older, and more widely used forms of forensic science evidence."[35]

The vast majority of the courts in which the admissibility of DNA evidence has been challenged have ruled in favour of its admission.[36]

---

27 M. Redmayne, "Expert Evidence and Scientific Disagreement" (1997) 30 U.C. Davis L. Rev. 1027, pp.1048-50.

28 *See e.g. Caldwell v. State*, 260 Ga. 278, 393 S.E.2d 436 (1990); *Commonwealth v. Curnin*, 409 Mass. 218, 565 N.E.2d 440 (1991).

29 Giannelli and Imwinkelried, *op. cit.* at §18.5(C); Redmayne, *op. cit.*, p.1050.

30 Thomson *op. cit.*, p.22.

31 *R v. Deen* [1994] T.L.R. 11; *R v. Doheny v. Adams* [1997] 1 Cr. App. R. 369.

32 For an overview of research sources *see* Kiely, *op. cit.,* pp.427-28.

33 National Research Council Committee on DNA Technology in Forensic Science, *DNA Technology in Forensic Science* (Washington, D.C., 1992); National Research Council Committee on DNA Technology in Forensic Science, *An Update: The Evaluation of Forensic DNA Evidence* (Washington, D.C., 1996).

34 Available at *www.fbi.gov.*

35 Saks and Koehler, *op. cit.*, p.362. This view has been echoed more recently on this side of the Atlantic. I.W. Evett *et al.,* "DNA Profiling: A Discussion of Issues Relating to the Reporting of Very Small Match Probabilities" [2000] Crim. L. R. 341, p.349: "No other area of forensic science has been explored statistically in anything remotely approaching the extent of the study of DNA profiling."

36 Giannelli and Imwinkelried, *op. cit.,* §18.5(A).

Some courts have even gone so far as to accept the reliability of particular DNA profiling techniques as a matter of judicial notice.[37] Several states have enacted statutes providing for the admissibility of DNA evidence and/or requiring persons convicted of certain offences to contribute samples to DNA databases.[38] Plea bargains and convictions are now routinely based partially or even wholly on DNA evidence and the diversity of the forensic practice is reflected in a burgeoning case law.[39] DNA evidence has also played a crucial but less obvious role in excluding individuals as suspects in criminal investigations. The exculpatory function of DNA evidence has a particular resonance in the United States because it has made possible the exoneration of countless individuals wrongly convicted and imprisoned, in some instances on death row.[40] The social ramifications of this remarkable development are most keenly reflected in a seachange in American attitudes to the propriety of the death penalty.[41]

DNA Evidence in Ireland

The use of DNA evidence in criminal investigation in Ireland dates back to the early 1990s (at least). Prior to that time, the Gardaí relied solely on other, traditional methods of criminal identification such as eyewitness testimony, confessions, fingerprinting and blood grouping. Recourse to DNA evidence was limited initially due to a lack of facilities within the State's Forensic Science Laboratory to conduct DNA analysis.[42] In the

---

37 *See e.g. United States v. Jakobetz,* 955 F.2d 786 (2d Cir. 1992).

38 Giannelli and Inwinkelried, *op. cit.* at §18.5(A); Kaye, *op. cit.*, p.358. For a detailed statement of the Illinois Supreme Court rule on discovery of DNA evidence *see* Kiely, *op. cit.*, p.426.

39 *See e.g. Id.*, p.431 *et seq.* (discussing cases); Giannelli and Imwinkelried, *op. cit.* at §18.5(A) (discussing cases).

40 Kiely, *op. cit.,* pp.451-54.

41 As evidenced by the decision of former Governor of Illinois, George Ryan, a former supporter of the death penalty, to halt executions in that State. *See e.g.*, J.C. Boger, "Acts of Capital Clemency: The Words and Deeds of Governor George Ryan" (2004) 82 N.C.L.Rev. 1279.

42 The Forensic Science Laboratory was established in 1975. *See* N. O'Connor, Cracking Crime: Jim Donovan–Forensic Detective, (O'Brien Press, Dublin, 2001) chaps.10 and 11; O'Donnell, *op. cit.*, p.63.

early years, the testing of DNA samples retrieved from Irish crime scenes and suspects was generally conducted in English laboratories. DNA analysis for purposes of criminal investigation is now conducted almost exclusively within the DNA section of the Forensic Science Laboratory.[43] That work focuses mainly on serious crimes such as murder, rape and armed robbery.[44]

The influential role which DNA evidence currently plays within the criminal justice system has gone relatively unobserved within the legal community because it has featured in relatively few reported cases. The prosecution tends to rely on DNA evidence in conjunction with other forms of evidence and its influence may be most keenly felt as a factor in the entry of guilty pleas.[45] DNA evidence has also played a role in the resolution of old, unsolved crimes, so-called "cold cases." The Forensic Science Laboratory maintains a crime stain database which stores DNA profiles taken from crime scenes. The number of profiles currently stored is around 1000.[46]

One of the first challenges to DNA evidence was raised in *People (DPP.) v. Lawlor*[47] which involved a charge of sexual assault. The prosecution presented evidence that the DNA extracted from semen stains on the victim's clothing matched the profile derived from a sample of the accused's blood. The match probability was estimated to be approximately 1 in 100 million of the general population. The admissibility of the evidence was challenged in a *voir dire* lasting several weeks and, ultimately, upheld by the trial judge. The chain of custody of the DNA samples was one of the issues which came under close judicial scrutiny in that case. As the use of DNA evidence has become more prevalent in the Irish criminal courts, defence counsel have mounted more robust and sophisticated challenges to its admission.

---

43 LRC Consultation Paper, *op. cit.*, pp.36-37.

44 *Id.*, p.38.

45 *Id.*, p.37; O'Donnell, *op. cit.*, p.65; E. Leahy, "Genetic Profiling and the Reasonable Doubt" (1995) 1 M.L.J.I. 66, p.66.

46 Communication with the Forensic Science Laboratory.

47 Central Criminal Court, December 2, 1995, Court of Criminal Appeal, February 19, 2001, discussed in LRC Consultation Paper, *op. cit.*, p.37; O'Donnell, *op. cit.*, p.65.

In *People (DPP.) v. Horgan*,[48] the court accepted the validity of DNA evidence in general as, indeed, counterpart courts have done throughout the common law world.[49] Proffers of DNA evidence have not always met with success in the Irish courts, however. In *People (DPP) v. Howe*,[50] Butler J. withdrew a case from the jury in which the prosecution had relied on DNA evidence. In *People (DPP) v. Allen*,[51] the Court of Criminal Appeal overturned a conviction for armed robbery and ordered a retrial on the ground that the statistical DNA evidence was insufficiently complete in one particular respect. More recently, the Court of Criminal Appeal rejected appellate challenges to DNA evidence in *People (DPP) v. Boyce*[52] and *People (DPP) v. Costigan*.[53] Though there exists a relative paucity of Irish case law on DNA evidence, it is collectively indicative of some of the more controversial issues that have been the subject of extended judicial discourse in other jurisdictions.

Classifying DNA Evidence

One of the more intriguing aspects of DNA evidence is its assimilation into the criminal trial process. As a species of expert evidence, its admission and the manner in which it is presented in court are governed by particular rules but, like any other form of evidence, its probative value is ultimately a matter for the jury. The jury must weigh the DNA evidence along with all other evidence in the trial in determining the ultimate issue of the innocence or guilt of the accused. The discussion in chapters 1 and 2 alluded to the traditional concern that expert evidence may mislead or unduly influence the jury and furthermore to the influence that this concern has exerted over judicial policy in this area; these

---

48 LRC Consultation Paper, *op. cit.*, p.231 (citing a report in the *Irish Examiner*, June 25, 2002).

49 *See e.g. R v. Pantoja* (1996) 88 A Crim. R. 554 (Australia); *R v. Krager* [2001] S.A.S.C. 64 (Australia); and *R v. Pengelly* [1992] 1 N.Z.L.R. 545, (1991) 7 C.R.N.Z. 333 (New Zealand).

50 Central Criminal Court, October 15, 2003; *Irish Times*, October 15, 2003.

51 [2003] 4 I.R. 295.

52 Unreported, December 21, 2005.

53 Unreported, April 28, 2006.

sensitivities over the relationship between the expert and the jury are heightened in the context of scientific evidence.[54]

In Ireland, as in most other common law jurisdictions, neither law nor practice recognises scientific evidence as a distinct subset within the general field of expert evidence and one best regulated by discrete rules and procedures. Undoubtedly this is due in part to the definitional difficulties that would stymie any attempt to distinguish scientific from other forms of expert evidence. But it also surely reflects the traditionally reactive (as opposed to proactive) development of the law of evidence. Part substantive and part adjectival, the law of evidence is omnipresent in the practice and academic analysis of the law and, perhaps for that reason, constitutes a particularly disparate and eclectic field within the general discipline. Reform of the law of evidence has tended to be *ad hoc* and piecemeal, in some instances the by-product of reforms in substantive areas such as family law or criminal law and, in others, a response to specific problems encountered at the coalface of legal practice.[55]

Against this backdrop, the decision of the Oireachtas to single out forensic evidence as a subject worthy of a distinct regime of governance assumes particular importance. The Criminal Justice (Forensic Evidence) Act 1990 is a relatively modest measure concerned more with the gathering of forensic evidence than with its presentation in court.[56] Nevertheless, some 16 years after its enactment, the statutory precedent of special treatment is entrenched, and the Act provides a foundation on which to construct a more robust, comprehensive legislative and administrative regime. Forensic evidence is a sufficiently concrete and discrete subset within the amorphous terrain of scientific evidence to be

---

[54] For general discussion on the limits of expert DNA evidence *see People (DPP) v. Boyce*, unreported, Court of Criminal Appeal, December 21, 2005.

[55] This characterisation of the development of the law of evidence can be overstated. On occasion, the Oireachtas has adopted legislation dedicated exclusively to reform of the law of evidence. An example is the Criminal Evidence Act 1992, No. 12 of 1992, an omnibus measure which introduced a miscellany of changes to various aspects of criminal evidence. In addition, the Law Reform Commission has examined specific aspects of the law of evidence over the years with a view to reform. *See e.g. Report on the Rule Against Hearsay in Civil Cases* (LRC 25-1998); *Report on the Competence and Compellability of Spouses and Witnesses* (LRC 13-1985).

[56] See chap.7 *supra*.

amenable to legal definition. As the present discussion seeks to demonstrate, the complexity of DNA evidence and its uniquely influential mystique are emblematic of the need for such special treatment.

Statistical DNA Analysis

The potential legal challenges to DNA evidence are many and varied. At each step along the route from crime scene to court, the validity of the evidence may be undermined by a myriad of occurrences. Common challenges include crime scene contamination,[57] chain of custody issues,[58] the unlawful taking of forensic samples,[59] laboratory error,[60] the qualifications of the expert witness,[61] and flawed scientific methodology.[62] This chapter is concerned primarily with another litigious aspect of DNA evidence, namely, its statistical presentation in court.[63]

The first step in DNA identification involves determining whether

---

57 *See* J. Donovan, "The Obtaining, Examining, Analysis and Retaining of Forensic Samples in Criminal Investigations" (2001) 7 M.L.J.I. 25.

58 *See e.g., People (DPP) v. Boyce*, unreported, Court of Criminal Appeal, December 21, 2005; *People (DPP.) v. Lawlor,* Central Criminal Court, December 2, 1995, Court of Criminal Appeal, February 19, 2001 (discussed in LRC Consultation Paper, *op. cit.*, p.37; O'Donnell, *op. cit.*, p.65); *Thomas v. State,* 1999 WL 1267801 (Ala. Crim. App. 1999).

59 *See supra* chap. 7. *See also e.g. Attorney General's Reference (No.3 of 1999)* [2001] 1 All E.R. 577; *R(S) v. Chief Constable of South Yorkshire* [2004] U.K.H.L. 39; [2003] 1 Cr. App. R. 16.

60 *See e.g. People v. Castro,* 545 N.Y.S.2d 985 (N.Y. Sup. Ct., Bronx County, 1989); Imwinkelried, *loc. cit.*

61 *People (DPP) v. Boyce*, unreported, Court of Criminal Appeal, December 21, 2005; *People (DPP.) v. Horgan* (*Irish Examiner*, June 25, 2002, cited in LRC Consultation Paper, *op. cit.*, p.231)*; People v. Miller,* 173 Ill.2d 167, 670 N.E.2d 721 (1996).

62 *See e.g. People (DPP) v. Allen* [2003] 4 I.R. 295; *R v. Doheny and Adams* [1997] 1 Cr. App. R. 369; E. Leahy, "Genetic Profiling and the Reasonable Doubt" (1995) 1 M.L.J.I. 66.

63 On the use of statistical means of proof, *see generally* P. Dawid, "Probability and Proof", online appendix to T. Anderson *et al., Analysis of Evidence,* 2nd ed. (Cambridge University Press, Cambridge, 2005) posted at *www.cambridge.org/9780521673167*; G. Williams, "The Mathematics of Proof – I and II" [1979] Crim. L. R. 297 & 340; M.M. Houck, "Statistics and Trace Evidence: The Tyranny of Numbers" (1999) 1 For. Sci. Comm. 1. For an example of the potential

the DNA profiles match.[64] Where that determination is made, the analyst moves on to the second step which is assessing the significance of the match, the so-called "match probability."[65] With the aid of statistical calculations, the analyst must estimate how common or rare the particular profile is in thc general population or, possibly, a substructure of the population.[66] The most common technique, sometimes styled the frequentist approach, is to determine the so-called "match probability" — the frequency of a random DNA match – using a product or multiplication rule *in tandem* with a population database.[67] Alternative methods of interpreting a DNA match, notably Bayesian analysis, rarely feature in court proceedings.[68]

The DNA expert is expected to couch his conclusions in far more precise terms than experts in other fields of forensic science. For example, courts have shown far greater willingness to accept the categoric identification of an accused on the basis of fingerprint evidence. Evett *et al.* note that "[paradoxically, DNA profiling represents the only forensic pursuit where the scientist, in the United Kingdom at least, is barred by precedent from expressing an opinion of identity of source."[69] Yet, from a legal perspective, the limitation is arguably intuitive; conversely, permitting the DNA analyst to express a subjective, categorical opinion might open a Pandora's box. For example, in a murder trial, the possible statement simpliciter of a DNA analyst that in his opinion blood found on the victim or at the crime scene belonged to the accused could be open

---

difficulties that judges may encounter when confronted with statistical evidence *see United States v. Shonubi,* 103 F.3d 1085 (2d. Cir. 1997). For an argument in favour of reliance on statistical data in preference to expert opinion *see* W. Meadow and C. Sunstein, "Statistics, Not Experts" (2001) 51 Duke L. Rev. 629.

64 On the possible significance of a non-match, *see R v. Mitchell, The Times*, July 8, 2004.

65 On probabilities in evidence *see* T. Anderson *et al., Analysis of Evidence,* 2nd ed. (Cambridge University Press, Cambridge, 2005), chap.9.

66 On calculating probabilities in relation to subgroups within the general population *see e.g. R v. Gordon* [1995] 1 Cr. App. R. 290; and the Australian case of *R v. Tran* (1990) 50 A Crim. R. 233.

67 See Robertson and Vignaux, *op. cit.,* chap.7.

68 *But see* Canadian cases *R v. Bourgignon*, January 14, 1991 (Ont. Ct.) (Gen. Div.); *R v. Baptiste*, July 15, 1991 (B.C. Sp. Ct.) (preferring qualitative statements over probability numbers); Leahy, *op. cit.*, p.67.

69 Evett *et al., op. cit.*, p.349.

to immediate challenge given the consensus among forensic scientists that a DNA match is not unique, and the reality that the witness's expertise does not extend beyond DNA analysis to the other evidentiary aspects of the case. The danger that the witness would be usurping the function of the jury could be very real, all the more so given the popular perception that DNA profiling is infallible. If DNA analysis is indeed subjected to more rigorous scrutiny than other forms of forensic science then arguably the imbalance should be redressed not by lowering the bar for DNA evidence but by applying stricter scrutiny across the board. In other words, the fault may lie, for example, in permitting the fingerprint expert to offer a conclusive opinion of identity of source. The fact that fingerprinting gained widespread acceptance in an era when the scrutiny of scientific evidence was far less rigorous than today provides at least one plausible explanation.

In the mid-1990s, the English Court of Appeal entertained a series of challenges to the statistical basis of DNA evidence. These cases may no longer represent the cutting edge of trial practice in this area, but they may hold lessons regarding the potential complexity surrounding the application of DNA analysis in the courtroom and therefore will be considered in some detail.

In *R v. Gordon*,[70] the court set aside the appellant's conviction on two counts of rape and ordered a retrial on foot of fresh expert evidence admitted for purposes of the appeal. The expert for the appellant conceded that there was a visual match between crime scene samples and the appellant's sample which showed a likelihood that the samples had emanated from the same source. However, he considered that the measurements and the basis they were arrived at was insufficiently precise to justify the use of a statistical database to calculate the match probability. It also emerged in the hearing before the Court of Appeal that the samples had been processed at two separate Home Office laboratories and by experts other that the witness on whom the prosecution had principally relied. The court concluded:

> "We do not doubt the validity and value of DNA evidence in general. However, in our view, the effect of the evidence in the present case was to raise some arguable questions on

70 [1995] 1 Cr. App. R. 290.

> whether the match probabilities put to the jury and summed up to them … could properly be sustained. Figures running into millions of the kind put before the jury have a dramatic quality which may well exert a strong influence upon them. We concluded that that we could not be sure the jury would necessarily have reached the same result had they heard the additional expert evidence which has been put before us."[71]

R v. Gordon was not the first case in which the Court of Appeal had set aside a conviction and ordered a retrial on the basis of flaws in the prosecution's DNA evidence. In the earlier landmark case of *R v. Deen*,[72] the Court had reached a similar result based on the manner in which the evidence was presented to the jury. Although strident in its criticism in *Deen,* the court offered no guidance to the trial courts as to the proper evidentiary practice to be followed in such cases. That guidance was to follow later when the Court of Appeal revisited the issue of probabilistic reasoning in *R v. Doheny and Adams*.[73] Doheny was convicted of rape and buggery and sentenced to concurrent terms of eight years' imprisonment, increased to 12 years by the Court of Appeal on a reference by the Attorney General. Adams was convicted of buggery and sentenced to five years' imprisonment. In each case, the prosecution had relied substantially on evidence of DNA match probabilities between a crime scene stain and a sample of the appellant's blood. The appeals, which were heard together, focused on the procedures that should govern the presentation of DNA evidence.[74]

The Court of Appeal accepted that a DNA match probability constitutes "highly probative" evidence when combined with sufficient additional evidence, provided there is no reason to doubt the matching data or statistical conclusion.[75] It concluded that the cogency of DNA

---

[71] *Id.*, at 296.

[72] [1994] T.L.R. 11.

[73] [1997] 1 Cr. App. R. 369.

[74] Leave to appeal had been given long out of time to enable the appellants to raise challenges to DNA evidence which had not been appreciated at the time of trial or in the period immediately thereafter. For purposes of the appeal, the Court of Appeal received fresh expert evidence from the prosecution and the defence. [1997] 1 Cr. App. R. at 371.

[75] [1997] 1 Cr. App. R. at 373.

evidence makes it "particularly important that DNA testing is rigorously conducted so as to obviate the risk of error in the laboratory, that the method of DNA analysis and the basis of subsequent statistical calculation should – so far as possible – be transparent to the Defence and that the true import of the resultant conclusion is accurately and fairly explained to the jury."[76]

With these objectives in mind, the Court endorsed certain standards relating to the use of DNA evidence. First, where DNA evidence is to be adduced, the prosecution should serve on the defence sufficient details as to the method whereby the match probability was calculated so as to enable the defence to scrutinise the basis for the calculations. Furthermore, if requested, the Forensic Science Service should make available to a defence expert the databases upon which the calculations have been based. Second, in terms of trial procedure, an issue of expert evidence should be identified and, if possible, resolved before trial. In particular, the court should explore this possibility when conducting the pre-trial review.[77]

Third, the Court turned to the role of the expert witness in the presentation of DNA evidence. When giving evidence, the scientist should not overstep the line which separates his province from that of the jury. He should explain to the jury the nature of the matching DNA characteristics between the DNA in the crime stain and the DNA in the blood sample taken from the Defendant. On the basis of empirical statistical data, he should give the jury the random occurrence ratio (*i.e.* the frequency with which the matching DNA characteristics are likely to be found in the population at large). For example, "[p]rovided that the expert has the necessary data, it may then be appropriate for him to indicate how many people with the matching characteristics are likely to be found in the United Kingdom or a more limited relevant sub-group, for instance, the Caucasian, sexually-active males in the Manchester area."[78] It will be for the jury to decide, having regard to all the relevant evidence, whether they are sure that it was the defendant who left the crime stain, or whether it is possible that it was left by someone else with the same matching DNA characteristics. Indeed, to avert the risk of the prosecutor's fallacy (discussed *infra*), the expert should not be asked his opinion on the

---

76 *Id.*, 373-374.
77 *Id.*, 374
78 *Id.*

likelihood that it was the defendant who left the crime stain, nor when giving evidence should he use terminology which may lead the jury to believe that he is expressing such an opinion.[79]

The elucidation of these standards provided beneficial guidance to the trial courts and assisted in dispelling some of the complexity surrounding the presentation of DNA evidence.[80] Some of the court's observations are no more than commonsense refinements of established practices relating to expert evidence. Others engage the specific challenge of DNA evidence but fail to fully grasp the nettle. For example, the court does not discuss the forensic scientist's use of population databases in constructing probabilities nor the need to account for complicating factors such as relatedness. The court has also been criticised for engaging in unnecessary terminological confusion.[81] DNA technology has advanced considerably in the years since the court's judgment and, almost a decade later, the guidelines fail above all to dispel the misconception that statistical analysis generates precise calculations that establish a DNA match as a conclusive fact.[82]

In light of these deficiencies, the Law Reform Commission decided against recommending the formal adoption of the guidelines in Ireland. Indeed, the Commission chose not to make any recommendation with regard to the statistical presentation of DNA evidence calling instead for the establishment of an expert group to examine the issue.[83] The Commission's recognition of the need for clear and comprehensive

---

79 *Id.* The Court also offered guidance in relation to the trial judge's summing up which is discussed *infra.*

80 M. Redmayne, "Presenting Probabilities in Court: The DNA Experience" (1997) 1 E & P 187; M. Redmayne, *Expert Evidence and Criminal Justice* (Oxford University Press, Oxford, 2001), chap. 4; C. McCartney, *Forensic Identification and Criminal Justice: Forensic Science, Justice and Risk* (Willan Publishing, Devon, 2006), pp.92-99.

81 Redmayne, (1997) 1 E & P p.210 (noting that the Court used the term "random occurrence ratio" when it likely had in mind the "match probability"); I.W. Evett *et al., op. cit.*,p.346 (suggesting that by "random occurrence ratio" the Court had been referring to a *relative frequency* and recommending the use of "match probability" as the preferred term).

82 This point was highlighted by the Court of Appeal of British Columbia in *Latch v. R.* (1998) 104 A Crim. R. 390.

83 Law Reform Commission, *Report on the Establishment of a DNA Database* (LRC 78–2005), paras.5.14-16; Consultation Paper, *op. cit.,* paras.9.41-42.

standards is welcome although it is regrettable that its lengthy discussion of statistical DNA analysis did not culminate in a substantive recommendation. The breadth of the Commission's examination of the forensic use of DNA is one of its strengths and it would be unfortunate if future policy in relation to this complex and dynamic field were to be directed piecemeal from disparate specialist groups or committees. The manner in which DNA statistical analysis is presented to juries should be examined at a minimum in the context of a broader review of the impact of DNA evidence on court practice and procedures. That said, there is considerable merit in the Commission's suggestion that the output of any expert study should take the form of a professional code of practice.[84] At the same time, it is essential to recognise the limitations of general guidelines in relation to this, and indeed any other form, of evidence. The jury must weigh the DNA evidence and the non-scientific evidence and their ultimate determination as to the innocence or guilt of the accused is necessarily grounded in the fact-specific context of the trial. The challenge lies in determining how best the forensic scientist, judge and lawyers can assist the jury in that task.[85]

THE PROSECUTOR'S FALLACY

In weighing a proffer of DNA evidence, the jury must assess two interrelated matters, namely, the significance of the DNA evidence and its relationship to the other evidence in the case. The use by the expert witness of probabilistic reasoning, though intended to enhance the jurors'

---

[84] LRC Report, *op. cit.,* para.5.16. A contemporary starting point is the contribution of the House of Commons Committee on Science and Technology which has placed particular emphasis on the need for clarity and simplicity in the manner in which DNA evidence is presented to juries. It has recommended that forensic scientists use the following form of words: "The probability that an unknown person, unrelated to the defendant, would have the same profile as the crime sample is 1 in X (the relevant figure)". House of Commons, Science and Technology Committee, *Forensic Science on Trial* (7th Report, 2004-05), p.71. It is the policy of both the UK Forensic Science Service and the Irish Forensic Science Laboratory to state a general figure (*e.g.* 1 in 1 billion) rather than a precise, categorical figure (*e.g.* 1 in 1,237,045).

[85] Evett *et al., op. cit.*, p.354.

comprehension of the significance of a DNA match, may counterintuitively complicate their task. One potential and well recognised pitfall into which the expert may inadvertently tread is to state the probabilistic reasoning in terms of the ultimate issue of the innocence or guilt of the accused. The so-called "prosecutor's fallacy" is not unique to DNA evidence but rather may occur in any proceedings involving a proffer of statistical evidence. A likely recent and well publicised example is *R v. Clark*,[86] which led to the wrongful conviction Sally Clark for the murder of her two children, each of whom had died in infancy when alone in the home with their mother. The principal prosecution evidence at trial was that of Sir Roy Meadow, an eminent paediatrician, who testified as to the extreme rarity of two infant deaths within the same family occurring from unexplained natural causes. He estimated the overall rate for double "sudden infant syndrome" (SIDS) deaths in families such as the Clarks to be 1 in 73 million. The jury were not warned against the reasoning of the prosecutor's fallacy and writers have speculated that they may have consciously or subconsciously treated the 1 in 73 million as measuring the probability that Clark might have been innocent.[87] Clark's appeal against her conviction was dismissed but her second appeal was allowed on the ground that newly discovered medical evidence of possible bacterial infection in one of the infants rendered her conviction unsafe.[88]

In the context of DNA evidence, the prosecutor's fallacy occurs where the matching probability is confused with the likelihood that the accused committed the offence.[89] The key to understanding the problem is an appreciation of two distinct questions:

---

[86] *R v. Clark* [2003] E.W.C.A. Crim. 1020.

[87] *See e.g.* Dawid, *op. cit.*, § 4.3.1 (noting that the press appears to have assumed this).

[88] Meadow was struck off the medical register by the medical council, a decision that was sensationally reversed by the English High Court. *Meadow v. General Medical Council* [2006] 1 W.L.R. 1452.

[89] On the prosecutor's fallacy *see generally* D.J. Balding and P. Donnelly, "The Prosecutor's Fallacy and DNA Evidence" [1994] Crim. L.R. 711; M. Redmayne, "Doubts and Burdens: DNA Evidence, Probability and the Courts" [1995] Crim. L. R. 464, p.474; M. Goode, "Some Observations on Evidence of DNA Frequency" (2002) 23 Adelaide L. Rev. 45, p.49 *et seq;* Wall, *op. cit.*, pp.93-95; Dawid, *op. cit.*, §.4.2.1. As Dawid notes, *id.*, § 4.2.2., fallacious statistical arguments are not the exclusive preserve of the prosecution.

(1) What was the probability that an individual would match the DNA profile from the crime sample given that he was innocent?
(2) What was the probability that an individual was innocent, given that he matched the DNA profile from the crime sample?

The prosecutor's fallacy consists of giving the answer to the first question in the form of the answer to the second; it is that "the statistics of the match necessarily translates into the *equivalent* chance of the accused being guilty."[90]

The gravity of the error embodied in the prosecutor's fallacy was demonstrated by *R v. Deen*[91] in which the English Court of Appeal set aside the appellant's convictions for three rapes.[92] DNA profiling constituted the principal evidence against the accused in relation to one of the rapes and, in the view of the Court of Appeal it was by extension crucial to the outcome of the entire trial.[93] The case was tried in February 1990 "when forensic application of DNA profiling was still in its infancy."[94] Mr. Michael Davey, a forensic scientist at the Home Office Forensic Science Laboratory, conducted the DNA analysis in the case using the RFLP technique.[95] He compared a DNA profile generated from semen contained in a vaginal swab taken from the victim with a profile generated from a blood sample taken from the appellant. Davey gave evidence that on a comparison of the two profiles he identified 10 matching bands on the autoradiographs and that he was satisfied that this constituted a match. As to his statistical evaluation of the probability of this match occurring in a person chosen randomly from the general population, he estimated that the bands in the area he concentrated on had an occurrence

[90] Goode, *op. cit.*, at p.50.
[91] [1994] T.L.R. 11. As noted, the prosecutor's fallacy can occur in any situation involving the use of statistical evidence (and thus is not limited to DNA statistics). One of the earliest and most frequently cited examples is *People v. Collins* 68 Cal.2d 319, 99 Cal. Rptr. 497, 439 P.2d 33 (1968).
[92] The appellant had been sentenced to 16 years' imprisonment.
[93] [1994] T.L.R. 11 at 12 ("Failure on that count would inevitably mean failure on all counts").
[94] *Id.*
[95] *See* chap.6 *supra.*

rate of approximately one in four of the population. He took the figure 0.26 and multiplied it by 10 (representing the 10 matching bands in the two profiles) to produce a figure of one in 700,000. Davey then took the additional step of factoring the appellant's blood type into the equation. That blood type was shared by about 25 percent of the population. Treating this as a discrete characteristic, Davey again multiplied his figure by 0.26 to reach a figure of 1 in 3,000,000.[96]

The appeal raised criticisms of the evidence at trial, the statistical formulae used, and the judge's summing up to the jury. The bulk of the Court of Appeal's concern related to Davey's statistical evaluation of the match and the judge's summing up on that issue. The prosecution conceded that on at least one occasion during his testimony, Davey had fallen into the trap of the prosecutor's fallacy. That error had been exacerbated by the judge's summing up in which he spoke of probability approximating "pretty well to certainty."[97] The Court of Appeal allowed the appeal, set aside the convictions and ordered a retrial.

The prosecutor's fallacy was again at issue before the court in *R v. Doheny and Adams*.[98] As in *Deen,* each appellant had been convicted of rape and the DNA profiling technique on which the evidence was based was RFLP, the profiles themselves being visualised on autoradiographs.[99] Phillips L.J., speaking for the Court, opened his judgment with a commentary on DNA testing in general and the prosecutor's fallacy in particular. He used the following example to demonstrate the fallacious reasoning sometimes presented to juries in support of prosecution DNA evidence:

> "(1) Only one person in a million will have a DNA profile which matches that of the crime stain.
> (2) The Defendant has a DNA profile which matches the crime stain.
> (3) Ergo there is a million to one probability that the

---

96 [1994] T.L.R. at 12.
97 *Id.*
98 [1997] 1 Cr. App. R. 369.
99 *See* chap. 6 *supra.*

> Defendant left the crime stain and is guilty of the crime."[100]

Having criticised this reasoning, Phillips L.J. then developed his example:

> "If one person in a million has a DNA profile which matches that obtained from the crime stain, then the suspect will be one of perhaps 26 men in the United Kingdom who share that characteristic. If no fact is known about the Defendant, other than that he was in the United Kingdom at the time of the crime the DNA evidence tells us no more than that there is a statistical probability that he was the criminal of 1 in 26.
>
> The significance of the DNA evidence will depend critically upon what else is known about the suspect. If he has a convincing alibi at the other end of England at the time of the crime, it will appear highly improbable that he can have been responsible for the crime, despite his matching DNA profile. If, however, he was near the scene of the crime when it was committed, or has been identified as a suspect because of other evidence which suggests that he may have been responsible for the crime, the DNA evidence becomes very significant."[101]

The relativism espoused by the court in this passage is a theme running through its discussion of DNA evidence. Although intent on providing general guidance to the trial courts relating to the presentation of such evidence, the court emphasised the need to assess each case in its own subjective context. This dimension to the judgment is particularly apparent in the court's ultimate determinations on the facts of the appeals of Doheny and Adams, respectively. In each case, the court concluded that the prosecution experts and the judges had propounded the prosecutor's fallacy but, in another relativist twist, held that such an error is not necessarily fatal depending upon the context.

---

[100] [1997] 1 Cr. App. R. 309 at 372-373

[101] *Id.*, p.373. Philips L.J. explicitly recognised the "highly probative" force of a DNA matching probability when combined with additional evidence.

Doheny was convicted of the rape and buggery of a 65 year old widow and sentenced to concurrent terms of 8 years increased to 12 years concurrent on each count on a reference by the Attorney General.[102] The complainant had been entering her home on a Friday afternoon when a man assaulted her, forced her into her home, threatened her with a knife which he claimed to have in his possession, raped and buggered her, and stole her purse. Semen stains found on the complainant's underclothes were forensically tested. At trial, the prosecution expert gave evidence that the appellant and the man who left the semen stains shared the same blood group along with approximately 14% of the population. The samples had been tested for DNA using both the mutilocus and the single locus probing techniques. The multilocus probe test produced 6 matching bands, one of which was disregarded, and the remaining 5 bands were each assigned a value of 0.26 and multiplied together to obtain a matching probability of 1 in 840. Three single locus probe tests produced a total of 5 matching bands which after applying appropriate formulae obtained a matching probability of 1 in 6,900. The expert then multiplied the results of the two tests to produce a figure of 1 in 5.7 million. Lastly, factoring in the blood group result, he multiplied this figure by 7 to produce a final matching probability of 1 in 40 million.[103]

The other evidence in the case included the complainant's description of her assailant which was generally consistent with the accused.[104] The appellant took the stand and testified that he had been playing pool in a public house that afternoon and had then driven straight home. His wife and other witnesses provided evidence generally supporting his movements and timings but the complainant's house was close to the appellant's route home and their evidence did not preclude the possibility that the appellant might have stopped there and committed the assault.[105]

---

[102] Pursuant to s.36 of the Criminal Justice Act 1988.

[103] [1997] 1 Cr. App. R. at 379

[104] The description was contained in her witness statement which was read to the jury. The victim never got a clear look at her assailant's face. The Court of Appeal said of her description: "While this did not match the appellant in every respect, there was no discrepancy that could not have been explained as an error of appreciation or recollection having regard to the complainant's description of her ordeal. She described her assailant as having a local accent. The appellant has a local accent." [1997] 1 Cr. App. R at 376.

[105] *Id.*

Forensic tests were also conducted on a pubic hair found on the bedspread and a second pubic hair found on the victim in the vicinity of her anus. These hairs originated neither from the appellant nor the complainant.

During examination-in-chief, counsel for the prosecution led the expert into the trap of the prosecutor's fallacy:

> "Q. What is the combination, taking all those into account?
> A. Taking them all into account, I calculated the chance of finding all of those bands and the conventional blood groups to be about 1 in 40 million.
> Q. The likelihood of it being anybody other than Alan Doheny?
> A. Is about 1 in 40 million.
> Q. You deal habitually with these things, the jury have to say, of course, on the evidence, whether they are satisfied beyond doubt that it is he. You have done the analysis, are you sure that it is he?
> A. Yes."[106]

The Court of Appeal was unequivocal in its conclusion that this series of questions and answers was "inappropriate and potentially misleading."[107] The second question and the answer thereto constituted a "classic example" of the prosecutor fallacy.[108] The third had invited the expert to trespass into the province of the jury, an invitation which he accepted by proffering an answer with a spurious evidentiary foundation. Simply put, the matching probability of 1 in 40 million left open the possibility of several individuals in the United Kingdom having the same DNA as the assailant and it was for the jury to decide on all the evidence whether it was the appellant who had left the stain. The Court concluded that these errors were exacerbated by the judge's summing up which gave the impression that if the jury accepted the expert's evidence the appellant's guilt would be conclusively established.

These forthright determinations might lead one to assume that the

---

[106] *Id.* at 377-378.
[107] *Id.* at 378.
[108] *Id.*

trial was irretrievably flawed. Perhaps the most interesting aspect of the judgment, however, is the court's conclusion that the significance of the prosecutor's fallacy is not automatically so great as to affect the safety of impugned convictions. Whether the prosecutor's fallacy distorts the DNA evidence in a given case will depend upon the remoteness of the matching probability. In the words of Phillips L.J.: "The more remote the random occurrence ratio [or matching probability], the less significant will be the adoption of the 'Prosecutor's Fallacy', until the point is reached where that fallacy does not significantly misrepresent the import of the DNA evidence."[109] Such was the position in Doheny's case; given what was then the uncontroverted expert evidence that the matching probability was 1 in 40 million, the court had "no doubt" that the jury would have reached the same verdict if it had been directed properly.[110] On the expert's figures, the prosecutor's fallacy was not sufficient standing alone to justify granting the appeal and setting aside the convictions. Fresh expert evidence presented on appeal, however, undermined the veracity of those figures and it was this error which resulted ultimately in the success of the appeal.

The court adopted a similar stance when assessing the prosecutor's fallacy that unfolded in the case of the second appellant. Gary Adams was convicted of the buggery of a 32 year old divorcee and sentenced to 5 years' imprisonment. The complainant, who was psychologically disturbed, frequently phoned the Samaritans for comfort and assistance and, on 4 October 1989, the night of the assault, spoke to the appellant, who worked as a volunteer. She testified at trial that the appellant asked if she wanted someone to come round to her house and about 10 or 15 minutes later, a man, whose voice she recognised as that of the appellant, arrived on his own (although the Samaritans' protocol called for visits to be made in pairs). The appellant hugged her and then sexually assaulted her, penetrating her anus and causing her excruciating pain. The complainant gave a description of her assailant's coat which was consistent with the coat the appellant had with him on the evening in question.[111]

---

[109] *Id.* at 379.

[110] *Id.*

[111] She also stated that her assailant was wearing Farrah trousers. The appellant denied that he was wearing Farrah trousers on the evening in question but admitted that he possessed a pair of such trousers. *Id.* at 382. The evening after the assault,

The appellant denied the allegations. He testified that his phone call with the complainant had ended when she became abusive and that that he had driven home directly at 10:35pm at the close of his session at the Samaritans Centre. The timing of his arrival home was corroborated by his mother and girlfriend. In December, the complainant signed a statement that she no longer wished to pursue the case but in January 1990 the Police searched the complainant's home for forensic evidence. A semen stain on a chair cushion was tested for DNA and declared to match the DNA taken from a sample of the appellant's blood.[112]

The prosecution expert testified that he had carried out four single locus probe tests which had resulted in 8 matching bands and that his statistical calculations had produced a matching probability of 1 in 27 million. Just as in Doheny's case, the Court of Appeal found that there was force to the appellant's complaint that the prosecution expert in presenting his evidence and the judge in summing up had propounded the prosecutor's fallacy.[113] However, just as in Doheny's case, "this fallacy does not significantly alter the picture if the random occurrence ratio is as extreme as 1 in 27 million."[114] Echoing the prosecution expert, the trial judge had estimated that there were probably no more than 27 million males in the United Kingdom which, he stated, rendered the match unique. Before the Court of Appeal, there was some conflict in the expert evidence regarding the accuracy of the prosecution expert's calculations and the possibility that the semen stain could have been left by one or more men other than the appellant. The Court of Appeal was not persuaded by the appellant's expert evidence but declared that the conflict between the experts was in any event beside the point:

---

the complainant told a friend about the incident and about 10 days later, accompanied by the friend, she went to the Samaritans Centre to complain about the appellant. One month after the assault, the complainant contacted the Police on discovering that the appellant was still working at the Samaritans Centre. *Id.* at 381-382.

[112] At this point, the appellant suggested an explanation that the Court of Appeal described as "fanciful", namely, that he had previously provided a semen specimen for fertility analysis which had been deposited at the Central Pathology Laboratory and that perhaps the complainant had obtained this sample from the hospital where she worked in order to frame him. *Id.* at 383.

[113] The relevant excerpt from the examination-in-chief and the summing up are set out in the Court of Appeal's judgment. *Id.* at 383-384.

[114] *Id.* at 384.

> "[I]n our view none of these issues have any significance in the context of the Adams appeal. The complainant had, quite comprehensively, identified one man – the Appellant – as her assailant: the telephone call, his voice, his appearance, his clothing. When to this was added the fact that his DNA profile matched the crime stain, no Jury could be in doubt that he it was who left the stain, whether the statistics suggested that there existed one other man, or ten, or even a hundred in the United Kingdom with the same DNA profile."[115]

Adams's appeal was thus rejected on this and, ultimately, all other grounds.

The popular perception of DNA evidence as the exclusive basis on which to convict an accused belies the subtle and complex evidentiary web that is weaved in most criminal trials. DNA evidence is by its very nature circumstantial and, as this case demonstrates, its ultimate value to the prosecution may lie in its potential to bolster the other more conventional evidence offered at trial. Nowhere is this more apparent that in the trial of sexual offences where, in the absence of evidence corroborating the complainant's account, the trial judge retains a discretion to caution the jury in his summing up about the dangers of convicting on what is according to historical perceptions, a slim evidentiary reed.[116] Thus, it is worthy of note that, in this case, the DNA evidence "strongly corroborated" [117] the complainant's story and not the other way around.

It is also interesting to compare the basis on which the Court of Appeal granted Doheny's appeal and rejected that of Adams. A statistical error on the part of the prosecution expert clearly distinguishes the former

---

[115] *Id.* at 385.

[116] *See* s.7(1) of the Irish Criminal Law (Rape) Amendment Act 1990. One of other unsuccessful grounds of appeal raised by Adams was that the judge had misdirected the jury as to the corroborative reach of the DNA evidence. The appellant contended that the direction should have specified that while the semen stain showed that there had been sexual activity, it did not corroborate the complainant's evidence that this activity amounted to buggery. The Court of Appeal considered that a corroboration warning was desirable in this case but that it was not necessary for the judge to direct that there should be corroboration of every element of the complainant's evidence. [1997] 1 Cr. App. R. at 387.

[117] *Id.*

case from the latter but in assessing the impact of that error on the safety of Doheny's convictions, the court engaged in same contextual assessment that characterised its reasoning in Adams's appeal, weighing the significance of the DNA evidence against the totality of the evidence as a whole.[118] From this perspective, the distinction between the two cases does not turn on any single point or neat formula. The court's determinations on the facts, no less than its reasoning on the principles, caution against generalised assumptions about the presentation at trial of DNA matching probabilities.

The Bayesian Alternative

Dissatisfaction with the presentation of DNA evidence in terms of match probabilities has prompted some writers to espouse the use of an alternative methodology, known as Bayesian analysis, which uses a mathematical formula, Bayes's theorem,[119] for calculating conditional

---

[118] The court concluded its assessment in *Doheny's* appeal thus: "The relevant position is this. If one excludes from the calculation the result of the multi locus probe test, in a population base of 800,000 suggested as constituting those within a reasonable proximity of the scene of the crime, there may well have been 20 or so individuals with the same DNA profile as the Appellant and as the crime stain. This figure still renders it an extremely unlikely coincidence that both the Appellant and another of this small cohort should have been in the vicinity of the crime at about the time that it was committed, the more so when one postulates that this other individual would also have had to share with the Appellant the other attributes – general appearance, age and local accent – that the complainant described in her assailant. Nevertheless we do not feel that we can say with confidence that these considerations demonstrate that the Appellant was rightly convicted, however compelling his evidence and that of his alibi witnesses may have been. Our doubts are augmented by the discovery of pubic hairs which had originated neither from the appellant nor from the complainant. For these reasons we have concluded that the conviction is unsafe and must be quashed." [1997] 1 Cr. App. R. at 380-381

[119] Originating in the work of Presbyterian minister, Reverend Thomas Bayes (1702-61). For an early discussion of the application of Bayesian analysis to evidence *see* M.O. Finkelstein and W.B. Fairley, "A Bayesian Approach to Identification Evidence" (1970) 83 Harv. L. Rev. 489. *See generally* R. Swinburne, ed., *Bayes's Theorem* (Oxford University Press, Oxford, 2002); Dawid, *op. cit.* at § 4.2.3; Robertson and Vignaux, *op. cit.,* chap.7.

probabilities. The weight of evidence is expressed in terms of likelihood ratios (*i.e.* statements of probability based on two alternative hypotheses).[120] As Redmayne explains, the likelihood ratio for an item of evidence can be depicted as the probability of finding the evidence given that the defendant is guilty divided by the probability of finding the evidence given that the defendant is innocent. This may be expressed in a simple notation:

$$\frac{P(E/G)}{P(E/I)}$$

Where P(E/G) is greater than P(E/I), the evidence favours the prosecution, where P(E/G) is less than P(E/I), the evidence favours the defence, and where P(E/G) equals P(E/I), the evidence is irrelevant.[121] Goode has offered this summation of the analysis:

> "Bayes' Theorem is a mathematical way of stating that an estimate of the probability of … the DNA match being a *guilty* match depends logically on an estimate, whether mathematically expressed or otherwise, of the *prior* evidence of the likelihood of the guilt of the accused. When the likelihood ratio derived from the DNA match is combined with the 'prior odds' one obtains a result which is usually called the '*posterior odds*'."[122]

The mathematical theory and formula of Bayes analysis is complex but its proponents contend that its application is simpler and easier to understand than traditional statistical analysis.[123] One of the advantages is that it provides a means of modifying knowledge in light of new data or, to put it another way, "a means of updating our belief in a hypothesis".[124] Bayesian analysis also assists the jury in placing the

---

[120] Redmayne [1995] Crim. L. R., p.467, n.21. *See supra* chap.6.
[121] Redmayne, (1997) 1 E & P. pp.190-91.
[122] Goode, *op. cit.*, pp.52-53.
[123] *See e.g.* Wall, *op. cit.*, p.84.
[124] Redmayne, E & P, p.190.

evidence in its ultimate context and, in the process, sidesteps the prosecutor's fallacy.[125] The cogent arguments against the use of Bayes's theorem include the difficulties juries may encounter in understanding Bayesian presentations and, in particular, the need to instruct juries in the estimation of prior odds.[126]

The application of Bayes's theorem in all its intricate complexity is beyond the scope of the present discussion. Although it has garnered considerable support in the academic literature, it has not gained a firm foothold in the courts. The English Court of Appeal, for example, has criticised its use in the presentation of DNA evidence in criminal trials. In *R v. Adams (Dennis)*,[127] the appellant was convicted of rape on the basis of expert testimony that his DNA profile matched the profile of DNA found on a swab taken from the victim. The DNA profile was calculated to occur in the general population with a frequency of 1 in 200 million. With the exception of geography (the appellant lived within a few miles of the scene of the crime), all of the non-scientific evidence supported the defence.[128] Thus, task facing the jury was how to reconcile the DNA and non-scientific evidence. An expert witness for the defence was permitted to outline the use of Bayes theorem to the jury, painstakingly explaining how to compose a likelihood ratio for each and every item of evidence.[129] The appellant's principal argument on appeal was that the trial judge had failed to explain the Bayesian method clearly to the jury during his summing up. Although the Court of Appeal quashed the conviction and ordered a retrial,[130] it criticised the use of Bayes theorem in criminal trials on several grounds: that it atomises the process of proof, that it dresses subjective analysis in apparently objective disguise, and

---

[125] R. Lempert, "Some Caveats Concerning DNA as Criminal Identification Evidence: With Thanks to the Reverend Bayes" (1991) 13 Cardozo L. Rev. 303, pp.314-15.

[126] *Id.* pp.330-31.

[127] [1996] 2 Cr. App. R. 467.

[128] The appellant had an alibi for the night in question. In addition, the complainant failed to identify him and he did not fit the description of the assailant she had given to the police.

[129] For a detailed discussion *see* Redmayne, (1997) 1 E & P pp.202-206

[130] The defence again presented expert testimony on Bayes theorem at the retrial. The appellant was convicted for a second time. *Id.*

that it potentially trespasses on the province of the jury.[131] The court concluded, in short, that "[t]o introduce Bayes Theorem, or any similar method, into a criminal trial plunges the Jury into inappropriate and unnecessary realms of theory and complexity deflecting them from their proper task."[132]

In the subsequent joint appeals of *Doheny and Adams*, the court reiterated its criticism of the Bayesian approach and omitted it from the general guidelines on the presentation of DNA evidence fashioned in its judgment.[133] As Dawid has argued, the Court of Appeal's criticisms of Bayesian analysis fail to address the problem that "common sense usually fares extremely badly when it comes to manipulating probabilities" and the further reality that "common experience simply does not encompass the tiny probabilities that arise with DNA matches."[134] Nevertheless, the court's reasoning in *Doheny and Adams* has been followed in other jurisdictions and Dawid concedes that "Bayesian arguments, while not formally banned from court, need to be presented with a good deal of circumspection."[135]

Statistical Issues

Although the judgment of the Court of Appeal in *Deen* speaks to the evidentiary impact of the prosecutor's fallacy, the case also illustrates the risk of statistical error inherent in DNA analysis.[136] An issue arose at trial as to the validity of the number of matching bands that the prosecution's expert had identified on the autoradiographs. Mr. Davey, for the prosecution, had referred to 10 matching bands but Professor Roberts, for the defence, had initially identified two discrepant bands in the profiles. After an adjournment to enable Roberts to examine the

---

131 [1996] 2 Cr. App. R. at 481. *See* Redmayne, (1997) 1 E & P pp.202-206

132 [1996] 2 Cr. App. R. at 482.

133 [1997] 1 Cr. App. R. at 375

134 Dawid, *op. cit.*, § 4.2.6.

135 *Id. See also R v. Krager* (1999) 103 A. Crim. R. 434, [2001] S.A.S.C. 64; Goode, *op. cit.*, p.54.

136 For a case involving an unsuccessful challenge to the terminology employed by an expert when explaining his methodology *see Thomas v. State,* 1999 WL 1267801 (Ala. Crim. App. 1999).

autoradiographs, Roberts had conceded that one of the discrepant bands could be explained. In summing up, the judge had stated that Davey said that there were 10 matching bands and that Roberts said that he was not satisfied about one of them. As the Court of Appeal noted, the judge had missed the point because the band which concerned Roberts was not one of the 10 said by Davey to match. The judge's error was compounded in two later passages which may have led the jury to believe that, even if there was a doubt in relation to one of the bands, 9 out of 10 matching bands was sufficient. Nowhere did the judge specifically state that even one unexplained discrepant band would be fatal to establishing a match.[137]

Statistical error provided the basis on which the Court of Appeal set aside the convictions for rape and buggery of Alan Doheny in the joint appeal in *R v. Doheny and Adams.*[138] As outlined above, the forensic scientist conducting the DNA analysis had employed both the mutilocus probing and the single locus probing techniques. His final matching probability of 1 in 40 million represented the combined results of these two techniques and the more basic blood grouping test. In fresh evidence before the Court of Appeal, the appellant challenged the legitimacy of combining the results of the multilocus and single locus probing tests. The challenge centred on the risk of overlap between the respective techniques:

> "[T]here is a risk that the multi locus probe test will identify bands which are the same as those identified by the single locus probes, or in such close proximity to them that there is a likelihood that they will be linked together, so that whenever one is found the other will be likely to be present also."[139]

There was consensus among the experts as to possibility of such a linkage between bands but divergence as to the likelihood of its occurrence. At trial, the prosecution expert had testified that he had included in his calculations of the matching probability only 5 rather than 6 of the bands identified by the multilocus probe because that band had been duplicated by one of the single locus probes. On the second day of the appeal, the

---

[137] [1994] T.L.R. at 12.
[138] [1997] 1 Cr. App. R. 369.
[139] *Id.* at 379.

experts for the Crown conceded that, on a re-examination of the material, there had been a second duplication, which had the effect of reducing the matching probability of 1 in 40 million to 1 in 10 million. They conceded further that they were unaware of other instances in which the results of the two techniques had been multiplied in this fashion nor of any empirical evidence supporting the independence of the results of the respective techniques. There was agreement among all of the experts in the appeal that the result of the multi locus probe test potentiated to a degree the results of the single locus probe tests. The Court of Appeal concluded that the extent, though uncertain, was likely to be significant, and that the methodology of the prosecution's expert at trial had not been demonstrated to be legitimate. The jury should have been given a matching probability based solely on the single locus probe tests and the blood grouping, though they could have been told that the result of the multi-locus probe test increased the probability to an indeterminate extent.[140]

One of the factors which the expert must incorporate into his calculations and the presentation of his evidence at trial is relatedness, *i.e.*, the fact that genetic similarities are far more likely among relatives than strangers.[141] A failure to comprehensively tease out the effects of relatedness prompted the Court of Criminal Appeal to set aside convictions and order a retrial in *People (DPP) v. Allen*.[142] The appellant was convicted of armed robbery and possession of a firearm with intent to commit an indictable offence as a result of a raid on a fast food restaurant. An expert from the Forensic Science Laboratory testified in relation to a comparison she had conducted between a DNA profile generated from a crime scene sample and the appellant's DNA profile. Basing her calculations on an Irish population database, she estimated that the chance of an unrelated person having the same profile was less than one in a thousand million. The appellant contended that the expert's evidence was misleading in

---

[140] *Id.* at 380. A second methodological challenge related to the prosecution expert's figure of 1 in 6,900 as the matching probability based on the results of the single locus probe tests. The challenge turned on the application of the data contained in the population data base used in the calculation. The court passed on the issue, noting that it was not sufficiently significant to affect the result of the appeal. *Id.*

[141] *See* Evett *et al., op. cit.*, p.346; Giannelli and Imwinkelried, *op. cit.,* §18.4(C).

[142] [2003] 4 I.R. 295.

that it did not disclose any probability figures in relation to siblings although there was evidence before the jury that the appellant had at least one brother.[143] McCracken J., delivering the judgment of the Court of Criminal Appeal, observed that the expert had dealt in general with the question of close relatives. For example, in response to a question on cross-examination, she conceded that "the pool of DNA" from which the appellant and his brothers were drawn was "obviously smaller than the population at large".[144] Whereas the jury had been appraised by this testimony that a match was more likely to occur between siblings than between members of the population at large, at no point was the extent of this greater likelihood quantified. McCracken J. continued:

> "When one starts from a statistic such as one in a thousand million, the phrase 'more likely' means very little without something more. It would not be unreasonable for a jury to assume that then perhaps it was twice as likely or even ten times as likely among brothers, but this would still give odds of one in five hundred million or one in one hundred million. This would be so far from the truth that the jury would be clearly misled."[145]

The Court of Criminal Appeal concluded that "the failure to elicit, either in direct or cross-examination, the actual statistics concerning brothers, had the potential to confuse or mislead the jury into believing that, even among brothers, an increased probability starting from a base of one in one thousand million would still be so improbable that they could disregard it."[146] While the court had no way of knowing the impact which additional statistical evidence in relation to brothers would have had on the jury, the lacuna in the evidence was such as to render the trial unsafe.[147]

---

[143] In fact, the appellant had three full brothers and two half brothers and at least one brother had been convicted of a criminal offence. This evidence, together with evidence that the probability of DNA profiles matching among siblings is 1 in 10,000, was not before the trial court and the Court of Appeal did not think it should be admitted at the appellate stage. [2003] 4 I.R. 295 at 300.

[144] Judgment of McCracken J. citing the trial transcript. [2003] 4 I.R. at 300.

[145] *Id.* at 300.

[146] *Id.* at 301.

[147] *Id. See also People (DPP.) v. Howe,* Central Criminal Court, October 15, 2003

The decision illustrates the challenges experts encounter when presenting their evidence within the confines of the trial process. It underscores the imperative that forensic scientists present match probabilities to the court in their full and complete context and, by extension, that prosecuting counsel put questions to forensic scientists during the course of examination-in-chief that facilitate this objective. As Evett *et al.* have astutely observed, "[t]here are many traps for the unwary in the dialogue between advocate and scientist".[148]

Jury Instructions

Where one of the parties challenges the relevance of expert evidence or the credentials of the expert witness, it is the trial judge who declares the evidence to be admissible or inadmissible. A challenge of this kind is usually made before or shortly after the witness takes the stand and the judge's determination is based on arguments and evidence submitted on a *voir dire,* outside the presence of the jury. During the course of the expert's testimony and throughout the remainder of the trial, the judge plays an important role as an intermediary between the expert witnesses and the jury. This role is exercised through the judge's supervision of the examination of the witnesses and, at the close of the trial, through his summary of the evidence in his instructions to the jury. In extreme instances, the judge's intervention may rise to the level of striking erroneous or misleading expert evidence from the record. The importance of the function lies in the ability of the judge to locate the expert evidence within the context of the overall trial and to enhance the jury's understanding of their function in interpreting and weighing that evidence. In relation to expert DNA evidence, the intermediary function can place the judge on a tightrope which he must tread with extreme care if he is to avoid the opposite perils of too much and too little intervention. In this area, as in other notable evidentiary contexts, the judge's summing up can be a particularly fertile ground for appellate challenge.

(discussed in the LRC Consultation Paper, *op. cit.*, p.240) in which a failure to take account of the effects of relatedness on a DNA match calculation was one of the grounds on which the trial judge withdrew the case from the jury.

[148] Evett *et al., op. cit.*, p.351.

Part of the conundrum presented by cases like *Deen* and *Doheny* is the potentially compounding effect that the judge's summing up can have on errors contained in the expert's testimony. Clearly, the judge must take care when summarising the expert's evidence not to mislead the jury but, as the Court of Appeal observed in *Doheny*, he must also strive "to dispel any obfuscation that may have been engendered in relation to areas of expert evidence where no real issue exists."[149] The Court emphasised that the judge should explain to the jury the relevance of the match probability and its relationship to the other evidence in the case. With regard to the match probability, the Court of Appeal approved the following direction:

> "Members of the Jury, if you accept the scientific evidence called by the Crown, this indicates that there are probably only four or five white males in the United Kingdom from whom that semen stain could have come. The Defendant is one of them. If that is the position, the decision you have to reach, on all the evidence, is whether you are sure that it was the Defendant who left that stain or whether it is possible that it was one of that other small group of men who share the same DNA characteristics."[150]

This direction has the merit of explaining the jury's task in a clear and simple manner. It describes the match probability in terms that avoid the prosecutor's fallacy and it draws the jury's attention to the existence of persons other than the accused whose DNA matches the crime scene profile. A further merit is the specific reference to the significance of the other evidence in the case although the direction does not go so far as to "bring out the relationship between any exculpatory evidence and the probability of someone else sharing the crime scene profile."[151] The simplicity of this direction is its strength but it also disguises certain weaknesses. As we have seen, the development of more sophisticated DNA profiling techniques has resulted in increasingly small match

---

[149] [1997] 1 Cr. App. R. at 375.

[150] *Id.*

[151] Redmayne, (1997) 1 E & P at p.211 (arguing that "[o]nly an explicitly Bayesian presentation seems to be able to bring out this relationship adequately").

probabilities and in some instances these probabilities outstrip the general population.[152]

A second example of a complexity not captured by the *Doheny* direction is the issue of relatedness: some of the defendant's relatives will be more likely to match the crime scene profile than a randomly selected member of the population. This issue was crucial to the Court of Criminal Appeal's decision to set aside the conviction in *People (DPP.) v. Allen.*[153]

The adequacy of the trial judge's charge to the jury in relation to DNA evidence was one of the grounds on which the applicant sought leave to appeal against his conviction for murder in the recent case of *People (DPP) v. Costigan.*[154] The victim had been stabbed approximately 35 times and a number of blood spatters had been found during the course of a forensic examination of the crime scene. Before the Court of Criminal Appeal, the applicant argued that the trial judge ought to have discharged the jury consequent upon his stating in his charge to the jury that the applicant's blood had been found on certain items at the crime scene. Instead, the trial judge had recharged the jury along the following lines:

> "I said, of course, in my charge that you must take no notice of anything I say about the facts. And I repeat that. But nevertheless I did, I did say during my charge, I made reference to the blood of Mark Costigan being on the duvet. Now I oughtn't to have put it like that because that indicates that I am of the view that it is Mark Costigan's blood, do you understand? And what I should have said was that it was blood with a DNA profile which matches the DNA of the blood sample taken from Mark Costigan. Because it's a matter entirely for you to decide on the basis of Mr. Burrington's evidence whether it is a match for the blood of Mark Costigan. So any suggestion from the way I put it that I had a view or I was entering into your territory, you must completely ignore.

---

[152] *Id.*; Evett *et al., loc. cit.*
[153] [2003] 4 I.R. 295.
[154] Unreported, Court of Criminal Appeal, Apr. 28, 2006.

> Because I don't have a view and it's a matter I can't have a view and that's a matter for yourselves."[155]

The Court of Criminal Appeal concluded that the concerns raised by defence counsel as to the original charge had been "very fully dealt with" by the judge and that the recharge itself had been "sufficiently clear." In holding that there was no error in the judge's failure to discharge the jury, the court observed that the applicant's concerns were capable of being remedied and had been so remedied in the circumstances.[156]

The result in *Costigan* aside, the case law suggests that the use of DNA evidence in a manner that respects the accused's right to a fair trial hinges to a considerable extent on the instructions which the judge delivers to the jury. The judge's summation of the evidence should be clear and comprehensible, providing the jury with a contextual explanation of the evidence, and curing rather than compounding any confusion that may have been sown during the examination of the expert witness. Above all, the jury weighing DNA evidence should be guided as to "the use that can and should be made of seemingly conclusive and unanswerable evidence."[157]

Additional Safeguards

The complexities involved in the use of scientific evidence in court and some proposed solutions were examined in chapters 1 and 2. Much of that general discussion spills over into the specific arena of DNA evidence. For example, whether the admissibility of DNA evidence should turn on the reliability of a particular DNA profiling technique or whether courts would benefit from the use of independent, court-appointed DNA experts are as much open to debate in this as in any other scientific field. DNA evidence nevertheless raises its own unique set of concerns which warrant individual consideration and particularised solutions. Some of these issues

---

[155] *Id.* at 13. A second related challenge was based on other aspects of the judge's charge and recharge concerning inferences that might be drawn from blood found on a soccer jersey.

[156] *Id.* at 14-15. *See also People (DPP) v. Murphy*, unreported, Court of Criminal Appeal, March 13, 2006).

[157] Goode, *op. cit.*, p.55.

have been discussed above but certain others should be mentioned in closing.

(a) Evidentiary hearings

The complexity of DNA evidence and the many potential traps into which experts, lawyers and judges may fall underscore the wisdom of convening special evidentiary hearings, outside the presence of the jury, either in advance of trial or immediately before the presentation of the evidence. The principal justification is the heightened potential for error in the gathering, processing and presentation of DNA evidence; a pre-trial hearing provides the court with an opportunity to examine the reliability of the evidence before admitting it. Where the evidence is subsequently admitted, the value of the hearing lies in narrowing issues of contention, reducing the potential for error, and enhancing the ultimate presentation of the evidence to the jury. This approach has found favour in other jurisdictions such as the United Kingdom,[158] the United States,[159] and Australia.[160]

The Irish courts lack a tradition of pre-trial procedure and operate on the general principle that the resolution of issues relating to the evidence or other aspects of the proceedings may be adequately dealt with during the course of the trial itself. Problems in relation to the evidence, for example, are generally dealt with *ad hoc* during the examination of witnesses or, if the need arises, by way of a *voir dire* or "trial within a trial" outside the presence of the jury.[161] In criminal proceedings, the constitutional imperative of a trial in due course of law[162] coupled with the increasing complexity and cost of litigation have cast doubt on the wisdom of this approach. There is growing support for the use of a *pre-trial* mechanism as a more effective means of resolving admissibility issues that are disposable in advance of trial.[163]

---

[158] *See e.g. R v. Doheny and Adams* [1997] 1 Cr. App. R. 369; Evett *et al., op. cit.*, p.354.

[159] Federal Rule of Evidence 702; *People v. Castro*, (1989) 545 NYS2d 985.

[160] *R v. Tran* (1990) 50 A Crim R 233. *See* Goode, *loc. cit.*

[161] *State v. Treanor* [1924] I.R. 193; *People (DPP.) v. Conroy* [1986] I.R. 460.

[162] Art.38.1 of the Constitution; art.6 of the European Convention on Human Rights.

[163] *See e.g.* Working Group on the Jurisdiction of the Courts, *The Criminal Jurisdiction of the Courts* (Courts Service, 2003), para.774.

The Law Reform Commission has added its voice to the debate by recommending the availability of a pre-trial mechanism in cases involving DNA evidence. Specifically, the Commission recommends that "if an issue as to the admissibility of DNA evidence is likely to arise or arises in a case, then consideration should be given to dealing with such an issue at a preliminary hearing or at an early hearing if this is just and convenient in the particular circumstances."[164] To this is added the suggestion that a written record of such a hearing be created and published so as to assist future judges in dealing with similar evidentiary difficulties.[165] Steps should be taken to implement these recommendations and introduce some form of pre-trial arrangement that would bring Ireland into line with international practice.

The Commission envisages that use of such a pre-trial mechanism would be entirely at the trial judge's discretion; clearly some evidentiary issues may surface only in the *denouement* of the trial but the Commission would also permit the judge to reserve for determination at trial even those issues that had been flagged in advance. This approach is less progressive than the trend in some other jurisdictions in favour of convening pre-trial hearings as a matter of routine practice.[166] It is, nevertheless, a step in the direction of American practice where the Federal Rules of Evidence require federal trial judges to assess the reliability of DNA evidence as a precondition to its admissibility, a task not infrequently conducted with the benefit of a pre-trial hearing.[167]

In Ireland, the admissibility of DNA evidence is not generally contingent on a demonstration by the party proffering the evidence of its reliability but, over time, heightened recourse to pre-trial hearings may render it increasingly so. Thus, it is interesting to speculate that this relatively discrete and beneficial development in practice may also presage an emergent doctrinal shift toward a more rigorous regime for the admissibility of this form of scientific evidence.[168]

---

[164] LRC Report, *op. cit.*, para.5.24. *See also* LRC Consultation Paper, *op. cit.*, pp.237-39.

[165] LRC Report, *op. cit.*, para.5.24.

[166] House of Commons Science and Technology Committee, *Forensic Science on Trial* (7th Rep. 2004-05), p.68.

[167] Federal Rule of Evidence 702.

[168] *See generally supra* chaps.1 and 2.

(b) Corroboration

In most cases, DNA profiling is just one of several items of evidence presented at trial. As the present discussion has sought to demonstrate, a crucial yet elusive aspect of DNA evidence is its relationship with that other evidence. A separate concern is whether the prosecution should be able to secure a criminal conviction on DNA evidence standing alone. Historically, the law singled out certain kinds of evidence as inherently suspect or problematic and required such evidence to be corroborated by some form of independent proof.[169] Strict corroboration requirements of this kind later gave way to the more flexible mechanism of corroboration warnings which are delivered by the trial judge to the jury on summing up. These warnings, which may be mandatory[170] or discretionary,[171] apply to specific, limited categories of evidence. In essence, they either oblige or permit the trial judge to draw the jury's attention as to the absence of corroboration in the case, to advise the jury that they may nevertheless convict if satisfied of the accused's guilt beyond a reasonable doubt, and to caution them about known risks of so doing.

The Irish courts have not squarely addressed the issue whether DNA evidence is sufficient to support a conviction standing alone. It surfaced before the Central Criminal Court in *People (DPP.) v. Howe*[172] when the prosecution rested its case solely on DNA analysis conducted on a bloodstain found on a piece of glass at the crime scene. Butler J. withdrew

---

[169] The last vestiges of the requirement of corroboration *per se* are found in a small but eclectic range of offences. These offences include treason, procuration of girls, and perjury. *See generally R v. Baskerville* [1916] 2 K.B. 658; *DPP. v. Hester* [1973] A.C. 296.

[170] In the case of accomplice evidence (*see e.g. People (AG) v. Carney* [1955] I.R. 324; *People (DPP.) v. Gilligan,* unreported, Court of Criminal Appeal, August 8, 2003), confession evidence (*see* s.10(1) of the Criminal Procedure Act 1993; *People (DPP.) v. Connolly* [2003] 2 I.R. 1), and identification evidence (*see e.g. People (AG) v. Casey (No.2)* [1963] I.R. 33; *People (DPP.) v. Christo*, unreported, Court of Criminal Appeal, January 31, 2005).

[171] In relation to the testimony of complainants in proceedings for sexual offences (*see* s.7(1) of the Criminal Law (Rape) (Amendment) Act 1990; *People (DPP.) v. J.E.M.* [2001] 4 I.R. 385; *People (DPP.) v. Gentleman* [2003] 4 I.R. 22) and the testimony of children (*see* s.28(1) of the Criminal Evidence Act 1992).

[172] Central Criminal Court, October 15, 2003; *Irish Times,* October 15, 2003. The case is discussed in the LRC Consultation Paper, *op. cit.*, pp.240-41.

the case from the jury because he concluded that the DNA evidence was flawed[173] but he left open the general question of the sufficiency of DNA evidence. More recently, the issue was raised before the Court of Criminal Appeal in *People (DPP) v. Boyce.*[174] In seeking leave to appeal against his conviction for sexual offences, the applicant contended that the prosecution's case rested solely on DNA evidence which was necessarily insufficient to support a conviction. The court did not reach a conclusion on the sufficiency of DNA evidence as a matter of principle because it was satisfied that the DNA evidence was not the only evidence which fell to be considered by the jury in this case.[175]

The English courts have approached the issue on a case-by-case basis. For example, in *R v. Watters*,[176] the Court of Appeal held that DNA evidence alone was insufficient to support the challenged conviction but emphasised that its determination was fact-specific. It reached the same conclusion in *R v. Lashley* and, while careful not to rule out the possibility, it emphasised "the difficulty in this particular case of relying on the DNA evidence alone in circumstances where there was absolutely no other evidence to set alongside it."[177] The ambivalence of the Court of Appeal and the cautious tenor of these cases imply that the possibility of the prosecution relying exclusively on DNA evidence may be more theoretical than real. Nevertheless, the decision to avoid a bright-line rule accords with the general trend away from the strait jacket of corroboration requirements.

Similarly, here in Ireland, it would seem counterintuitive for the Oireachtas or the courts to stipulate that DNA evidence must always be corroborated at a time when the law has shaken off all but the last vestiges of this approach to suspect evidence. There are arguably more effective

---

[173] Specifically, the judge concluded that the forensic scientist was not qualified as an expert in statistics and that the prosecution had not disproved the possibility that the accused had a brother who could have had similar DNA.

[174] Unreported, Court of Criminal Appeal, December 21, 2005.

[175] *Id.* at 28.

[176] Court of Appeal, unreported, October 19, 2000.

[177] Court of Appeal, unreported, February 8, 2000. *See also R v. Smith,* Court of Appeal, unreported, February 8, 2000, in which an appeal on similar grounds was dismissed . In addition to the DNA evidence, the jury had been presented with the appellant's own testimony and with evidence that the appellant had been arrested in the locality.

ways of dealing with those rare instances in which the prosecution advances DNA profiling as the sole basis on which to prove its case. The nub of the issue is whether DNA evidence should join the ranks of seemingly inherently suspect evidence which attract mandatory or discretionary corroboration warnings.

In its Consultation Paper on the *Establishment of a DNA Database*, the Law Reform Commission recommended the introduction of a mandatory corroboration warning. This would mean that in all cases where the prosecution seeks to rely on DNA evidence alone, the trial judge would be obliged to warn the jury of the dangers of convicting on this evidence in the absence of supporting evidence while, at the same time, reminding them that they are at liberty to do so provided they are satisfied beyond a reasonable doubt of the accused's guilt.[178] However, the Commission subsequently had a partial change of heart and, in its final Report, recommended the introduction of a discretionary corroboration warning on the basis "that a standard warning is unnecessary, that it could unduly fetter the trial judge's discretion and may have the effect of adding further complexity to the case."[179]

This final recommendation is the wiser choice although at the same time not an entirely satisfactory solution. Certainly, it is more in tune with the general trend in the law on corroboration away from mandatory warnings in favour of discretionary warnings. The existence of a discretion would obviate some of the hazards associated with such warnings, including the definition of corroboration and the form of words in which the warning is set. At the same time, experience in other areas, such the evidence of complainants in proceedings for sexual offences, suggests that seemingly discretionary warnings may crystallise into routine practice over time. Given that the presentation of DNA evidence is still an evolving phenomenon in the Irish courts, it seems likely that trial judges, armed with such a discretion, would err on the side of caution and deliver the warning. Before legislating on foot of the Commission's recommendation, the Oireachtas should give careful consideration to the propriety of corroboration warnings in general and their possible application to DNA evidence in particular. Addressing misconceptions about DNA evidence under the rubric of corroboration may not be the most sensible strategy.

---

[178] LRC Consultation Paper, *op. cit.*, p.244.

[179] LRC Report, *op. cit.* , paras. 5.27-28.

Given the particular need for juries to locate DNA evidence in the context of the other evidence at trial (even where that other evidence emanates only from the defence), corroboration warnings may thwart a holistic assessment of the evidence. As the Court of Criminal Appeal observed in *People (D.P.P) v. Boyce*[180] "the extent to which forensic evidence is central or peripheral to the prosecution case will depend upon the facts of each case." Trial judges must necessarily tackle the complexity of DNA evidence in their summing up. Emphasis on the formulation of general standards in jury instruction, sufficiently flexible to be tailored to fit the individual case, might prove a more profitable avenue for future practice.

---

[180] Unreported, Court of Criminal Appeal, December 21, 2005 at 27.

APPENDIX 1

S.I. No. 114/1955: Regulations as to the Measuring and Photographing of Prisoners, 1955

REGULATIONS 3, 4, 5, 8

3. A convicted prisoner may be photographed and measured and his finger and palm prints may be taken at any time during his imprisonment.

4.—(1) Subject to paragraph (3), an untried prisoner shall not, while in prison, be measured or photographed nor shall his finger or palm prints be taken except with the authority of the Minister for Justice or upon the application in writing of a member of the Garda Síochána of not lower rank than Inspector approved by a Justice of the District Court, or, in the Dublin Metropolitan District, by the Commissioner or a Deputy Commissioner of the Garda Síochána.

(2) The application shall set forth that from the character of the offence with which the prisoner is charged or for other specified reasons there are grounds for suspecting that he has been previously convicted or has been engaged in crime or that for other specified reasons the particulars are required for the purposes of justice.

(3) If the prisoner, on being informed of his right to object, does not do so, his height may be measured, and his photograph, finger and palm prints taken, on the application in writing of a member of the Garda Síochána of not lower rank than Inspector.

(4) This regulation is without prejudice to the provisions of any special enactment.

5. Where, in the case of an untried prisoner not previously convicted of any crime, photographs, prints or measurements have been taken under these regulations, all such photographs (both negatives and copies), print impressions and records of measurements so taken shall, upon his discharge or acquittal, be forthwith destroyed or handed over to him.

8. The external filaments of the fingers and thumbs and palms of both hands are to be taken by pressing them first upon an inked plate and then upon paper or cardboard, so as to leave a clear print of the skin surface.

Appendix 2

Criminal Law Act, 1976

Section 7

Power of Garda Síochána in relation to certain arrested persons
7.—(1) Where a person is in custody under the provisions of section 30 of the Act of 1939 or section 2 of the Emergency Powers Act, 1976, a member of the Garda Síochána may do all or any of the following in respect of him:

(*a*) demand of him his name and address;
(*b*) search him or cause him to be searched;
(*c*) photograph him or cause him to be photographed;
(*d*) take, or cause to be taken, his fingerprints and palm prints;
(*e*) make or cause to be made any test designed for the purpose of ascertaining whether he has been in contact with any firearm (within the meaning of the Firearms Acts, 1925 to 1971) or with any explosive substance (within the meaning of the Explosive Substances Act, 1883) and for that purpose take swabs from his skin or samples of his hair;
(*f*) seize and retain for testing anything that he has in his possession.

(2) Any person who obstructs or attempts to obstruct any member of the Garda Síochána or any other person acting under the powers conferred by subsection (1) of this section, or who fails or refuses to give his name and address when demanded, or gives a name or address which is false or misleading, shall be guilty of an offence and shall be liable—

(*a*) on summary conviction, to a fine not exceeding £500 or to imprisonment for a term not exceeding 12 months, or to both, or (*b*) on conviction on indictment, to imprisonment for a term not exceeding 5 years.

APPENDIX 3

Criminal Justice Act, 1984

SECTION 6, 8, 9, 28

Powers of Garda Síochána in relation to detained person.

6.—(1) Where a person is detained pursuant to *section 4*, a member of the Garda Síochána may—

(*a*) demand of him his name and address;
(*b*) search him or cause him to be searched;
(*c*) photograph him or cause him to be photographed;
(*d*) take, or cause to be taken, his fingerprints and palm prints;
(*e*) make or cause to be made any test designed for the purpose of ascertaining whether he has been in contact with any firearm (within the meaning of the Firearms Acts, 1925 to 1971) or with any explosive substance (within the meaning of the Explosive Substances Act, 1883) and for that purpose take swabs from his skin or samples of his hair;
(*f*) seize and retain for testing anything that he has in his possession.

(2) The powers conferred by *subsection (1)(c)* and *(1)(d)* shall not be exercised except on the authority of a member of the Garda Síochána not below the rank of superintendent.

(3) *Subsection (1)(b)* does not empower a member of the Garda Síochána to require a person to remove his underclothing, except where such member, with reasonable cause, suspects that he has concealed on his person a controlled drug (within the meaning of section 2 of the Misuse of Drugs Act, 1977) or an explosive substance and a member of the Garda Síochána not below the rank of superintendent so authorises.

(4) Any person who obstructs or attempts to obstruct any member of

the Garda Síochána or any other person acting under the powers conferred by *subsection (1)* or who fails or refuses to give his name and address when demanded, or gives a name or address which is false or misleading, shall be guilty of an offence and shall be liable on summary conviction to a fine not exceeding £1,000 or to imprisonment for a term not exceeding 12 months or to both.

(5) Section 7 (2) of the Criminal Law Act, 1976, is hereby amended by the substitution in paragraph (*a*), for "£500", of "£1,000" and by the deletion of paragraph (*b*).

Destruction of records

8.—(1) Every photograph (including a negative), fingerprint and palm print of a person taken in pursuance of the powers conferred by *section 6* and every copy and record thereof shall, if not previously destroyed, be destroyed as this section directs.

(2) Where proceedings for an offence to which *section 4* applies are not instituted against the person within the period of six months from the date of the taking of the photograph or print and the failure to institute such proceedings within that period is not due to the fact that he has absconded or cannot be found, the destruction shall be carried out on the expiration of that period.

(3) Where proceedings have been so instituted and the person is acquitted or discharged or the proceedings are discontinued, the destruction shall be carried out on the acquittal, discharge or discontinuance.

(4) (*a*) Where a person is the subject of an order under subsection (1) or (2) of section 1 of the Probation of Offenders Act, 1907, the destruction shall be carried out at the expiration of three years from the making of the order provided that he has not been charged with an offence during that period.

(*b*) *Paragraph (a)* shall not apply to an order under section 1 (2) of that Act discharged on the appeal of a person against conviction if on appeal his conviction is affirmed.

(5) The person concerned, his solicitor or some other person authorised

by him in writing to act on his behalf shall be entitled, on request, to witness the destruction.

(6) Where civil proceedings are instituted before a particular photograph or print is required to be destroyed under this section and a party to the proceedings serves notice on the Commissioner of the Garda Síochána that it may be required in connection with the proceedings, then, notwithstanding anything in this section, the photograph or print shall be preserved until six months from the conclusion of the proceedings or until the conclusion of any proceedings on appeal, whichever is the later.

(7) Notwithstanding anything in the foregoing provisions of this section, a justice of the District Court may, on the application of the Director of Public Prosecutions, authorise the preservation of a photograph or print for a period not exceeding six months on being satisfied that it may be required for the purpose of further proceedings in relation to the offence.

Application to persons in custody under section 30 of Offences against the State Act, 1939

9.—*Sections 4 (8)*, *5*, *6 (2)* and *6 (3)* shall apply, with the necessary modifications, in relation to persons in custody under section 30 of the Act of 1939 and to the powers conferred by section 7 of the Criminal Law Act, 1976, as they apply to persons detained pursuant to *section 4* of this Act.

Taking of fingerprints of person dealt with under Probation of Offenders Act, 1907, or convicted.

28.—(1) Where a person, on being prosecuted for an indictable offence, is the subject of an order under subsection (1) or (2) of section 1 of the Probation of Offenders Act, 1907, or is convicted and otherwise dealt with, his fingerprints may be taken by a member of the Garda Síochána either within the precincts of the court or at any other convenient place.

(2) The power to take a person's fingerprints pursuant to this section shall cease on the expiration of one week beginning on the date on which

he is dealt with under the Probation of Offenders Act, 1907, or convicted, unless he has made it impracticable for his fingerprints to be taken pursuant to this section in that period.

(3) The provisions of *section 8* shall apply to the fingerprints taken pursuant to this section of a person who is the subject of an order under subsection (1) or (2) of section 1 of the Probation of Offenders Act, 1907, as they apply to fingerprints taken in pursuance of the powers conferred by *section 6*.

(4) Any person who refuses to allow his fingerprints to be taken pursuant to this section shall be guilty of an offence and shall be liable on summary conviction to a fine not exceeding £1,000 or to imprisonment for a term not exceeding twelve months or to both.

APPENDIX 4

S.I. No. 119/1987: Criminal Justice Act, 1984 (Treatment of Persons in Custody in Garda Síochána Stations) Regulations, 1987

REGULATIONS 3 AND 18

General

3. (1) In carrying out their functions under these Regulations members shall act with due respect for the personal rights of persons in custody and their dignity as human persons, and shall have regard for the special needs of any of them who may be under a physical or mental disability, while complying with the obligation to prevent escapes from custody and continuing to act with diligence and determination in the investigation of crime and the protection and vindication of the personal rights of other persons.

(2) There shall be no unnecessary delay in dealing with persons in custody

Fingerprints, etc.

18.(1)(*a*) Fingerprints, palm prints or photographs shall not be taken of, or swabs or samples taken from, a person in custody (otherwise than pursuant to a power conferred on a member by law) except with his written consent and, where he is under the age of seventeen years, the written consent of an appropriate adult.

(*b*) A consent shall be signed and be recorded in the custody record or a separate document.

(2) The fact that fingerprints, palm prints, photographs, swabs or samples have been taken of or from a person in custody shall be recorded.

(3) Where the authority of a member of the Garda Síochána of a specified rank is required for the taking of fingerprints, palm prints or photographs of a person in custody, the name and rank of the member giving the authority shall be recorded.

APPENDIX 5

Criminal Justice (Forensic Evidence) Act, 1990

ARRANGEMENT OF SECTIONS

ACTS REFERRED TO

Criminal Justice Act, 1960	1960, No. 27
Criminal Justice Act, 1984	1984, No. 22
Criminal Law Act, 1976	1976, No. 32
Dentists Act, 1985	1985, No. 9
Medical Practitioners Act, 1978	1978, No. 4
Offences against the State Act, 1939	1939, No. 13
Prisons Acts, 1826 to 1980	
Probation of Offenders Act, 1907	1907, c. 17

AN ACT TO AMEND AND EXTEND THE LAW TO AUTHORISE THE TAKING OF BODILY SAMPLES FOR FORENSIC TESTING FROM PERSONS SUSPECTED OF CERTAIN CRIMINAL OFFENCES. [24*th December*, 1990]

BE IT ENACTED BY THE OIREACHTAS AS FOLLOWS:

Interpretation.

1.—In this Act

"appropriate consent" has the meaning assigned to it by *section 2 (10)* of this Act;

"the Minister" means the Minister for Justice;

"prescribed" means prescribed by regulations made by the Minister under *section 5* of this Act;

"prison" means any place for which rules or regulations may be made under the Prisons Acts, 1826 to 1980, or *section 13* of the Criminal Justice Act, 1960;

"registered dentist" means a person whose name is entered for the time being on the Register of Dentists maintained under the Dentists Act, 1985;

"registered medical practitioner" has the meaning assigned to it by section 2 of the Medical Practitioners Act, 1978;

"samples" means the samples or other things referred to in *section 2 (1) (a)* to *(e)* of this Act.

Power to take bodily samples.

2.—(1) Subject to the provisions of *subsections (4)* to *(8)* of this section, where a person is in custody under the provisions of section 30 of the Offences against the State Act, 1939, or section 4 of the Criminal Justice Act, 1984, a member of the Garda Síochána may take, or cause to be taken, from that person for the purpose of forensic testing all or any of the following samples, namely—

(*a*) a sample of—
- (i) blood,
- (ii) pubic hair,
- (iii) urine,

(iv) saliva,
(v) hair other than pubic hair,
(vi) a nail,
(vii) any material found under a nail,

(*b*) a swab from any part of the body other than a body orifice or a genital region,
(*c*) a swab from a body orifice or a genital region,
(*d*) a dental impression,
(*e*) a footprint or similar impression of any part of the person's body other than a part of his hand or mouth.

(2) Subject to the provisions of *subsections (3)* to *(8)* of this section, where a person is in prison, a member of the Garda Síochána may take, or cause to be taken, from that person for the purpose of forensic testing all or any of the samples specified in subsection (1) of this section.

(3) The power conferred by *subsection (2)* of this section shall only be exercisable—

(*a*) where the sample to be taken is required in connection with an offence other than the offence in respect of which the person is in prison or an offence of which he could be convicted on an indictment alleging that offence, and
(*b*) where the sample to be taken is required in connection with an investigation in respect of the commission of an offence under the Offences against the State Act, 1939, or an offence which is for the time being a scheduled offence for the purposes of Part V of that Act or an offence to which section 4 of the Criminal Justice Act, 1984, applies.

(4) A sample may be taken under this section only if—

(*a*) a member of the Garda Síochána not below the rank of superintendent authorises it to be taken, and
(*b*) in the case of a sample mentioned in *subparagraph (i), (ii), (iii)* or *(iv)* of *paragraph (a)* of *subsection (1)* of this section, or in *paragraph (c)* or (*d*) of the said subsection *(1)*, the appropriate consent has been given in writing.

(5) An authorisation to take a sample under this section shall not be given unless the member of the Garda Síochána giving it has reasonable grounds—

(*a*) for suspecting the involvement of the person from whom the sample is to be taken—
   (i) in a case where the person is in custody, in the offence in respect of which he is in custody, or
   (ii) in a case where the person is in prison, in the commission of an offence under the Offences against the State Act, 1939, or an offence which is for the time being a scheduled offence for the purposes of Part V of that Act or an offence to which section 4 of the Criminal Justice Act, 1984, applies,

and

(*b*) for believing that the sample will tend to confirm or disprove the involvement of the person from whom the sample is to be taken in the said offence.

(6) Before a member of the Garda Síochána takes, or causes to be taken, a sample under *subsection (1)* of this section, or seeks the consent of the person from whom the sample is required to the taking of such a sample, the member shall inform the person—

(*a*) of the nature of the offence in which it is suspected that that person has been involved,
(*b*) that an authorisation has been given under *subsection (4) (a)* of this section and of the grounds on which it has been given, and
(*c*) that the results of any tests on the sample may be given in evidence in any proceedings.

(7) An authorisation under *subsection (4) (a)* of this section may be given orally but, if it is given orally, it shall be confirmed in writing as soon as is practicable.

(8) A sample of a kind specified in *subparagraph (i)* or *(ii)* of paragraph (a) of *subsection (1)* of this section or in *paragraph (c)* of the said *subsection (1)* may be taken only by a registered medical practitioner

and a dental impression may be taken only by a registered dentist or a registered medical practitioner.

(9) A person who obstructs or attempts to obstruct any member of the Garda Síochána or any other person acting under the powers conferred by *subsection (1)* of this section shall be guilty of an offence and shall be liable on summary conviction to a fine not exceeding £1,000 or to imprisonment for a term not exceeding 12 months or to both.

(10) In this Act "appropriate consent" means—

(*a*) in the case of a person who has attained the age of 17 years, the consent of that person,

(*b*) in the case of a person who has not attained the age of 17 years but has attained the age of 14 years, the consent of that person and of a parent or guardian of that person, and

(*c*) in the case of a person who has not attained the age of 14 years, the consent of a parent or guardian of that person.

(11) The powers conferred by this section are without prejudice to any other powers exercisable by a member of the Garda Síochána.

Inferences from refusal to consent to taking a sample.

3.—(1) Where a consent required under *section 2* of this Act is refused without good cause, in any proceedings against a person for an offence—

(*a*) the court, in determining—

(i) whether to send forward that person for trial, or

(ii) whether there is a case to answer, and

(*b*) the court (or, subject to the judge's directions, the jury), in determining whether that person is guilty of the offence charged (or of any other offence of which he could lawfully be convicted on that charge),

may draw such inferences, if any, from the refusal as appear proper; and the refusal may, on the basis of such inferences, be treated as, or as being capable of amounting to, corroboration of any evidence in relation to which the refusal is material, but a person shall not be convicted of an offence solely on an inference drawn from such refusal.

(2) The reference in *subsection (1)* of this section to evidence shall, in relation to the preliminary examination of a charge, be taken to include a statement of the evidence to be given by a witness at the trial.

(3) *Subsection (1)* of this section shall not have effect in relation to an accused unless he has been told in ordinary language by a member of the Garda Síochána when seeking his consent that the sample was required for the purpose of forensic testing, that his consent was necessary and, if his consent was not given, what the effect of a refusal by him of such consent could be.

(4) This section shall not apply—

(*a*) to a person who has not attained the age of 14 years, or

(*b*) in a case where an appropriate consent has been refused by a parent or guardian.

Destruction of records and samples.

4.—(1) Subject to *subsection(5)* of this section, every record identifying the person from whom a sample has been taken pursuant to *section 2* of this Act shall, if not previously destroyed, be destroyed as this section directs and every sample identified by such record shall be destroyed in like manner.

(2) Where proceedings for any offence in respect of which a person could be detained under section 30 of the Offences against the State Act, 1939, or section 4 of the Criminal Justice Act, 1984, are not instituted against the person from whom the sample was taken within six months from the taking of the sample and the failure to institute the proceedings within that period is not due to the fact that he has absconded or cannot be found, the destruction of the record and the sample identified by such record shall be carried out on the expiration of that period unless an order has been made under *subsection (5)* of this section.

(3) Where proceedings have been so instituted and the person is acquitted or discharged or the proceedings are discontinued, the destruction of the record and the sample identified by such record shall be carried out on the expiration of twenty-one days after the acquittal, discharge or discontinuance unless an order has been made under *subsection (5)* of this section.

(4)(*a*) Where a person from whom a sample has been taken is the subject of an order under subsection (1) or (2) of section 1 of the Probation of Offenders Act, 1907, the destruction of the said sample and every record identifying such sample shall be carried out on the expiration of 3 years from the making of the order; provided that he has not been convicted of an offence to which section 4 of the Criminal Justice Act, 1984, applies during that period.

(*b*) *Paragraph (a)* of this subsection shall not apply to an order under section 1 (2) of the Probation of Offenders Act, 1907, discharged on the appeal of a person against conviction if on appeal his conviction is affirmed.

(5) If a court is satisfied, on an application being made to it by or on behalf of the Director of Public Prosecutions or the person from whom the sample was taken, that there is good reason why records and samples to which this section applies should not be destroyed under this section, it may make an order authorising the retention of such records and samples for such purpose or period as it may direct.

Regulations regarding taking of samples.

5.—(1) The Minister shall make regulations relating to the taking of samples for the purposes of this Act.

(2) Without prejudice to the generality of *subsection (1)* of this section, the regulations shall—

(*a*) make provision for the recording in the records of a Garda Síochána station of—

(i) an authorisation to take a sample given under *section 2 (4) (a)* of this Act and any consent given under *section 2 (4) (b)* of this Act,

(ii) a refusal to consent to the taking of a sample in cases where consent is to be given under *section 2 (4) (b)* of this Act,

(iii) particulars of the time and manner of the taking of a sample pursuant to this Act, and (*b*) make provision for the taking of samples from persons who have not attained the age of 17 years.

(3) Every regulation made under this section shall be laid before each House of the Oireachtas as soon as may be after it is made and, if a resolution annulling the regulation is passed by either such House within the next twenty-one days on which that House has sat after the regulation has been laid before it, the regulation shall be annulled accordingly, but without prejudice to the validity of anything previously done thereunder.

Repeals.

6.—Section 7 (1)*(e)* of the Criminal Law Act, 1976, and section 6 (1) *(e)* of the Criminal Justice Act, 1984, are hereby repealed.

Expenses.

7.—The expenses incurred by the Minister in the administration of this Act shall, to such extent as may be sanctioned by the Minister for Finance, be paid out of moneys provided by the Oireachtas.

Short title and commencement.

8.—(1) This Act may be cited as the Criminal Justice (Forensic Evidence) Act, 1990.

(2) This Act shall come into operation on such day as may be fixed therefor by order of the Minister.

APPENDIX 6

S.I. No. 130/1992: Criminal Justice (Forensic Evidence) Act, 1990 Regulations, 1992

I, PÁDRAIG FLYNN, Minister for Justice, in exercise of the powers conferred on me by section 5 of the Criminal Justice (Forensic Evidence) Act, 1990 (No. 34 of 1990), hereby make the following Regulations:

Citation and commencement.

1. (1) These Regulations may be cited as the Criminal Justice (Forensic Evidence) Act, 1990, Regulations, 1992.

(2) These Regulations shall come into operation on the 5th day of June, 1992.

Interpretation.

2. (1) In these Regulations:—

"the Act of 1990" means the Criminal Justice (Forensic Evidence) Act, 1990 (No. 34 of 1990);

"custody record" means a record kept under Regulation 6 of the Criminal Justice Act, 1984 (Treatment of Persons in Custody in Garda Síochána Stations) Regulations, 1987 (S.I. No. 119 of 1987);

"member" means a member of the Garda Síochána;

"member in charge" has the same meaning as in Regulation 4 (1) of the Criminal Justice Act, 1984 (Treatment of Persons in Custody in Garda Síochána Stations) Regulations, 1987;

"prison record" means a record kept in a prison in respect of a person in custody in that prison;

"station" means a Garda Síochána station.

(2) In these Regulations a reference to a person signing a document shall include, in the case of a person unable to write, a reference to the person making his mark.

General.

3. In carrying out their functions under these Regulations members or other persons concerned shall act with due respect for the personal rights of persons in custody and their dignity as human persons, and shall have regard for the special needs of any of them who have not attained the age of 17 years or who may be under a physical or mental disability.

Record of authorisation for taking of sample.

4. Where an authorisation is given under section 2 (4) (*a*) of the Act of 1990 for the taking of a sample from a person, the member in charge shall as soon as practicable make or cause to be made an entry in the custody record or prison record, as the case may be, relating to that person of the giving of the authorisation, of the name and rank of the member who gave it and of the date and time when it was given, and the entry shall be signed by the person making it.

Record of information given under s. 2(6) of Act of 1990.

5. Where a member gives to a person from whom it is proposed that a sample should be taken the information which he is required by section 2 (6) of the Act of 1990 to give to that a person, the member in charge shall as soon as practicable make or cause to be made in the custody record or prison record, as the case may be, relating to that person an entry recording the giving of the information, together with the name and rank of the member who gave it and the date and time when it was given, and the entry shall be signed by the person making it.

Record of consent or refusal of consent to taking of sample.

6. Where a person whose consent to the taking of a sample is required by section 2 (4) (b) of the Act of 1990 gives or refuses his consent, the member in charge shall as soon as practicable make or cause to be made in the custody record or prison record, as the case may be, relating to the person from whom the sample is proposed to be taken an entry recording the giving or refusal of the consent, together with the date and time of the giving or refusal, and where consent is given the document containing it shall be attached to the custody record or prison record.

Record of sample taken.

7. The member in charge shall as soon as practicable enter the following particulars, or cause them to be entered in the custody record or prison record, as the case may be, of the person concerned—

(i) the name of the person from whom the sample was taken;
(ii) the offence in respect of which the sample was taken;
(iii) the nature of the sample;
(iv) the name of the person who took the sample;
(v) the date and time the sample was taken and the manner in which it was taken;

and the entry shall be signed by the person making it.

Taking of sample from persons under 17 years of age.

8. A sample shall not be taken from a person who has not attained the age of seventeen years, nor shall the consent of such a person to the taking of a sample be sought, except in the presence of a parent or guardian of that person.

Forms.

9. (1) The forms in the Appendices to these Regulations, or forms to the like effect shall be used for the purpose of providing a record of the matters stated in the forms.

(2) When each form is signed it shall as soon as practicable be attached to the custody record or prison record relating to the person concerned.

Appendix A. Criminal Justice (Forensic Evidence) Act, 1990.

SECTION 2 (4)(*b*) AND (10)(*a*).
Consent by person aged 17 years or over to taking of sample from him.

1. I..
of ....
being aged 17 years or over have been informed:

(*a*) of the nature of the offence in which it is suspected I have been involved,
(*b*) that an authorisation has been given under section 2(4)(*a*) of the Criminal Justice (Forensic Evidence) Act, 1990, for the taking of a sample from me for the purpose of forensic testing of the sample, the sample being one or more of the following samples, namely—
  (I) a sample of
    (i) blood []
    (ii) pubic hair[]
    (iii) urine[]
    (iv) saliva[]
  (II) a swab from a body orifice mentioned in box opposite[]

Tick box as appropriate.

  (III) a swab from a genital region mentioned in box opposite[]
  (IV) a dental impression[]
(*c*) that my consent is necessary for the taking of the sample;
(*d*) that the results of any tests on the sample may be given in evidence in any proceedings against me for an offence;
(*e*) that, if I refuse without good cause to consent to the taking of the sample, then in any proceedings against me for an offence evidence of the refusal may be given and may result in inferences being drawn against me and that the

refusal may be treated as, or as capable of amounting to, corroboration of any evidence in relation to which the refusal is material, but that I shall not be able to be convicted of an offence solely on an inference drawn from the refusal.

2. I hereby consent to the taking of the sample.
Signed: ....
Date: ....

APPENDIX B. CRIMINAL JUSTICE (FORENSIC EVIDENCE) ACT, 1990.

SECTION 2 (4) (*b*) AND (10) (*b*).
Consent by person aged 14, 15 or 16 years, and consent of his parent or guardian, to taking of sample from him.

A.1. I ....
of..
who was born on ....
have been informed:

(*a*) of the nature of the offence in which it is suspected I have been involved,
(*b*) that an authorisation has been given under section 2(4)(*a*) of the Criminal Justice (Forensic Evidence) Act, 1990, for the taking of a sample from me for the purpose of forensic testing of the sample, the sample being one or more of the following samples, namely—
 (I) a sample of
  (i) blood []
  (ii) pubic hair[]
  (iii) urine[]
  (iv) saliva[]
 (II) a swab from a body orifice mentioned in box opposite[]

Tick box as appropriate.

 (III) a swab from a genital region mentioned in box

opposite[]

(IV) a dental impression[]

(*c*) that my consent and the consent of my parent or guardian is necessary for the taking of the sample;

(*d*) that the results of any tests may be given in evidence in any proceedings against me for an offence;

(*e*) that, if I refuse without good cause to consent to the taking of the sample, then (unless my parent or guardian also refuses to consent) in any proceedings against me for an offence, evidence of my refusal may be given and may result in inferences being drawn against me and that my refusal may be treated as, or as capable of amounting to, corroboration of any evidence in relation to which my refusal is material, but that I shall not be able to be convicted of an offence solely on an inference drawn from my refusal.

2. I hereby consent to the taking of the sample.

Signed: ....

Date: ....

B. I ....

of..

a parent/guardian of ....

....

have been informed of the matters stated in paragraph 1 above and I hereby consent to the taking of the sample from him.

Signed:

....

Date:

....

APPENDIX C. CRIMINAL JUSTICE (FORENSIC EVIDENCE) ACT, 1990.

SECTION 2 (4)(*b*) AND (10)(*c*).

Consent of parent or guardian of person aged less than 14 years to taking of sample from him.

1. I ....
of ....
a parent/guardian of ....
of ....
who was born on ....
have been informed:

(*a*) of the nature of the offence in which it is suspected that he has been involved,

(*b*) that an authorisation has been given under section 2(4)(a) of the Criminal Justice (Forensic Evidence) Act, 1990, for the taking of a sample from him for the purpose of forensic testing of the sample, the sample being one or more of the following samples, namely—

(I) a sample of

(i) blood []

(ii) pubic hair[]

(iii) urine[]

(iv) saliva[]

(II) a swab from a body orifice mentioned in box opposite[]

Tick box as appropriate.

(III) a swab from a genital region[]

(IV) a dental impression[]

(*c*) that the consent of a parent or guardian of .... is necessary for the taking of the sample;

(*d*) that the results of any tests on the sample may be given in evidence in any proceedings against .... for an offence.

2. I hereby consent to the taking of the sample.
Signed: ....
Date: ....

APPENDIX D. CRIMINAL JUSTICE (FORENSIC EVIDENCE) ACT, 1990.

REGULATIONS, 1992.

Form to be completed by member or other person who took the sample under section 2 of the Act of 1990.

1. Name and address of the person from whom the sample to which this form relates was taken:
....
....
....
2. Nature of sample:
....
3. Garda station or prison at which sample was taken:
....
....
4. Date on and time at which sample was taken:
....
5. Manner in which sample was taken:
....
....

I, the undersigned, took from the person named at 1. above the sample referred to at 2. above.
Signature of member or other person concerned.
....
Date: ....

GIVEN under my Official Seal, this 29th day of May, 1992.
PÁDRAIG FLYNN,
Minister for Justice.

EXPLANATORY NOTE.

These regulations specify the procedures to be followed by the Garda Síochána relating to the taking of samples for forensic testing under the Criminal Justice (Forensic Evidencc) Act, 1990.

APPENDIX 7

Criminal Justice (Drug Trafficking) Act, 1996

AMENDMENT OF ACT OF 1990

Sections 3 and 5

3.—The Act of 1990 is hereby amended—

(*a*) in section 2—

(i) by the substitution in subsection (1) for "or section 4 of the Criminal Justice Act, 1984," of "section 4 of the Criminal Justice Act, 1984, or *section 2* of the *Criminal Justice (Drug Trafficking) Act, 1996,*", and

(ii) by the insertion in paragraph *(b)* of subsection (3) after "applies" of "or a drug trafficking offence within the meaning of section 3 (1) of the Criminal Justice Act, 1994",

and

(*b*) in section 4, by the substitution in subsection (2) thereof for "or section 4 of the Criminal Justice Act, 1984," of "section 4 of the Criminal Justice Act, 1984, or *section 2* of the *Criminal Justice (Drug Trafficking) Act, 1996,*".

Application of certain provisions of Act of 1984.

5.—Sections 4 (4), 4 (7), 4 (8), 4 (11), 5, 6 (1) to (4) and 8 of the Act of 1984 shall apply with any necessary modifications in relation to persons detained under *section 2* as they apply to persons detained under section 4 of the Act of 1984

APPENDIX 8

Criminal Justice (Miscellaneous Provisions) Act, 1997

SECTIONS 11 AND 12

Electronic recording of fingerprints and palmprints.

11.—(1) A power under any enactment, whether passed before or after the passing of this Act, to take the fingerprints or palmprints of any person shall include the power to record an image of that person's fingerprints or palmprints by electronic means or in any other manner.

(2) A photograph, or an image of any fingerprint or palmprint attached to or contained in a certificate purporting to be signed by the member who took such photograph or recorded such image and stating that—

(*a*) the said photograph is that of a specified person, or
(*b*) the said image is that of the fingerprint or palmprint, as the case may be, of a specified person,

and was taken or recorded, as the case may be, by the said member, shall, unless the contrary is proved, be evidence of the matters stated in the certificate.

Amendment of section 28 of Criminal Justice Act, 1984.

12.—The Criminal Justice Act, 1984, is hereby amended by the substitution of the following section for section 28:

> 28. "Taking of fingerprints, palmprints or photographs of person dealt with under Probation of Offenders Act, 1907, or convicted.
>
> (1) Where a person, on being prosecuted for an indictable offence, is the subject of an order under subsection (1) or (2)

of section 1 of the Probation of Offenders Act, 1907, or is convicted and otherwise dealt with, a member of the Garda Síochána may—

(*a*) at any convenient place, take the fingerprints, palmprints or photograph of that person, within 7 days of the making of such order or his being convicted, or

(*b*) require, in writing, that person to attend, within 7 days of the making of such order or his being convicted, at a named Garda Síochána station for the purpose of having his fingerprints, palmprints or photograph taken:

Provided that where a person has made it impracticable for his fingerprints, palmprints or photograph to be taken within the said period of 7 days, a member of the Garda Síochána may require (or in the case of a person attending a Garda Síochána station pursuant to a requirement under this section, further require) in writing, that person to attend at a named Garda Síochána station on a specified day for the purpose of having his fingerprints, palmprints or photograph taken.

(2) A member of the Garda Síochána may take the fingerprints, palmprints or photograph of a person on his attendance at a Garda Síochána station pursuant to a requirement under this section.

(3) The provisions of section 8 shall apply to fingerprints, palmprints or photographs taken pursuant to this section of a person who is the subject of an order under subsection (1) or (2) of section 1 of the Probation of Offenders Act, 1907, as they apply to fingerprints, palmprints or photographs taken in pursuance of the powers conferred by section 6.

(4) Any person who refuses to comply with a requirement under this section or to allow his fingerprints, palmprints or photograph to be taken pursuant to this section shall be guilty of an offence and shall be liable on summary conviction to a fine not exceeding £1,500 or to imprisonment for a term not exceeding 12 months or to both."

APPENDIX 9

Criminal Justice Act, 2006

(as signed by the President, July 16, 2006)

SECTIONS 13 AND 14

Amendment of Act of 1984

13.—The Act of 1984 is amended—

(*a*) in section 6(4), by the substitution of "€3,000" for "£1,000",

(*b*) in section 8—

(i) in subsection (2), by the substitution of "within the period of twelve months" for "within the period of six months",

(ii) by the substitution of the following subsections for subsection (3):

"(3) Where proceedings have been so instituted and—

(*a*) the person is acquitted,

(*b*) the charge against the person in respect of the offence concerned is dismissed under 30 section 4E of the Criminal Procedure Act 1967, or

(*c*) the proceedings are discontinued, the destruction shall be carried out on the expiration of a period of 21 days after the acquittal, dismissal or 35 discontinuance, as the case may be.

(3A) For the purposes of subsection (3)(*b*), a charge against the person in respect of the offence concerned shall be regarded as dismissed when—

(*a*) the time for bringing an appeal against the dismissal has expired,

(*b*) any such appeal has been withdrawn or

abandoned, or

(*c*) on any such appeal, the dismissal is upheld.",

and

(iii) in subsection (7)—

(I) by the substitution of "for a period not exceeding twelve months" for "for a period not exceeding six months", and

(II) by the substitution of "for the purpose of proceedings or further proceedings" for "for the purpose of further proceedings",

and

(*c*) in section 28(4), by the substitution of "€3,000" for "£1,500".

Amendment of Criminal Justice (Forensic Evidence) Act 1990.

14.—The Criminal Justice (Forensic Evidence) Act 1990 is amended—

(*a*) in section 2—

(i) in subsection (1)—

(I) by the substitution of "the provisions of subsections (4) to (8A)" for "the provisions of subsections (4) to (8)",

(II) by the substitution of the following paragraph for paragraph (*b*):

"(*b*) a swab from any part of the body including the mouth but not from any other body orifice or a genital region,",

(III) by the substitution of the following paragraph for paragraph (*c*):

"(*c*) a swab from a body orifice, other than the mouth, or a genital region,",

(IV) in paragraph (*e*), by the deletion of "or mouth",

(ii) by the insertion of the following subsection after subsection (1):

"(1A) A reference in subsection (1) of this section to the mouth shall be read as including a reference to the inside of the mouth.",

(iii) in subsection (2), by the substitution of "the provisions of subsections (3) to (8A)" for "the provisions of subsections (3) to (8)",

(iv) in subsection (4)(*b*), by the substitution of "subparagraph (i), (ii) or (iii) of paragraph (*a*) of subsection (1) of this section" for "subparagraph (i), (ii), (iii) or (iv) of paragraph (*a*) of subsection (1) of this section",

(v) in subsection (5), by the insertion in paragraph (*a*)(ii) after "applies" of "or a drug trafficking offence" within the meaning of section 3(1) of the Criminal Justice Act 1994",

(vi) by the insertion of the following subsection after subsection (8):

"(8A) Where a sample of hair other than pubic hair is taken in accordance with this section—

(*a*) the sample may be taken by plucking hairs with their roots and, in so far as it is reasonably practicable, the hairs shall be plucked singly, and

(*b*) no more hairs shall be plucked than the person taking the sample reasonably considers to be necessary to constitute a sufficient sample for the purpose of forensic testing.",

(vii) in subsection (9), by the substitution of "•3,000" for "£1,000",

(*b*) in section 4—

(i) in subsection (2), by the substitution of "within twelve months from the taking of the sample" for "within six months from the taking of the sample", and

(ii) by the substitution of the following subsections for subsection (3):

"(3) Where proceedings have been so instituted and—

(*a*) the person is acquitted,

(*b*) the charge against the person in respect of the

offence concerned is dismissed under section 4E of the Criminal Procedure Act 1967, or

(*c*) the proceedings are discontinued, the destruction of the record and the sample identified by such record shall be carried out on the expiration of twenty-one days after the acquittal, dismissal or discontinuance, as the case may be, unless an order has been made under subsection (5) of this section.

(3A) For the purposes of subsection (3)(*b*) of this section, a charge against the person in respect of the offence concerned shall be regarded as dismissed when—

(*a*) the time for bringing an appeal against the dismissal has expired,

(*b*) any such appeal has been withdrawn or abandoned, or

(*c*) on any such appeal, the dismissal is upheld.",

(*c*) in section 5(2), by the deletion of "and" at the end of paragraph (a) and the insertion of the following paragraph after paragraph (*a*):

"(*aa*) make provision for—

(i) the manner in which samples may be taken,

(ii) the location and physical conditions in which samples may be taken, and

(iii) the persons (including members of the Garda Síochána), and the number of such persons, who may be present when samples are taken, and".

Index